LOL!
OPS!
22:33
Chats
Mother
last seen 12 minutes ago
MO
May 7
Mom,why have you blacklisted my number ?
09:15
I had to , because of all that spam .
09:16
What spam ??
09:17
Things like Mom,put some money on my phone ,Mom ,I need a new jacket !and Mom , I need some cash,pronto!
09:18
Message

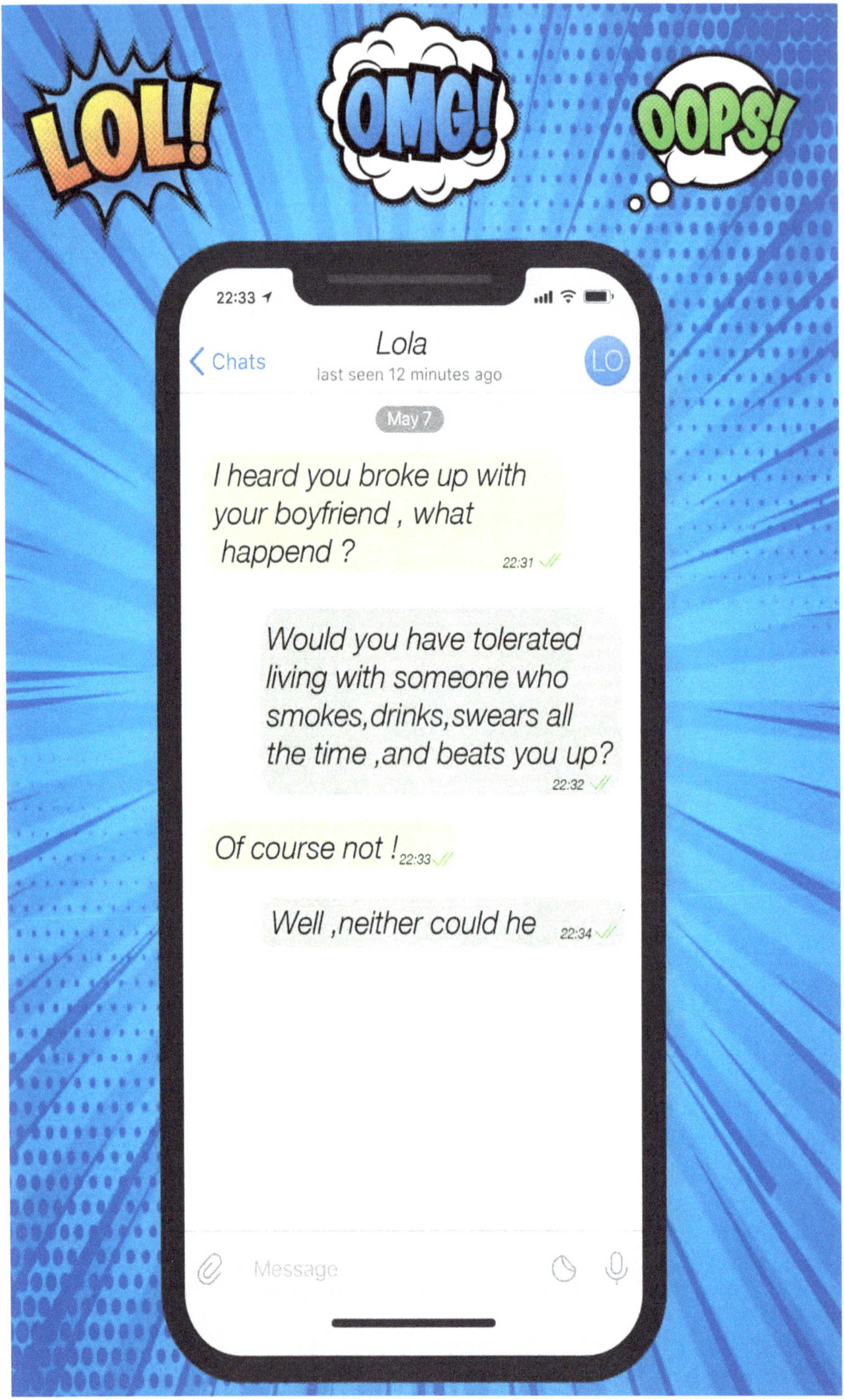
LOL!
OMG!
OOPS!
22:33
Chats
Lola
last seen 12 minutes ago
LO
May 7
I heard you broke up with your boyfriend , what happend ?
22:31
Would you have tolerated living with someone who smokes,drinks,swears all the time ,and beats you up?
22:32
Of course not !
22:33
Well ,neither could he
22:34
Message

LOL!
OMG!
OOPS!
22:33
Mom
Chats
last seen 12 minutes ago
MO
May 7
Mom , tel me the truth :
was i adopted ?
22:33
Do you think that , given a choice,your dad and I would have picked someone like you ?
22:34
Message

LOL!
OMG!
OOPS!
22:33
Chats
Dad.
last seen 12 minutes ago
DA
May 7
Uh , Daddy , i got Suspended 11:11
WTH???WHAT DID YOU DO ?? 11:11
Well,my ex,BF was being a dick,so I told him off and he said "Sticks and stones may break my bones ,but words can never hurt me" So I grabbed a dictionary, 11:12
Threw it at his face and screamed "HOWS THAT FOR WORDS HURTING YOU BITCH " Then ran away. 11:13
You are totaly my daughter. I'll be right there! 11:13
Message

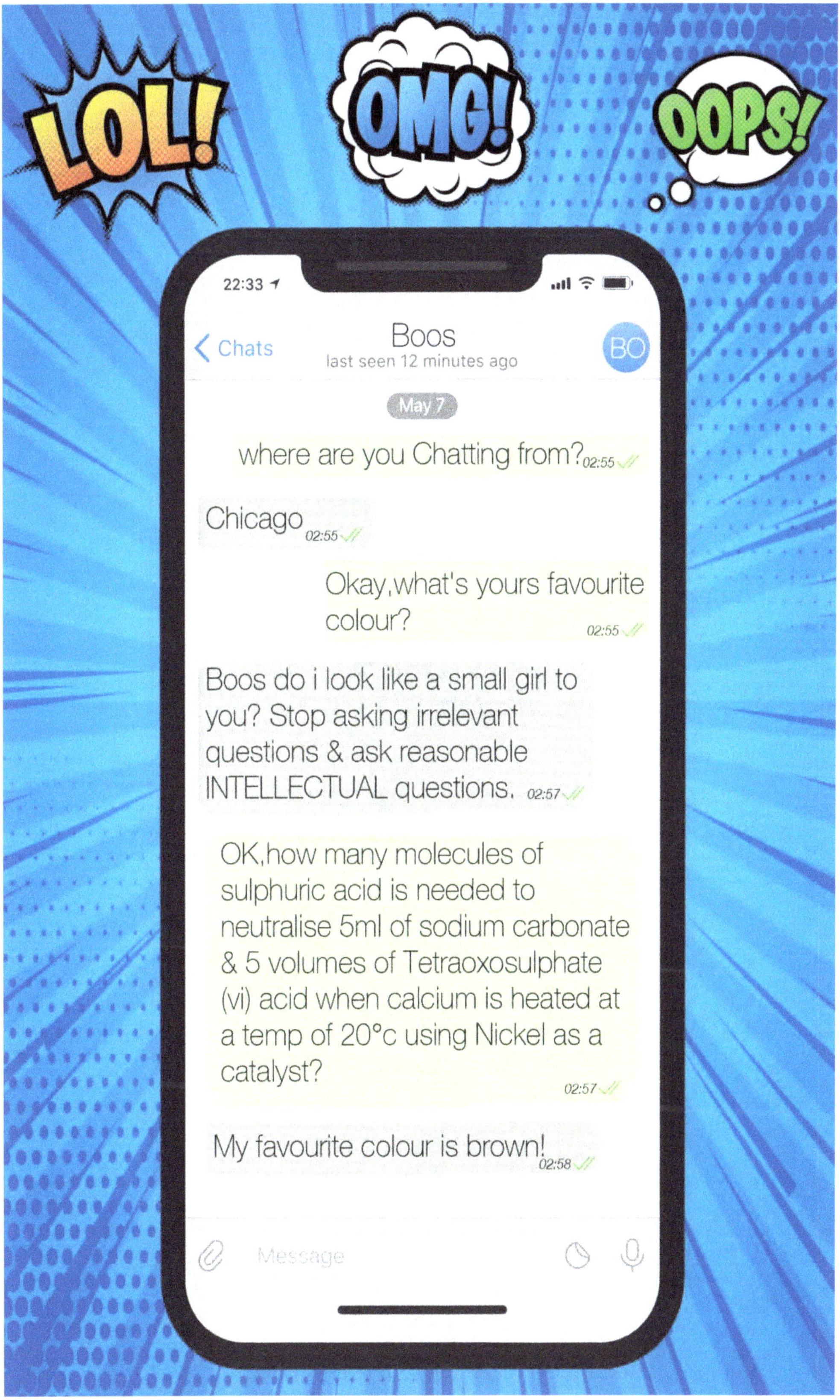

LOL!
OMG!
OOPS!
22:33
Chats
Boos
last seen 12 minutes ago
BO
May 7
where are you Chatting from? 02:55
Chicago 02:55
Okay,what's yours favourite colour? 02:55
Boos do i look like a small girl to you? Stop asking irrelevant questions & ask reasonable INTELLECTUAL questions. 02:57
OK,how many molecules of sulphuric acid is needed to neutralise 5ml of sodium carbonate & 5 volumes of Tetraoxosulphate (vi) acid when calcium is heated at a temp of 20°c using Nickel as a catalyst? 02:57
My favourite colour is brown! 02:58
Message

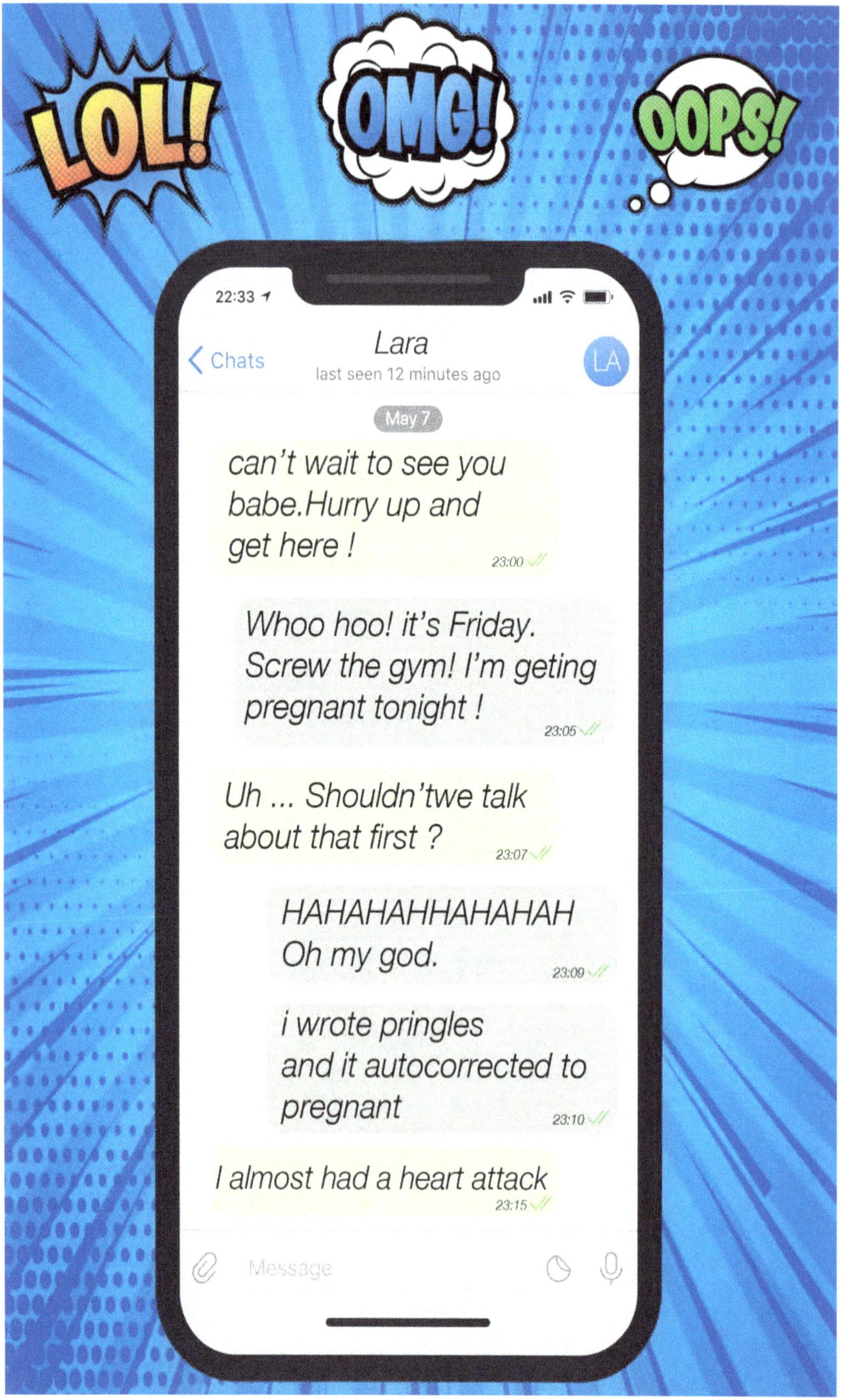
LOL!
OMG!
OOPS!
22:33
Chats
Lara
last seen 12 minutes ago
LA
May 7
can't wait to see you babe.Hurry up and get here !
23:00
Whoo hoo! it's Friday. Screw the gym! I'm geting pregnant tonight !
23:05
Uh ... Shouldn'twe talk about that first ?
23:07
HAHAHAHHAHAHAH Oh my god.
23:09
i wrote pringles and it autocorrected to pregnant
23:10
I almost had a heart attack
23:15
Message

LOL!
OMG!
OOPS!
22:33
Chats
Oliver
last seen 12 minutes ago
OL
May 7
Where are you ??
20:31
I'll be there in five minutes.
22:34
If I'm not , just read previous message over again.
22:34
Message

LOL!
OMG!
OOPS!
22:33
Chats
Amie
last seen 12 minutes ago
AM
May 7
My inner things hurt ... 13:23
Mine are good ... I have genital soreness ..My arms are tired ... 13:24
Genital soreness?!?!Lol 13:25
GENERAL...GENERAL... fml..Auto correct is a DAMN dirty bitch ... 13:26
Oh my god . I can't breathe 13:26
I'm dying over here!!! I just read it to everyone ...they're laughing too!!!That was epic!! HAHHAHAHAHAH 13:27
Message

LOL!
OMG!
OOPS!
22:33
Chats
Crush
last seen 12 minutes ago
CR
May 7
Good night don't let the demons drag you into hell and devour your soul ;) 07:12
Um.. Excuse me? O.o 07:12
OMG... I'm so sorry that was for my friend Ashley! 07:13
Lol its ok 07:13
Omg ashley I texted Josh the wrong text... Now he thinks I'm a freak and I have no chance with him now :(07:14
Kate? Still wrong person. But you still have a chance with me :)
good night don't let the demons drag you into hell or else we can never go on a date :) 07:15
Message

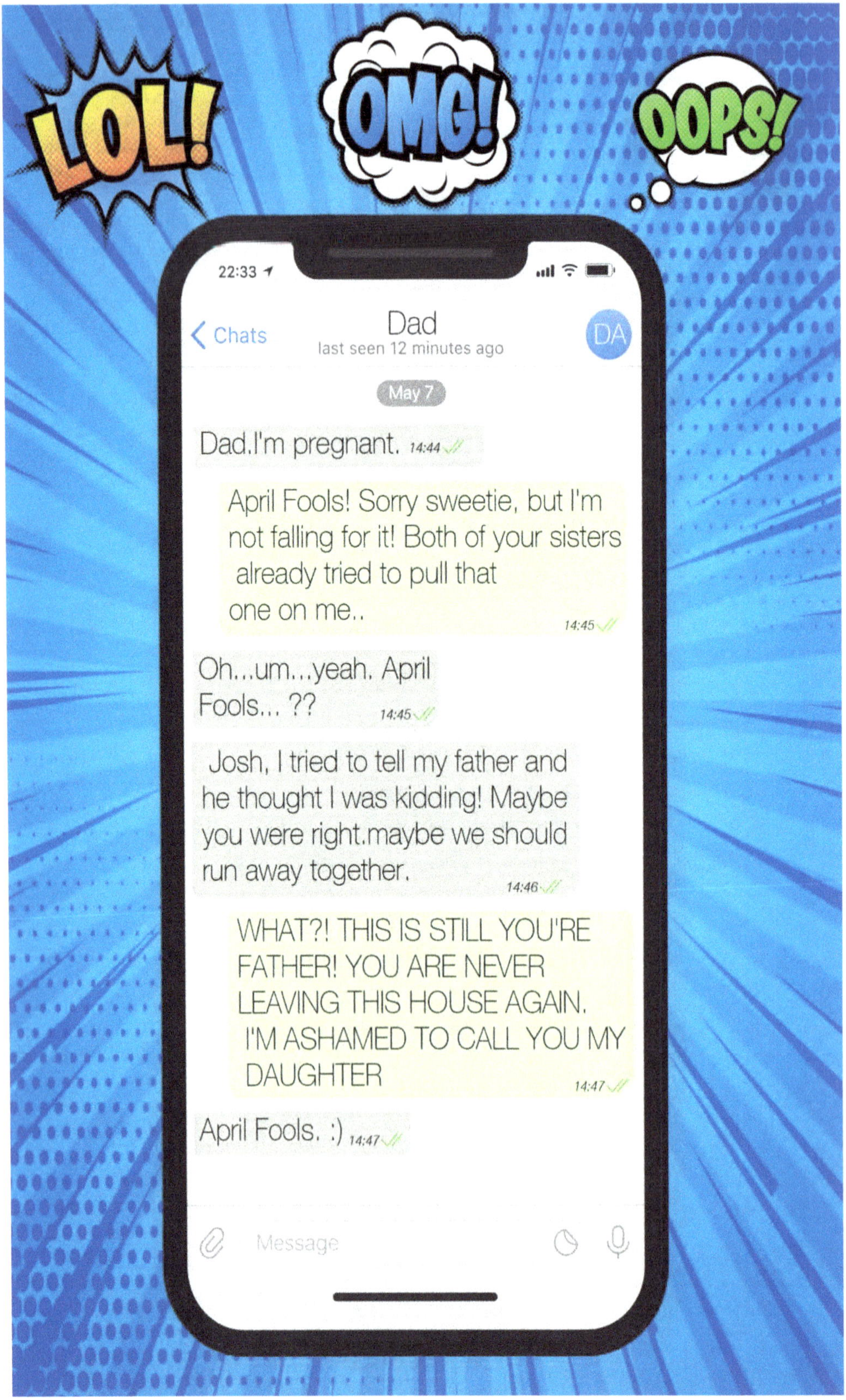
LOL!
OMG!
OOPS!
22:33
Chats
Dad
last seen 12 minutes ago
DA
May 7
Dad.I'm pregnant. 14:44
April Fools! Sorry sweetie, but I'm not falling for it! Both of your sisters already tried to pull that one on me.. 14:45
Oh...um...yeah. April Fools... ?? 14:45
Josh, I tried to tell my father and he thought I was kidding! Maybe you were right.maybe we should run away together. 14:46
WHAT?! THIS IS STILL YOU'RE FATHER! YOU ARE NEVER LEAVING THIS HOUSE AGAIN. I'M ASHAMED TO CALL YOU MY DAUGHTER 14:47
April Fools. :) 14:47
Message

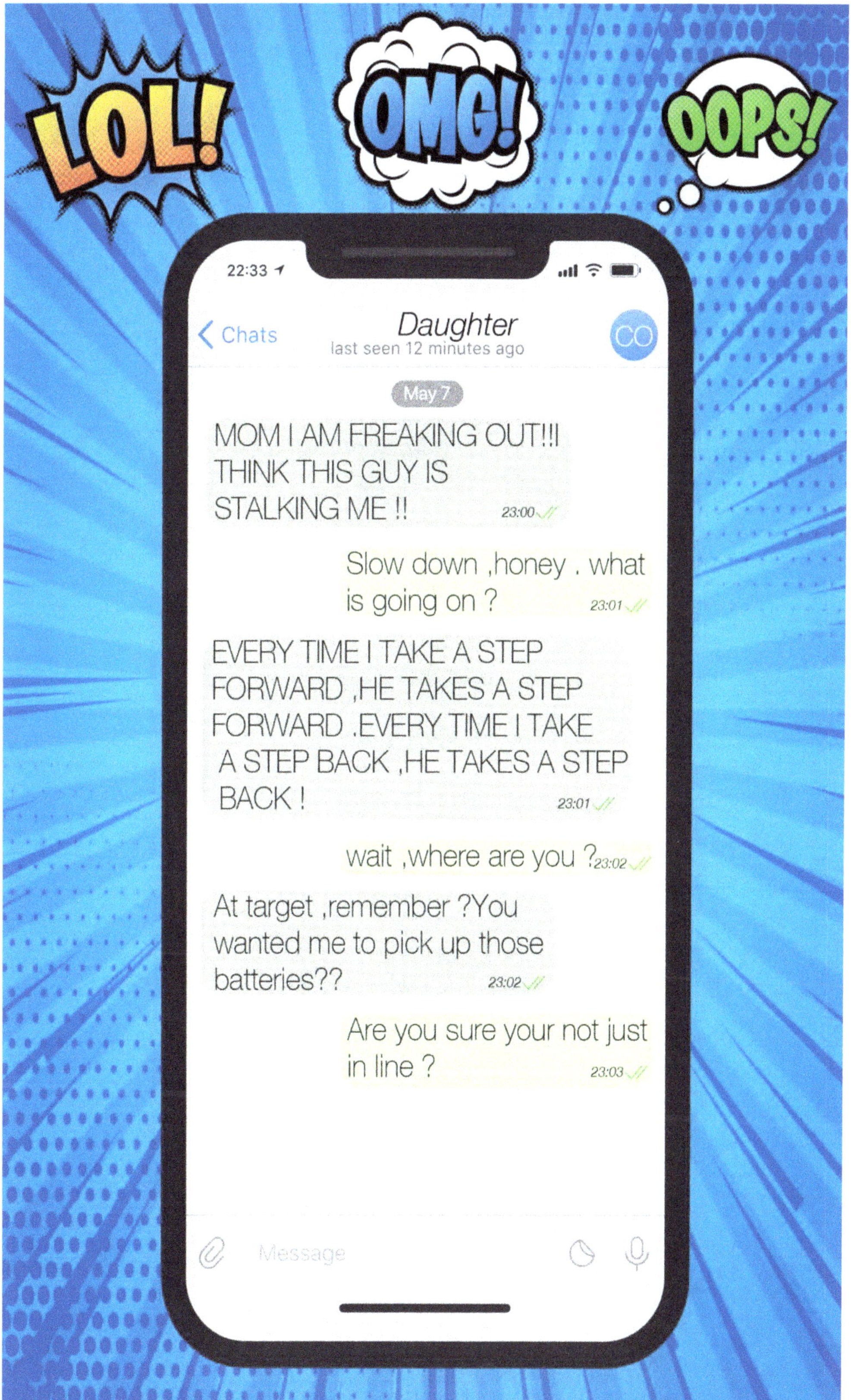
LOL!
OMG!
OOPS!
22:33
Chats
Daughter
last seen 12 minutes ago
CO
May 7
MOM I AM FREAKING OUT!!I THINK THIS GUY IS STALKING ME !! 23:00
Slow down ,honey . what is going on ? 23:01
EVERY TIME I TAKE A STEP FORWARD ,HE TAKES A STEP FORWARD .EVERY TIME I TAKE A STEP BACK ,HE TAKES A STEP BACK ! 23:01
wait ,where are you ? 23:02
At target ,remember ?You wanted me to pick up those batteries?? 23:02
Are you sure your not just in line ? 23:03
Message

LOL!
OMG!
OOPS!
22:33
Chats
Mom
last seen 12 minutes ago
MO
May 7
Mom! I think there's a theif in the house! COME HOME ! 11:42
Go hide in your closset! NOW! I'll be home in 15 minutes! 11:43
I can hear steps mom! IM SCARED! 11:44
Just be quiet honey! 11:44
Okay, I think he's gone now.. phew! But I can't get out of the closset! OMG, HE LOCKED ME IN! 11:45
No he didn't, I did. And I came early home from the meeting. Omg, you are easy to scare! PS. Hope you still talking to me! Love you. Mom. :-) 11:47
Message

LOL!
OMG!
OOPS!
22:33
Chats
Kyle
last seen 12 minutes ago
KY
May 7
Our house for Christmas this year .You are coming right? 13:23
Yea! 13:24
You cooking? Or Alison?? 13:24
Me .I am gonna dry hump the roast 3 days before. 13:25
Okay that's a bid visual. On secound thought maybe I wil stay home.Lol. 13:26
Dry humping 13:26
Dry rub 13:27
Message

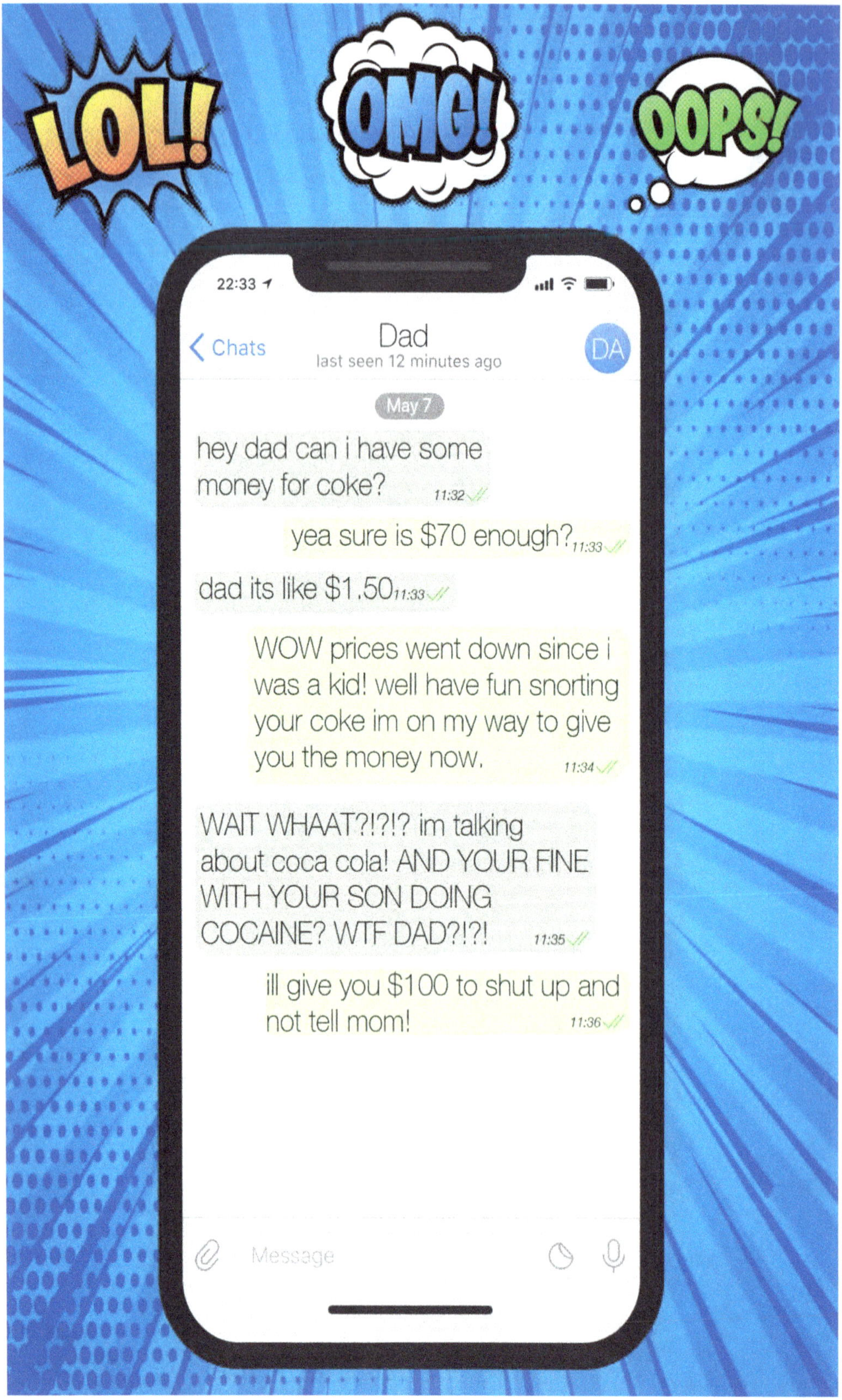
LOL!
OMG!
OOPS!
22:33
Chats
Dad
last seen 12 minutes ago
DA
May 7
hey dad can i have some money for coke? 11:32
yea sure is $70 enough? 11:33
dad its like $1.50 11:33
WOW prices went down since i was a kid! well have fun snorting your coke im on my way to give you the money now. 11:34
WAIT WHAAT?!?!? im talking about coca cola! AND YOUR FINE WITH YOUR SON DOING COCAINE? WTF DAD?!?! 11:35
ill give you $100 to shut up and not tell mom! 11:36
Message

LOL!
OMG!
OOPS!
22:33
Chats
Mom
last seen 12 minutes ago
Mo
May 7
your great aunt just passed away , LOL
16:11
why is that funny ?
16:15
its not funny David! what do you mean ?
16:16
Mom lol means laughing out loud!
16:17
ohmg goodness!! I sent that to everyone i thought it meant lots of love , I have to call everyone back oh god
16:17
Message

LOL!
OMG!
OOPS!
22:33
Chats
Terri
last seen 12 minutes ago
TE
May 7
I dont know how to start. I hate you. Ive never loved you. I want you to leave, tonight. Dont tell anyone, just pack your bags and go, and dont come back! 04:30
WHAT?? what did i do? please let me stay! 04:30
No, my decision is made, goodbye. 04:31
MOM, WHAT THE HELL, WHERE AMISUPPOSED TO GO :(04:31
Oh shit honey, sorry, i meant to send that to your father. 04:32
WHAT! what did dad do?! MOM! 04:33
Message

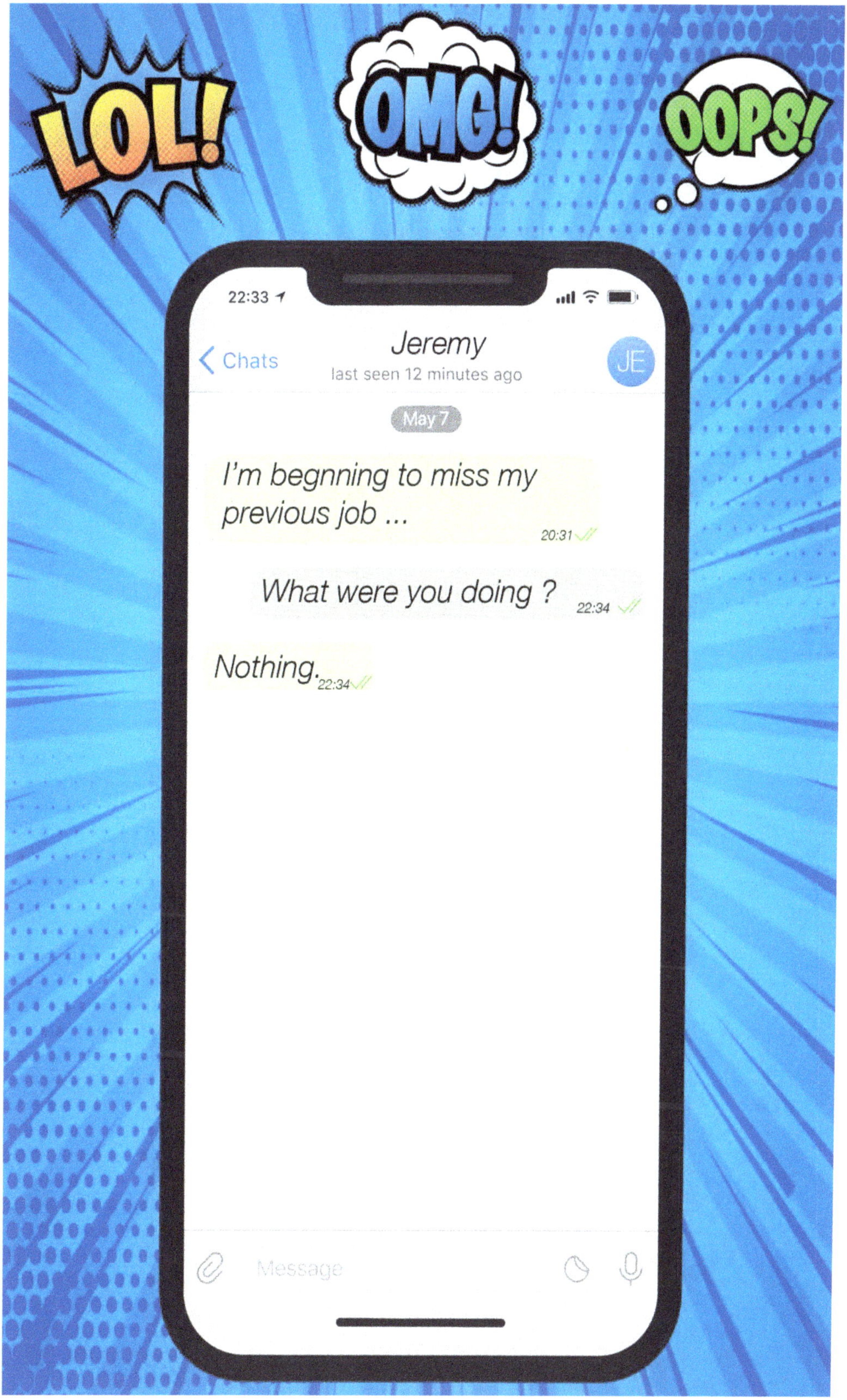
LOL!
OMG!
OOPS!
22:33
Chats
Jeremy
last seen 12 minutes ago
JE
May 7
I'm begnning to miss my previous job ...
20:31
What were you doing ?
22:34
Nothing.
22:34
Message

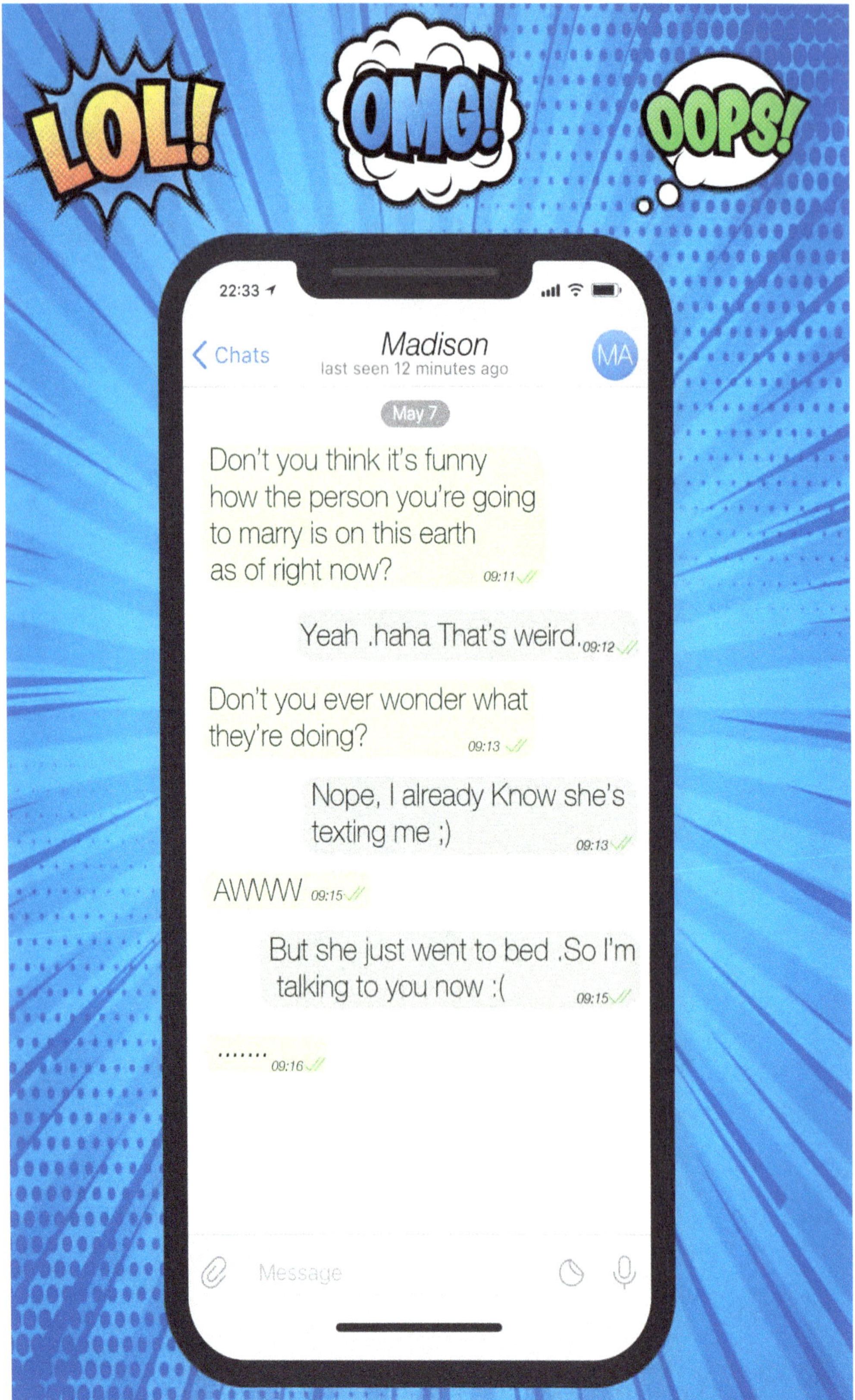
LOL!
OMG!
OOPS!
22:33
Chats
Madison
last seen 12 minutes ago
MA
May 7
Don't you think it's funny how the person you're going to marry is on this earth as of right now? 09:11
Yeah .haha That's weird. 09:12
Don't you ever wonder what they're doing? 09:13
Nope, I already Know she's texting me ;) 09:13
AWWW 09:15
But she just went to bed .So I'm talking to you now :(09:15
.... 09:16
Message

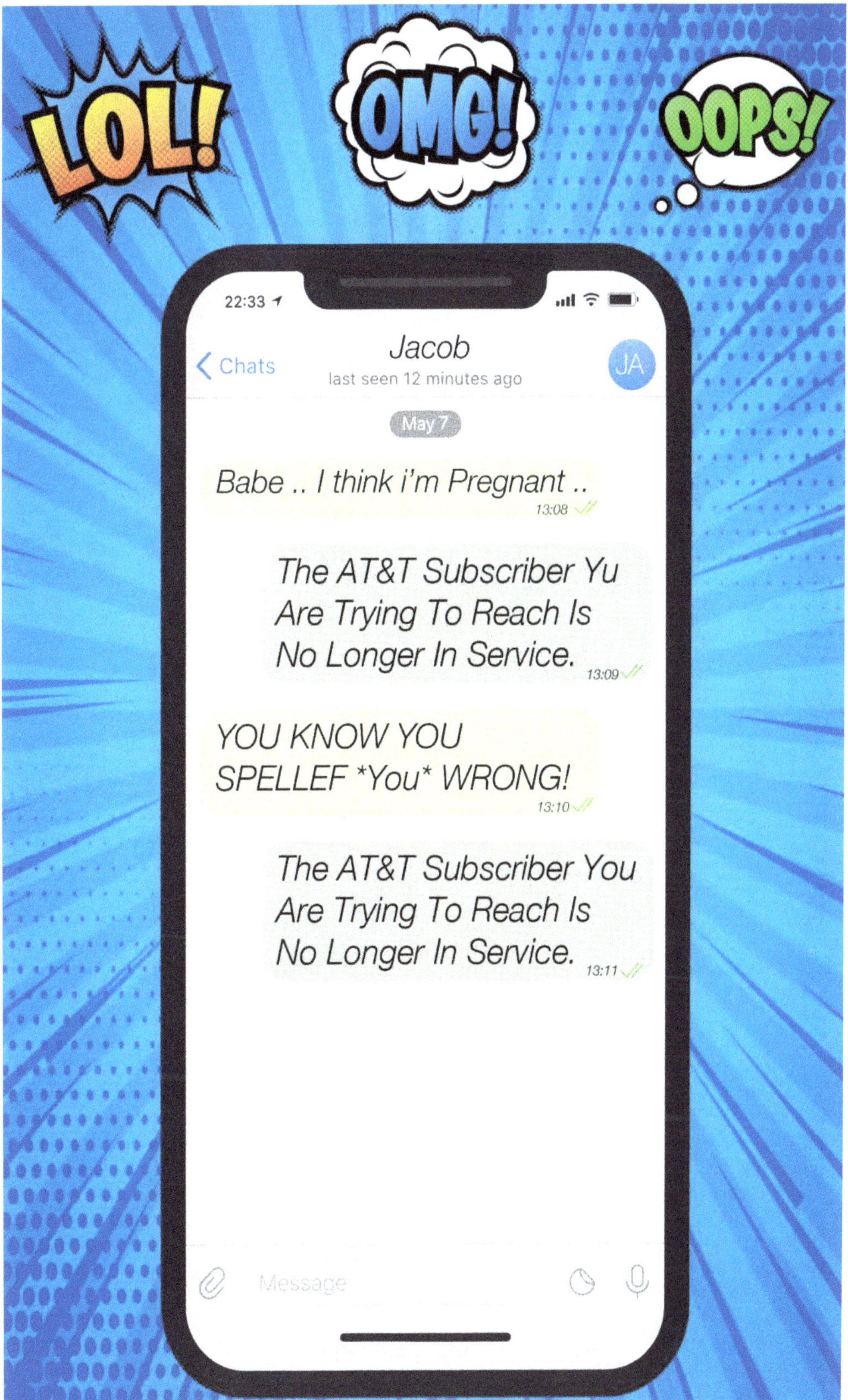
LOL!
OMG!
OOPS!
22:33
Chats
Jacob
last seen 12 minutes ago
JA
May 7
Babe .. I think i'm Pregnant ..
13:08
The AT&T Subscriber Yu Are Trying To Reach Is No Longer In Service.
13:09
YOU KNOW YOU SPELLEF *You* WRONG!
13:10
The AT&T Subscriber You Are Trying To Reach Is No Longer In Service.
13:11
Message

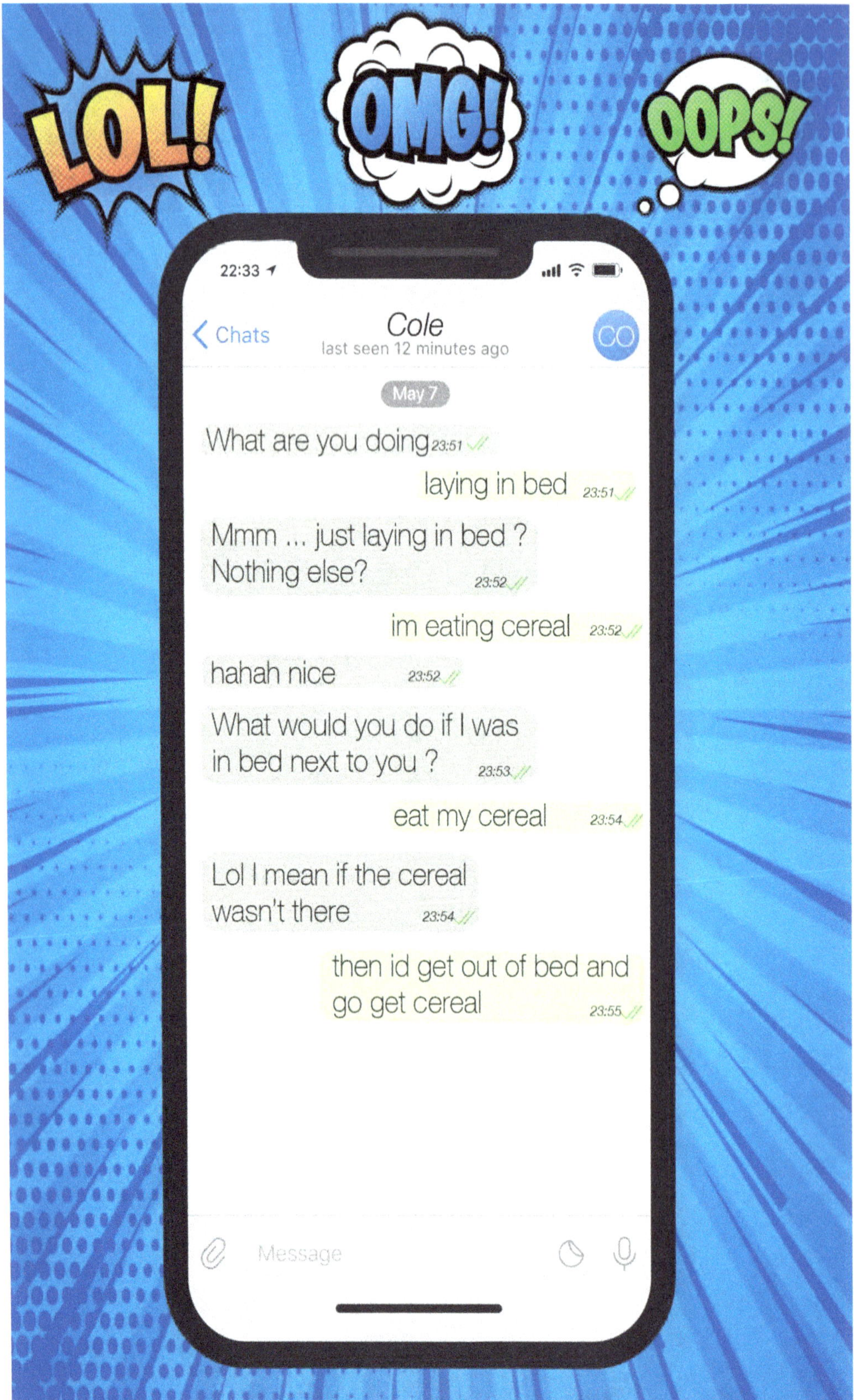

LOL!
OMG!
OOPS!
22:33
Chats
Cole
last seen 12 minutes ago
CO
May 7
What are you doing 23:51
laying in bed 23:51
Mmm ... just laying in bed ? Nothing else? 23:52
im eating cereal 23:52
hahah nice 23:52
What would you do if I was in bed next to you ? 23:53
eat my cereal 23:54
Lol I mean if the cereal wasn't there 23:54
then id get out of bed and go get cereal 23:55
Message

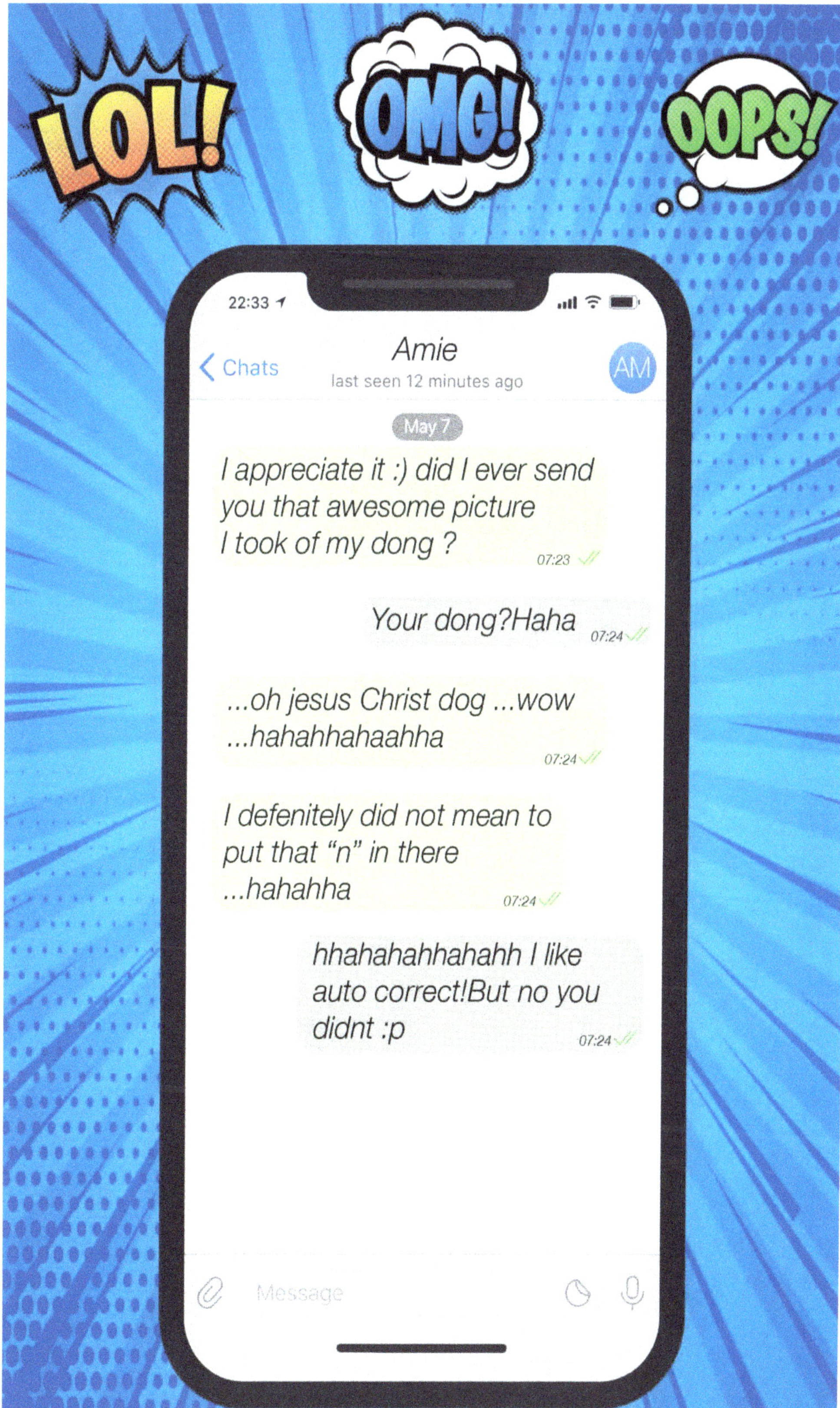
LOL!
OMG!
OOPS!
22:33
Chats
Amie
last seen 12 minutes ago
AM
May 7
I appreciate it :) did I ever send you that awesome picture I took of my dong ? 07:23
Your dong?Haha 07:24
...oh jesus Christ dog ...wow ...hahahhahaahha 07:24
I defenitely did not mean to put that "n" in there ...hahahha 07:24
hhahahahhahahh I like auto correct!But no you didnt :p 07:24
Message

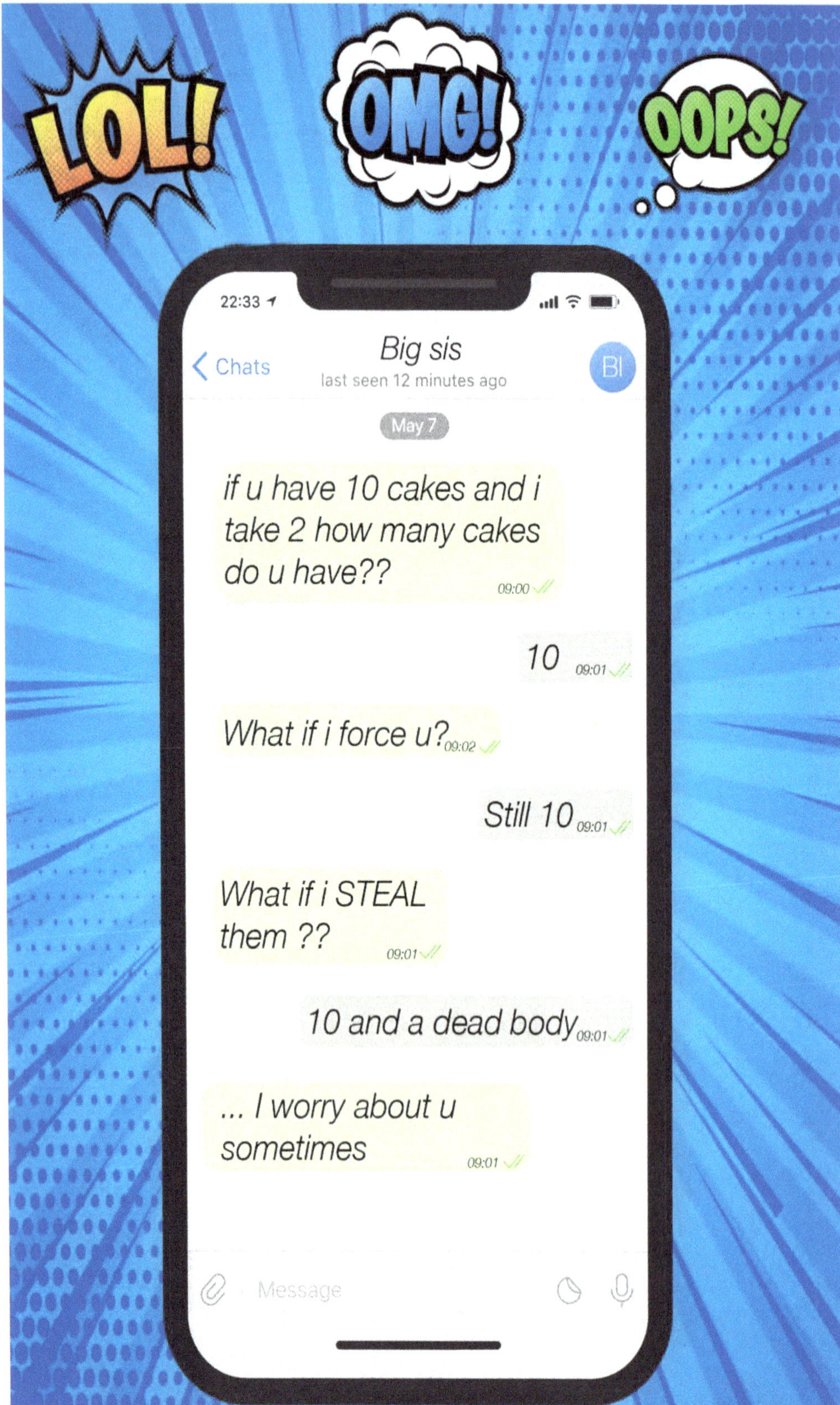
LOL!
OMG!
OOPS!
22:33
Chats
Big sis
last seen 12 minutes ago
BI
May 7
if u have 10 cakes and i take 2 how many cakes do u have?? 09:00
10 09:01
What if i force u? 09:02
Still 10 09:01
What if i STEAL them ?? 09:01
10 and a dead body 09:01
... I worry about u sometimes 09:01
Message

LOL!
OMG!
OOPS!
22:33
Chats
Dad
last seen 12 minutes ago
DD
May 7
hey honey, how's your day ?
23:35
Good I'm having the best weed of my life.
23:36
oh me too ... where did you get your's from.
23:40
NO NO NO I meant WEEK!!!! wait what dad?
23:42
Lets not tell mom about this conversation...
23:42
Message

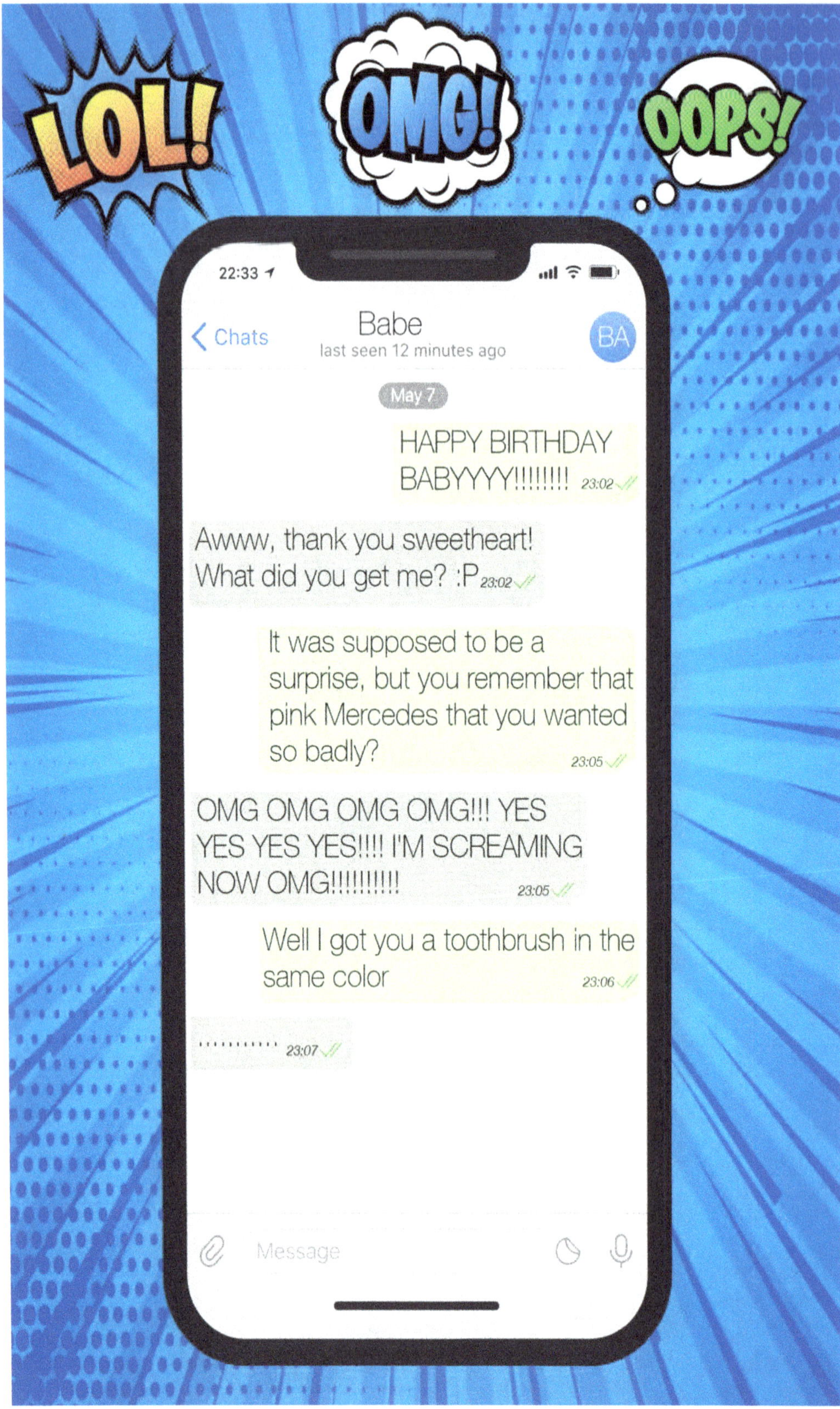
LOL!
OMG!
OOPS!
22:33
Chats
Babe
last seen 12 minutes ago
BA
May 7
HAPPY BIRTHDAY BABYYYY!!!!!!!! 23:02
Awww, thank you sweetheart! What did you get me? :P 23:02
It was supposed to be a surprise, but you remember that pink Mercedes that you wanted so badly? 23:05
OMG OMG OMG OMG!!! YES YES YES YES!!!! I'M SCREAMING NOW OMG!!!!!!!!!! 23:05
Well I got you a toothbrush in the same color 23:06
.... 23:07
Message

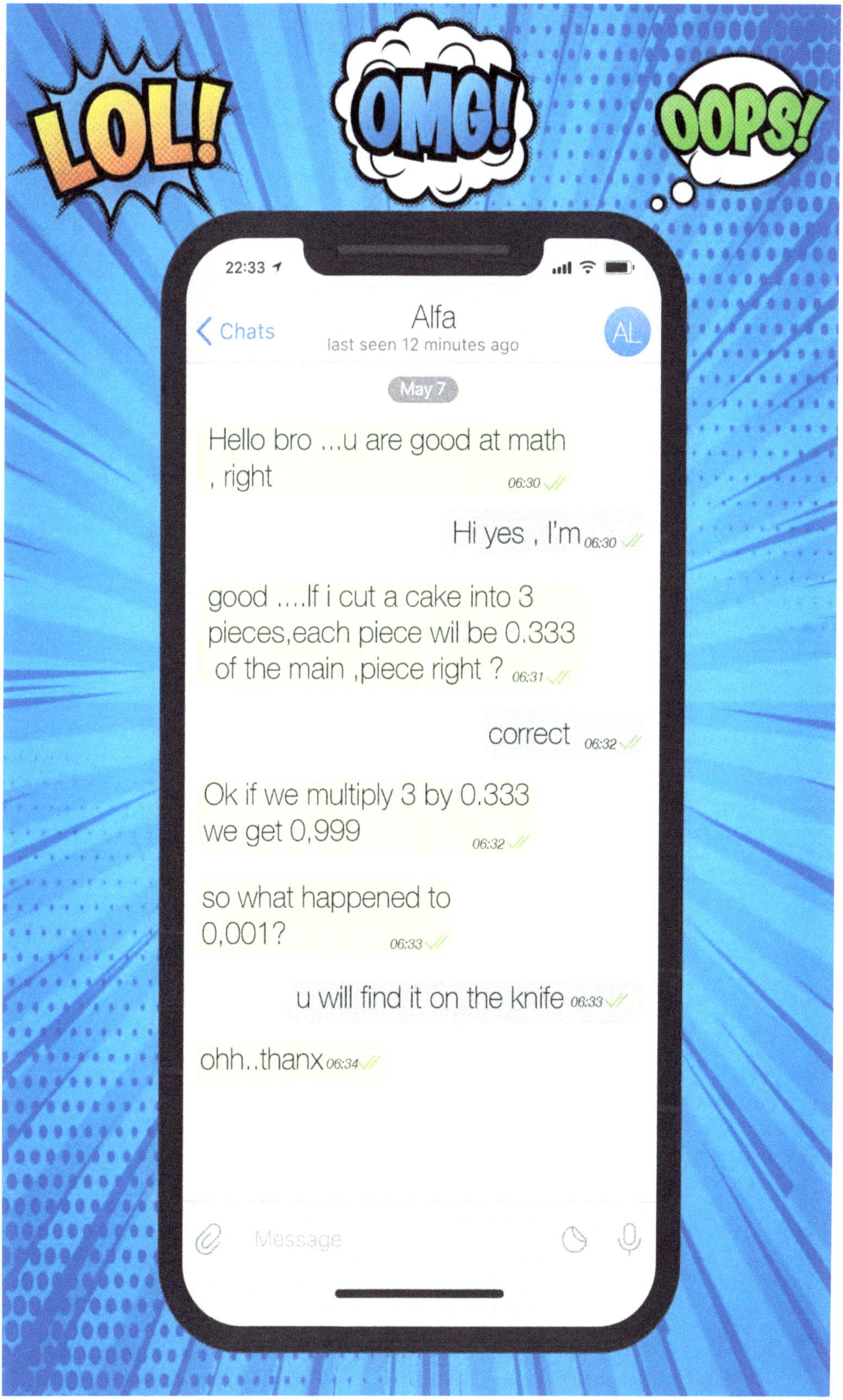
LOL!
OMG!
OOPS!
22:33
Chats
Alfa
last seen 12 minutes ago
AL
May 7
Hello bro ...u are good at math , right 06:30
Hi yes , I'm 06:30
good ....If i cut a cake into 3 pieces,each piece wil be 0.333 of the main ,piece right ? 06:31
correct 06:32
Ok if we multiply 3 by 0.333 we get 0,999 06:32
so what happened to 0,001? 06:33
u will find it on the knife 06:33
ohh..thanx 06:34
Message

LOL!
OMG!
OOPS!
22:33
Chats
Crush
last seen 12 minutes ago
CR
May 7
Hey, Amanda, will u go out with me? :) 01:17
Error 32332: Message could not send. 01:17
Hey, Amanda, will u go out with me? :) 01:18
Error 32332: Message could not send. 01:18
Hey, Amanda, will u go out with me? :) 01:19
34256: This person doesn't want to go out with you. Try someone else. 01:20
Message

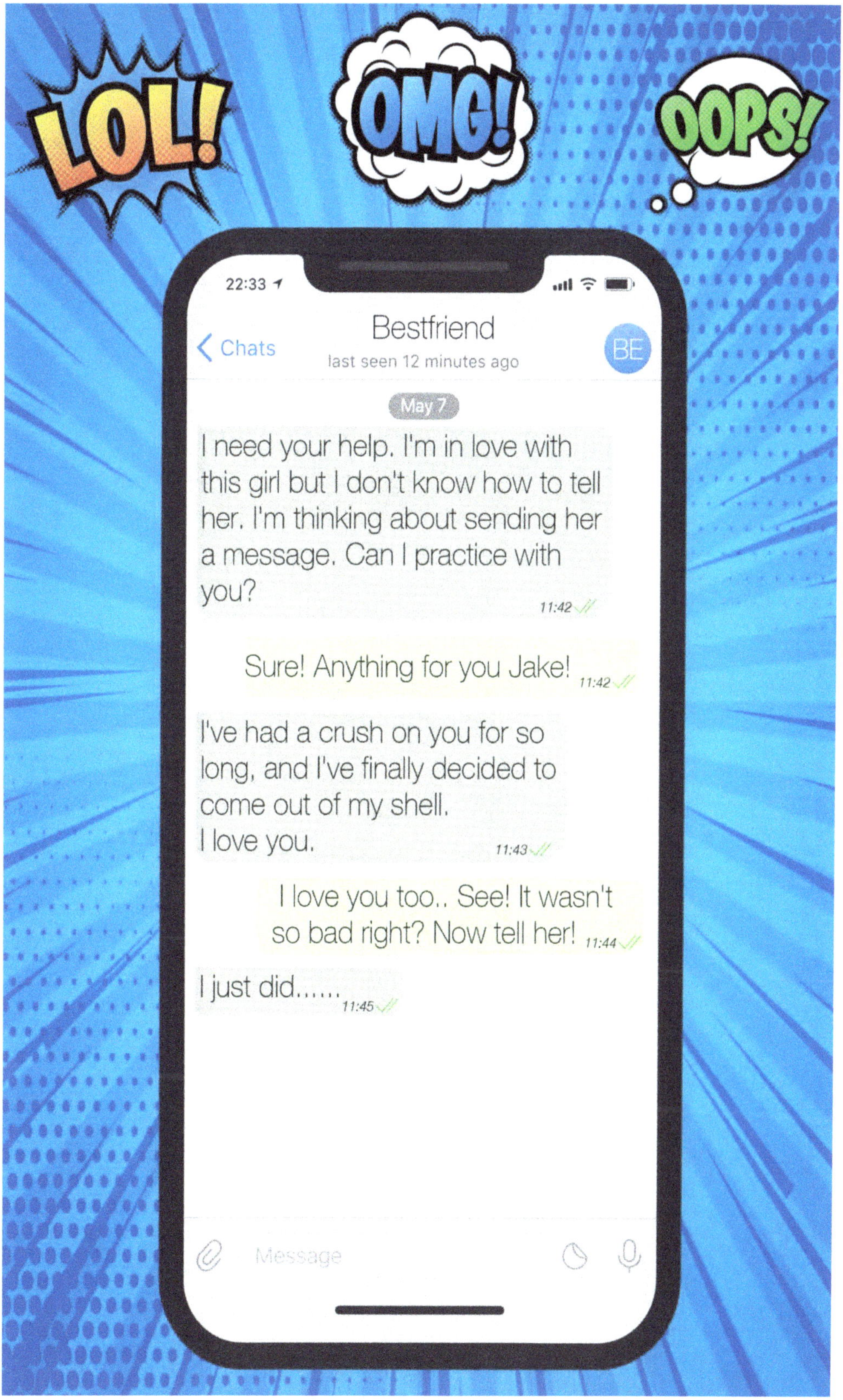

LOL!
OMG!
OOPS!
22:33
Chats
Bestfriend
last seen 12 minutes ago
BE
May 7
I need your help. I'm in love with this girl but I don't know how to tell her. I'm thinking about sending her a message. Can I practice with you? 11:42
Sure! Anything for you Jake! 11:42
I've had a crush on you for so long, and I've finally decided to come out of my shell.
I love you. 11:43
I love you too.. See! It wasn't so bad right? Now tell her! 11:44
I just did...... 11:45
Message

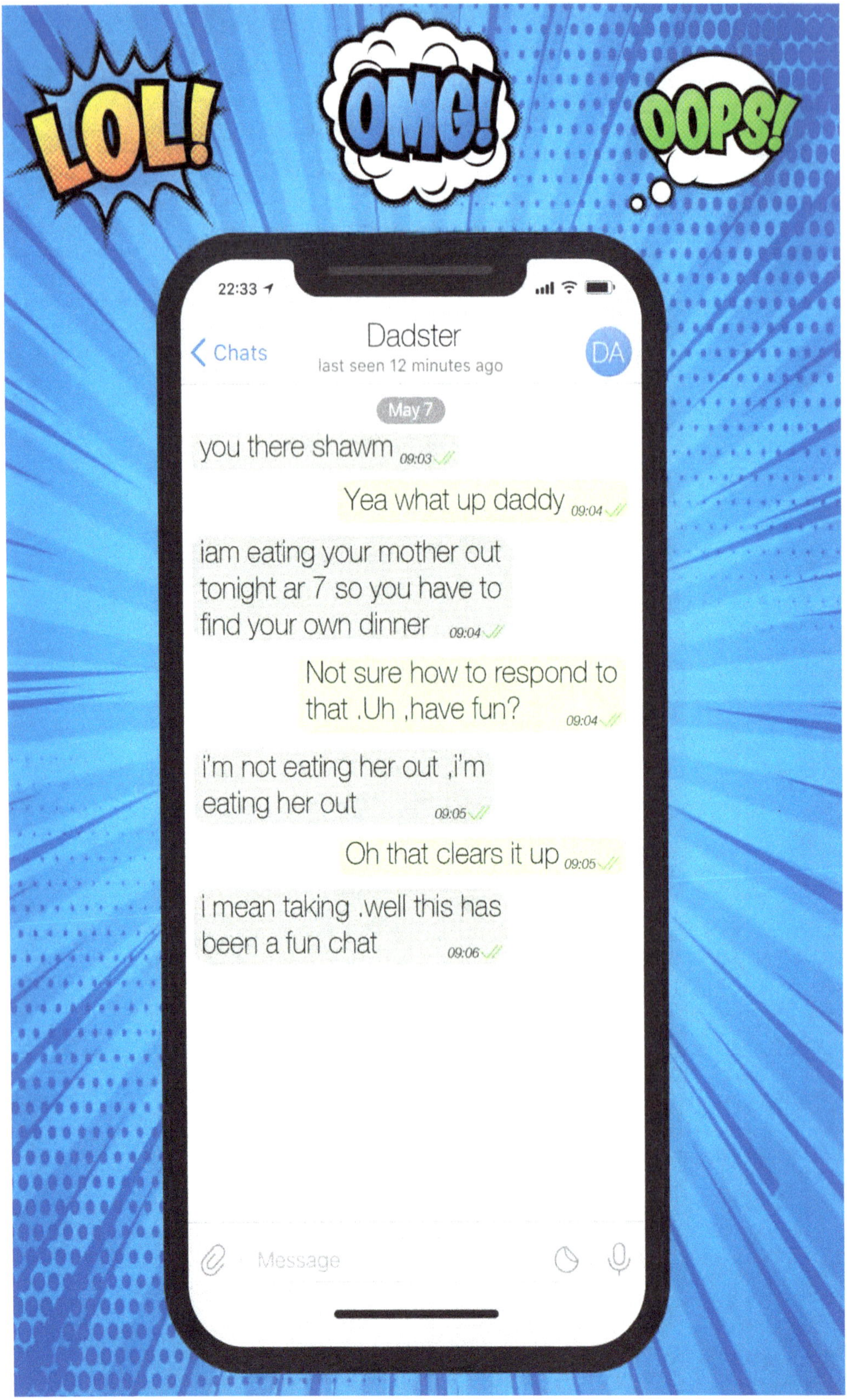
LOL!
OMG!
OOPS!
22:33
Chats
Dadster
last seen 12 minutes ago
DA
May 7
you there shawm 09:03
Yea what up daddy 09:04
iam eating your mother out tonight ar 7 so you have to find your own dinner 09:04
Not sure how to respond to that .Uh ,have fun? 09:04
i'm not eating her out ,i'm eating her out 09:05
Oh that clears it up 09:05
i mean taking .well this has been a fun chat 09:06
Message

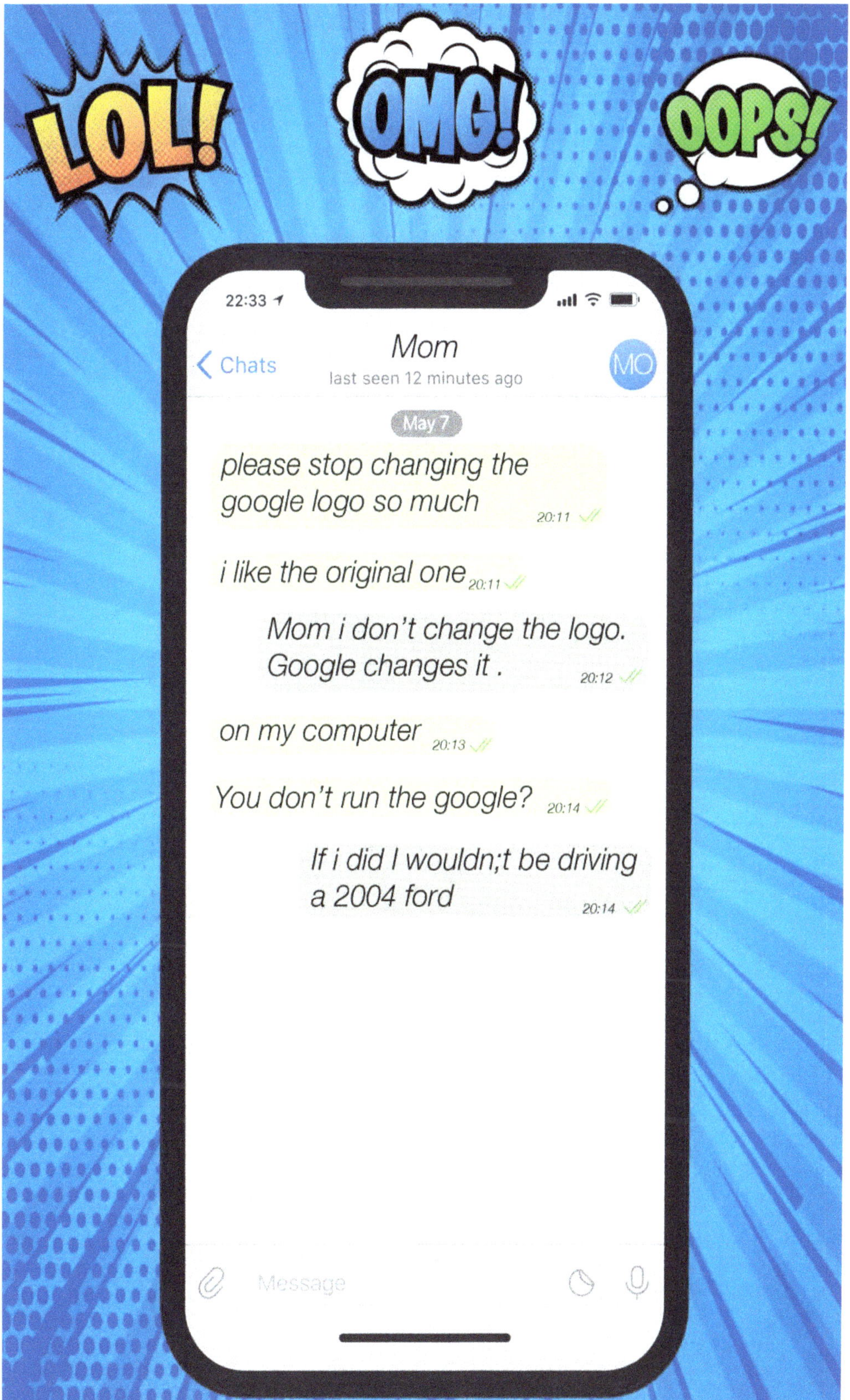
LOL!
OMG!
OOPS!
22:33
Chats
Mom
last seen 12 minutes ago
MO
May 7
please stop changing the google logo so much 20:11
i like the original one 20:11
Mom i don't change the logo. Google changes it . 20:12
on my computer 20:13
You don't run the google? 20:14
If i did I wouldn;t be driving a 2004 ford 20:14
Message

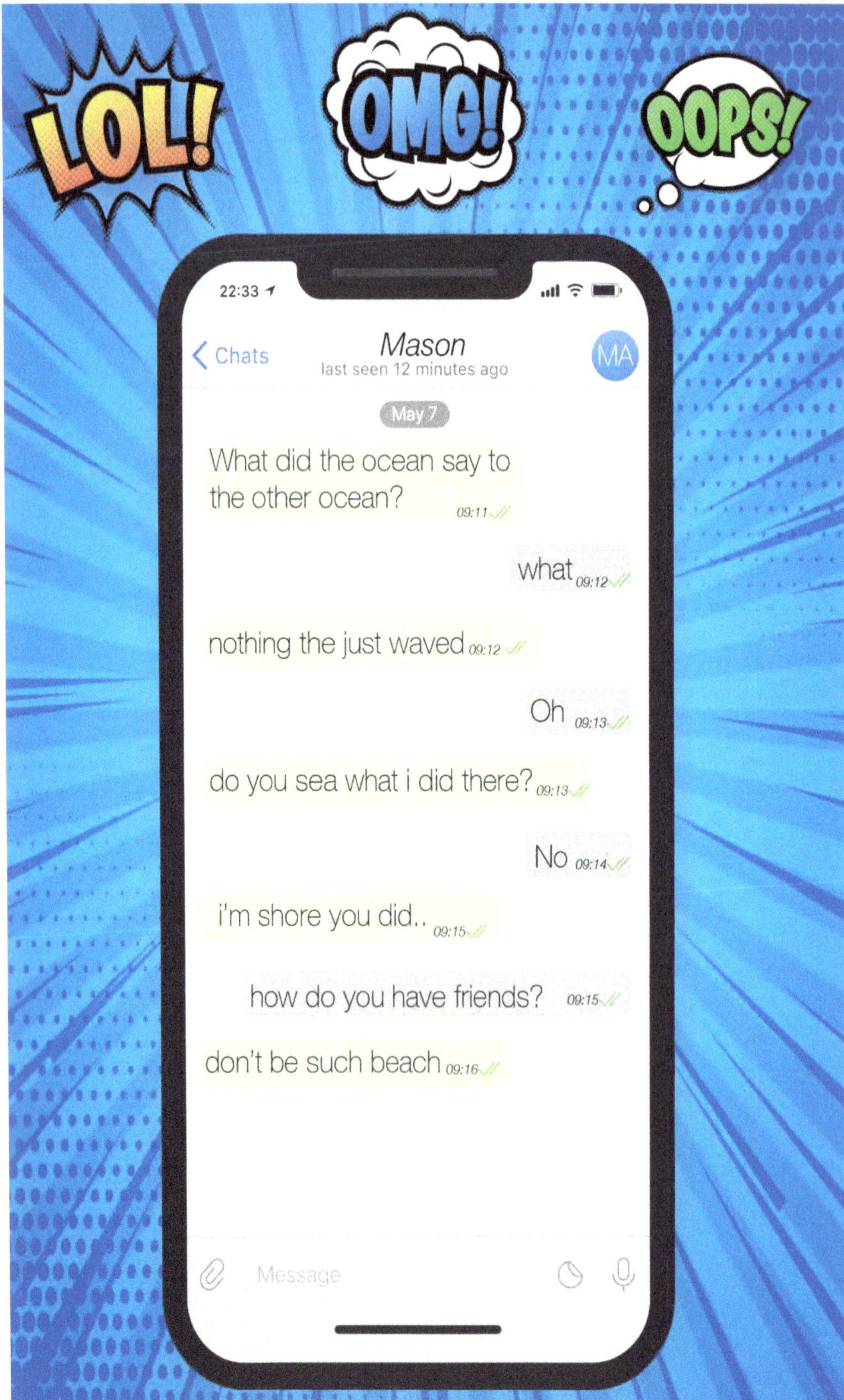
LOL!
OMG!
OOPS!
22:33
Chats
Mason
last seen 12 minutes ago
MA
May 7
What did the ocean say to the other ocean? 09:11
what 09:12
nothing the just waved 09:12
Oh 09:13
do you sea what i did there? 09:13
No 09:14
i'm shore you did.. 09:15
how do you have friends? 09:15
don't be such beach 09:16
Message

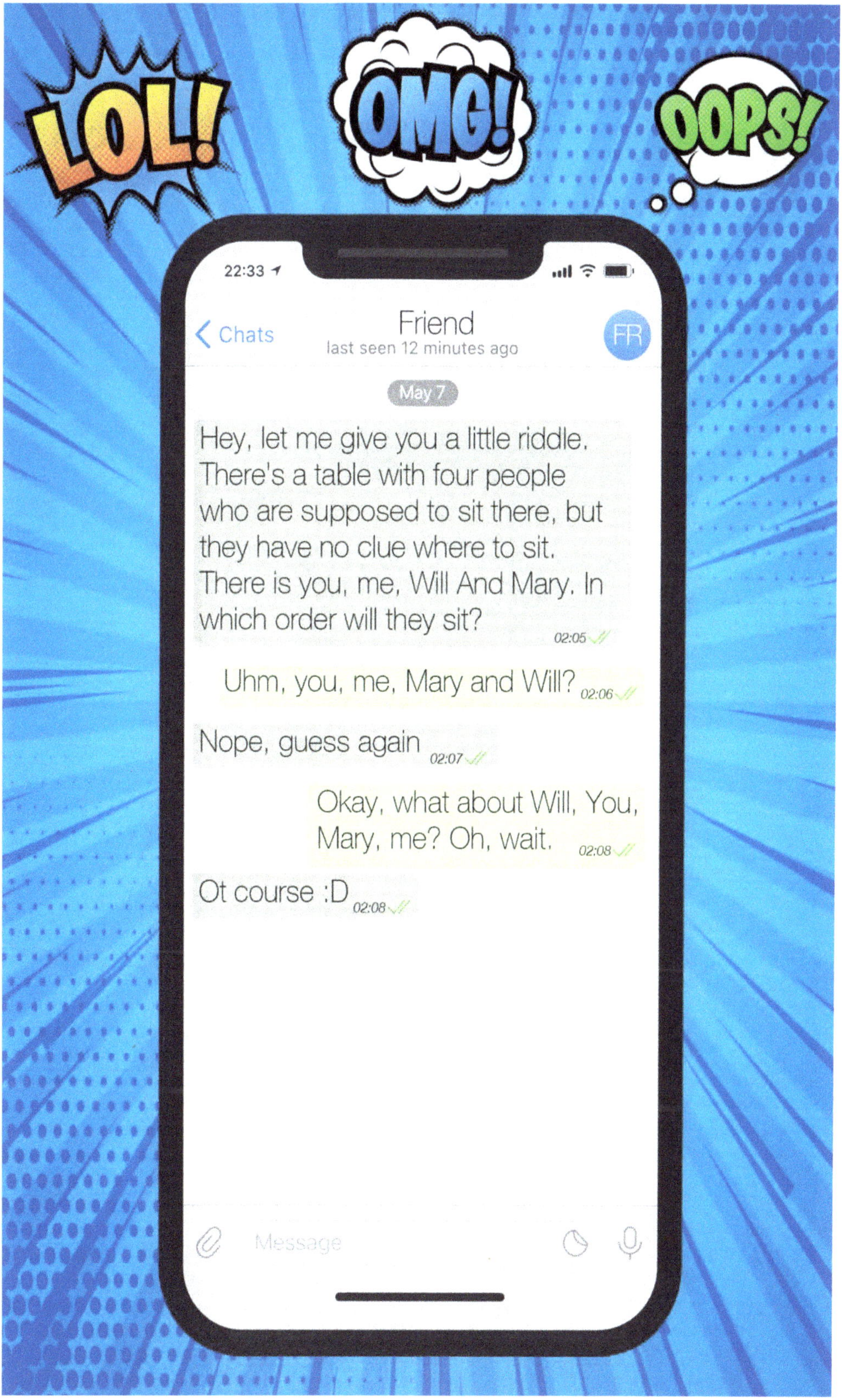
LOL!
OMG!
OOPS!
22:33
Chats
Friend
last seen 12 minutes ago
FR
May 7
Hey, let me give you a little riddle. There's a table with four people who are supposed to sit there, but they have no clue where to sit. There is you, me, Will And Mary. In which order will they sit? 02:05
Uhm, you, me, Mary and Will? 02:06
Nope, guess again 02:07
Okay, what about Will, You, Mary, me? Oh, wait. 02:08
Ot course :D 02:08
Message

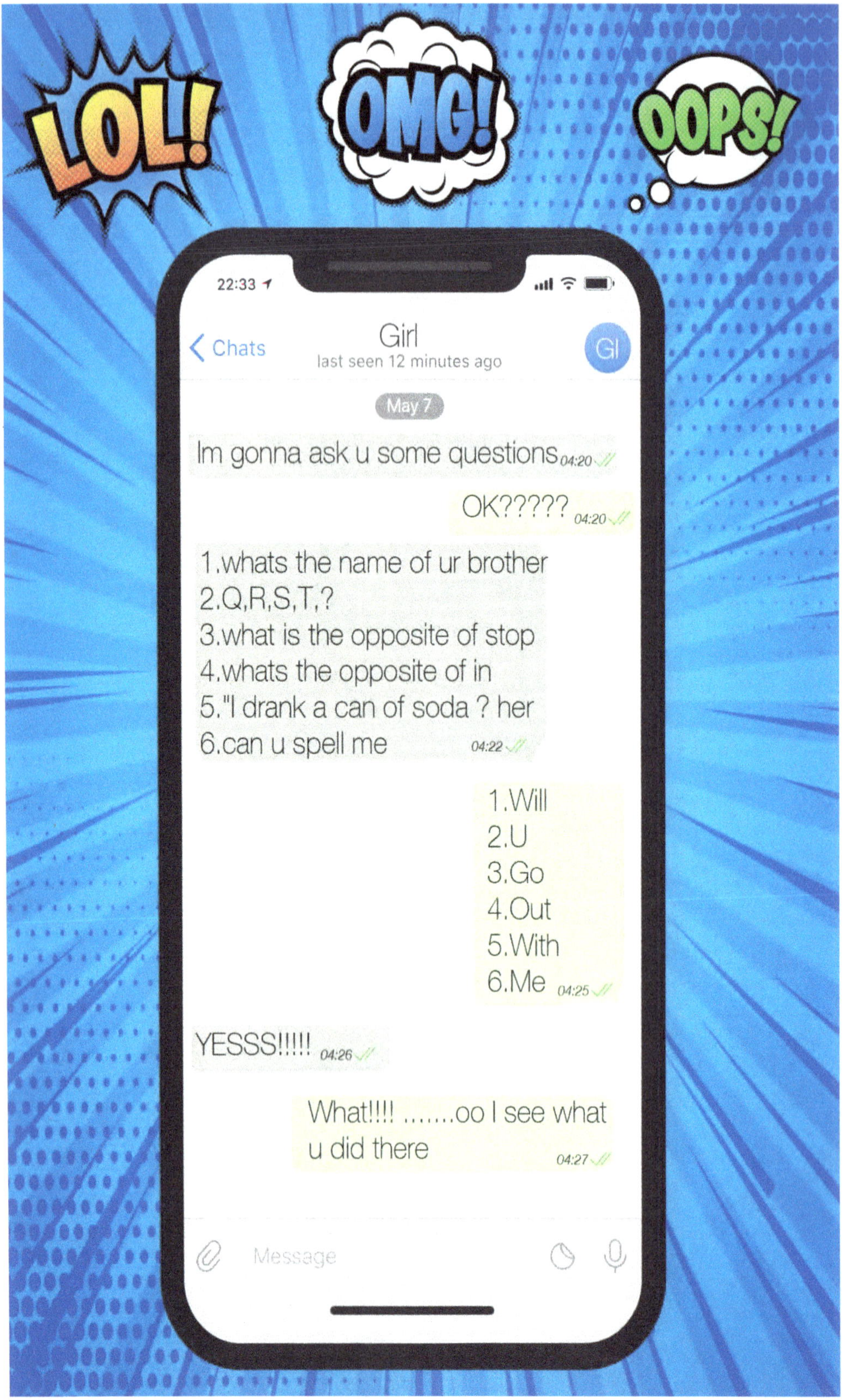
LOL!
OMG!
OOPS!
22:33
Chats
Girl
last seen 12 minutes ago
Gl
May 7
Im gonna ask u some questions 04:20
OK????? 04:20
1.whats the name of ur brother
2.Q,R,S,T,?
3.what is the opposite of stop
4.whats the opposite of in
5."I drank a can of soda ? her
6.can u spell me 04:22
1.Will
2.U
3.Go
4.Out
5.With
6.Me 04:25
YESSS!!!!! 04:26
What!!!! ....oo I see what u did there 04:27
Message

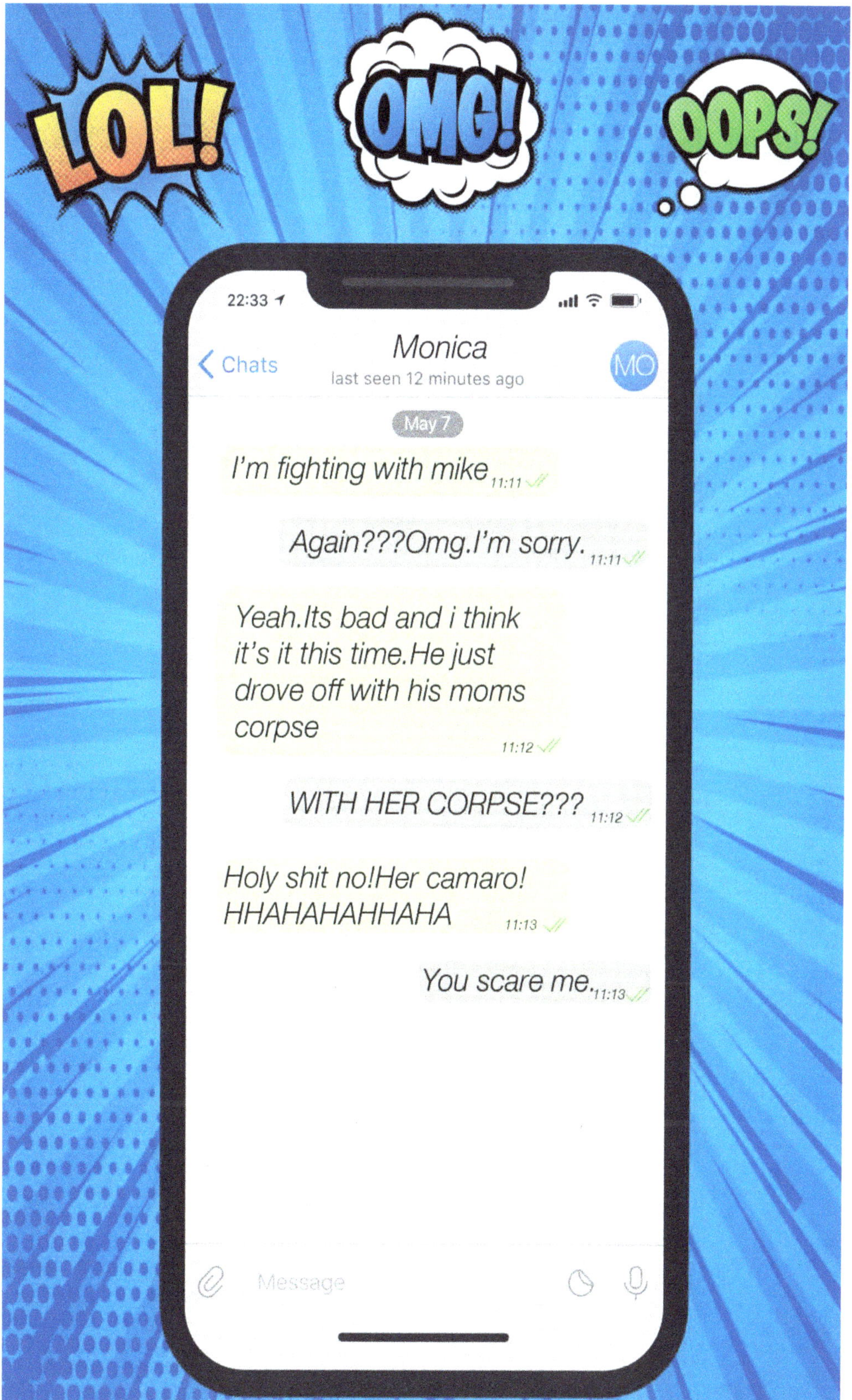
LOL!
OMG!
OOPS!
22:33
Chats
Monica
last seen 12 minutes ago
MO
May 7
I'm fighting with mike 11:11
Again???Omg.I'm sorry. 11:11
Yeah.Its bad and i think it's it this time.He just drove off with his moms corpse 11:12
WITH HER CORPSE??? 11:12
Holy shit no!Her camaro! HHAHAHAHHAHA 11:13
You scare me. 11:13
Message

LOL!
OMG!
OOPS!
22:33
Chats
Sonny
last seen 12 minutes ago
SO
May 7
Mom , Dad ! I've decided to live on my own! 15:07
We congratulate you on starting your independent life , darling ! 15:08
Thank you. 15:09
By the way _ I've already packed your bags! 15:09
Message

LOL!
OMG!
OOPS!
22:33
Chats
Babe
last seen 12 minutes ago
BA
May 7
Hey. you ready for tonight? 12:59
I guess. Im really nervous though, cause it is my first time. 13:01
Dont worry. You can scream if you want, alot of people do on their first time. Its ok ill be right there, holding you tight. 13:01
Thanks baby :) im still kinda scared though. I dont know if I can do it. 13:02
The roller coasters not that scary babe. 13:03
Message

LOL!
OMG!
OOPS!
22:33
Chats
Dad
last seen 12 minutes ago
DA
May 7
Hey sarah , you're boyfriend is really nice , he's really good at fucking too . 23:15
WTF DAD?ARE YOU SERIOUS? 23:15
I MEANT COOKING !SWEAR COOKING COKING COOKING 23:16
Omg Dad , call me next time. I practically died. 23:18
Ok . Well mom liked him too. 23:18
Go away 23:18
Message

LOL!
OMG!
OOPS!
22:33
Chats
Dad
last seen 12 minutes ago
DA
May 7
Hey babe, we need to talk.. 12:59
What is it? 13:01
Actually 'm pregnant): idk what to do/: 13:01
I feel like you should tell your father because if not and he finds out in text message he might kick your ass, and kick my ass as well. 13:02
check your name on the phone honey 13:02
....dad we need to talk. 13:03
Message

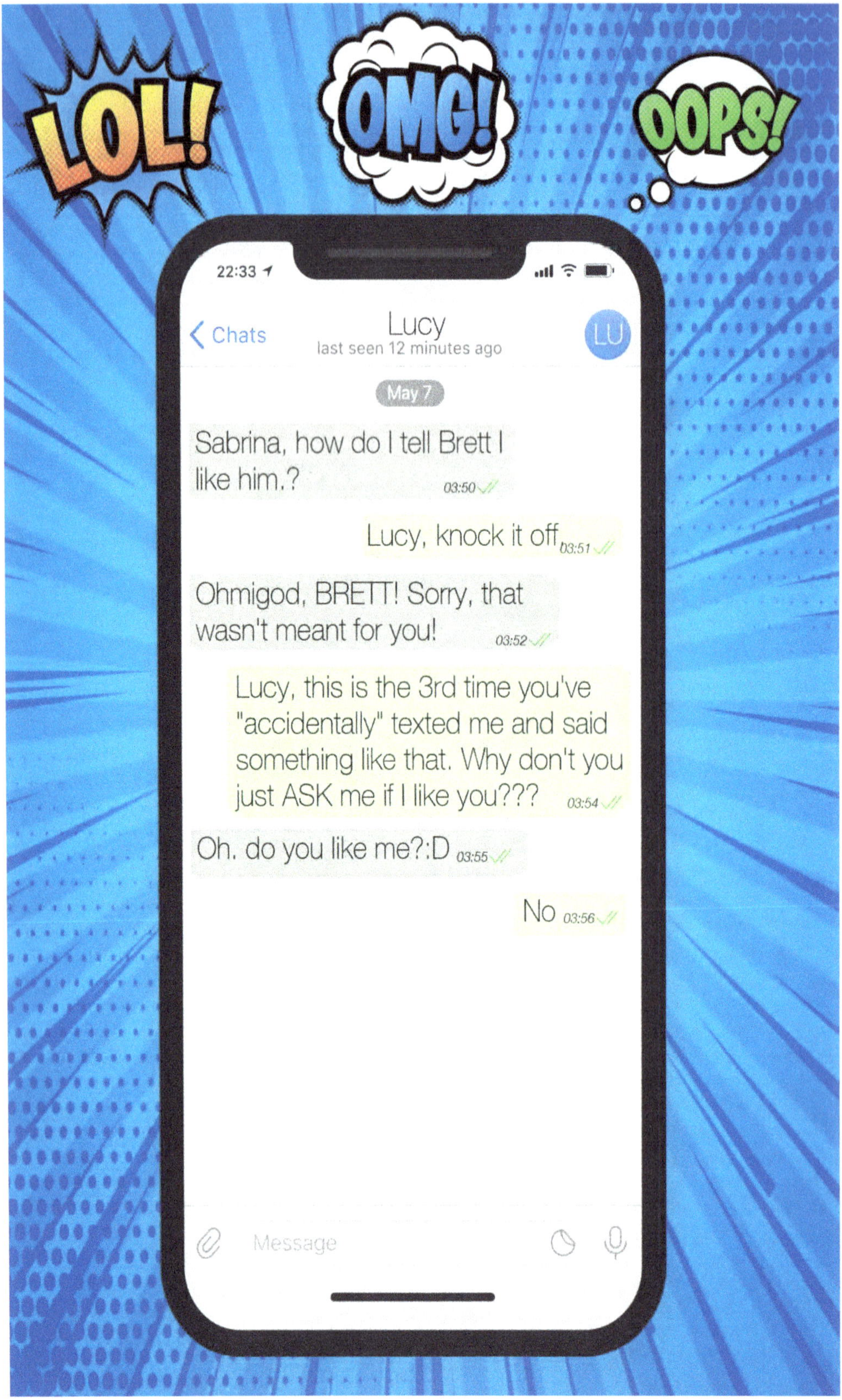
LOL!
OMG!
OOPS!
22:33
Chats
Lucy
last seen 12 minutes ago
LU
May 7
Sabrina, how do I tell Brett I like him.? 03:50
Lucy, knock it off 03:51
Ohmigod, BRETT! Sorry, that wasn't meant for you! 03:52
Lucy, this is the 3rd time you've "accidentally" texted me and said something like that. Why don't you just ASK me if I like you??? 03:54
Oh. do you like me?:D 03:55
No 03:56
Message

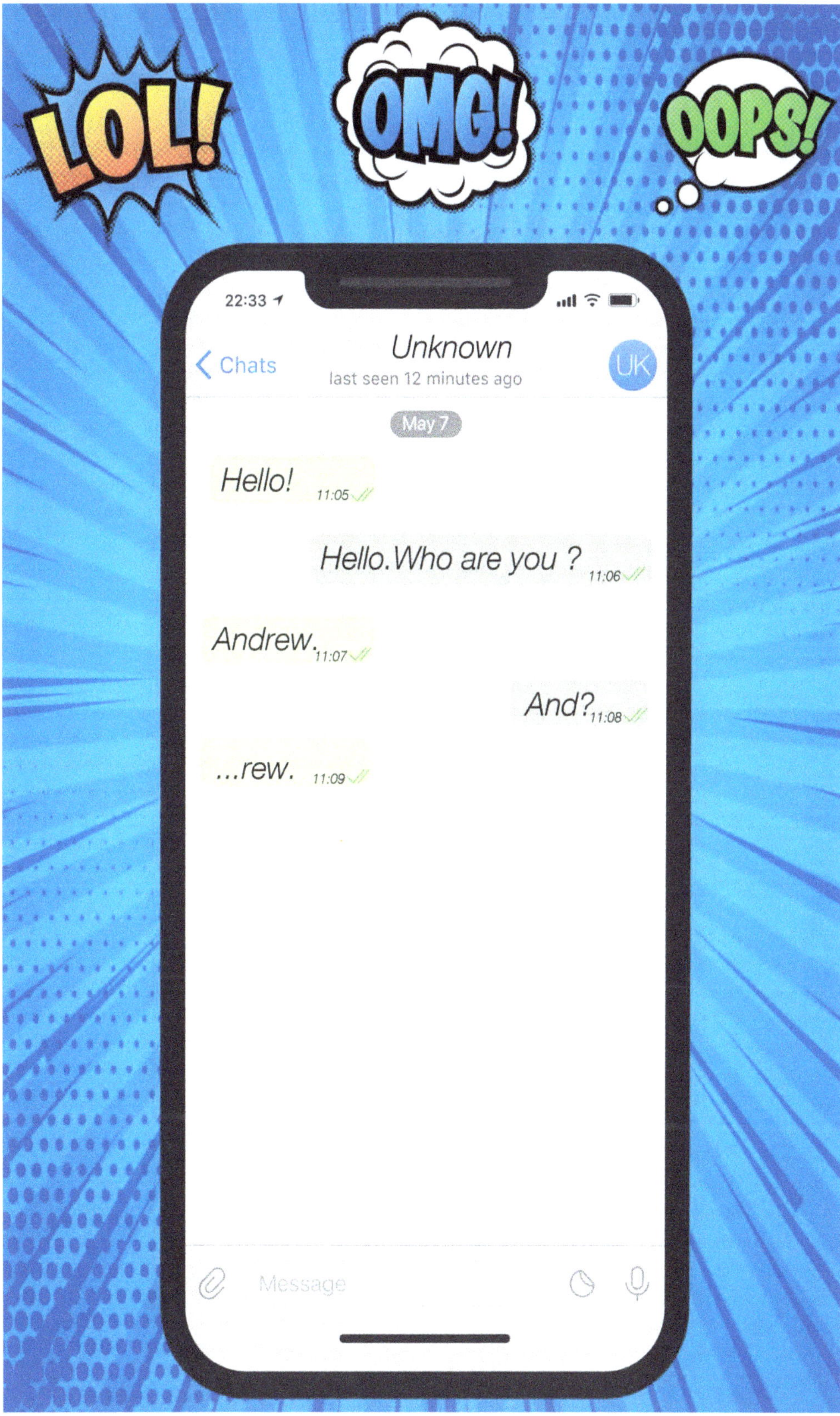
LOL!
OMG!
OOPS!
22:33
Chats
Unknown
last seen 12 minutes ago
UK
May 7
Hello! 11:05
Hello.Who are you ? 11:06
Andrew. 11:07
And? 11:08
...rew. 11:09
Message

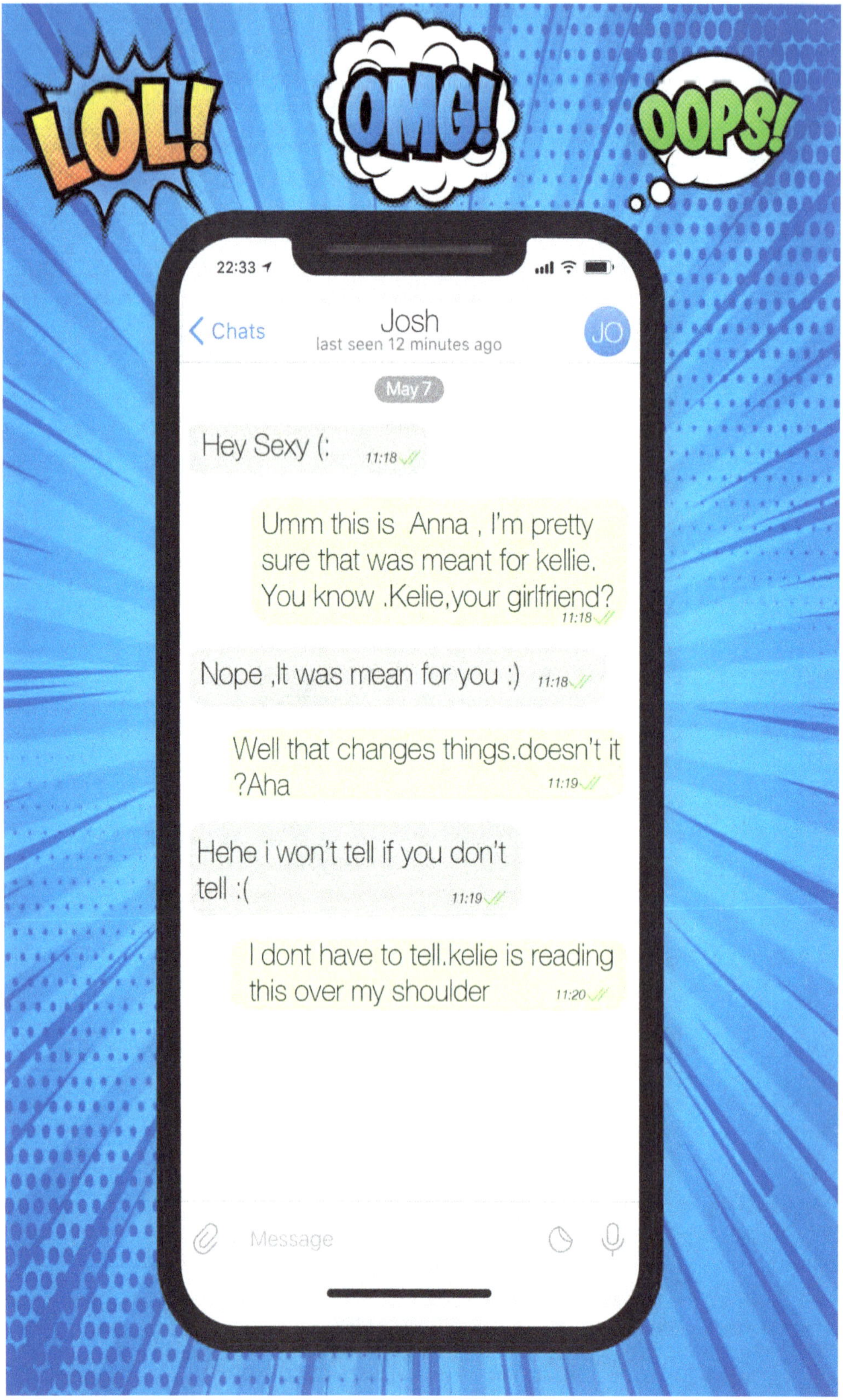
LOL!
OMG!
OOPS!
22:33
Chats
Josh
last seen 12 minutes ago
JO
May 7
Hey Sexy (: 11:18
Umm this is Anna , I'm pretty sure that was meant for kellie. You know .Kelie,your girlfriend? 11:18
Nope ,It was mean for you :) 11:18
Well that changes things.doesn't it ?Aha 11:19
Hehe i won't tell if you don't tell :(11:19
I dont have to tell.kelie is reading this over my shoulder 11:20
Message

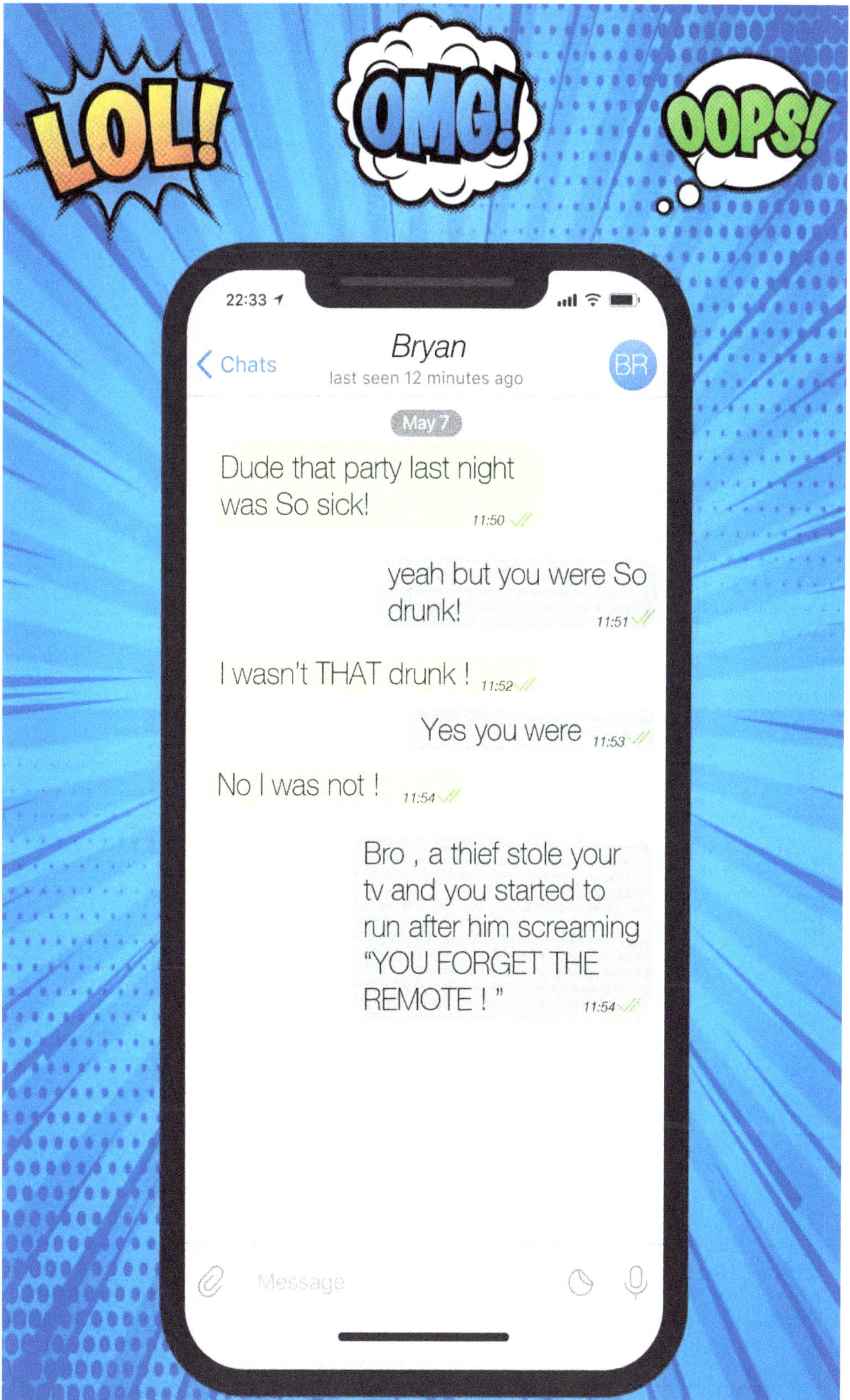
LOL!
OMG!
OOPS!
22:33
Chats
Bryan
last seen 12 minutes ago
BR
May 7
Dude that party last night was So sick! 11:50
yeah but you were So drunk! 11:51
I wasn't THAT drunk ! 11:52
Yes you were 11:53
No I was not ! 11:54
Bro , a thief stole your tv and you started to run after him screaming "YOU FORGET THE REMOTE ! " 11:54
Message

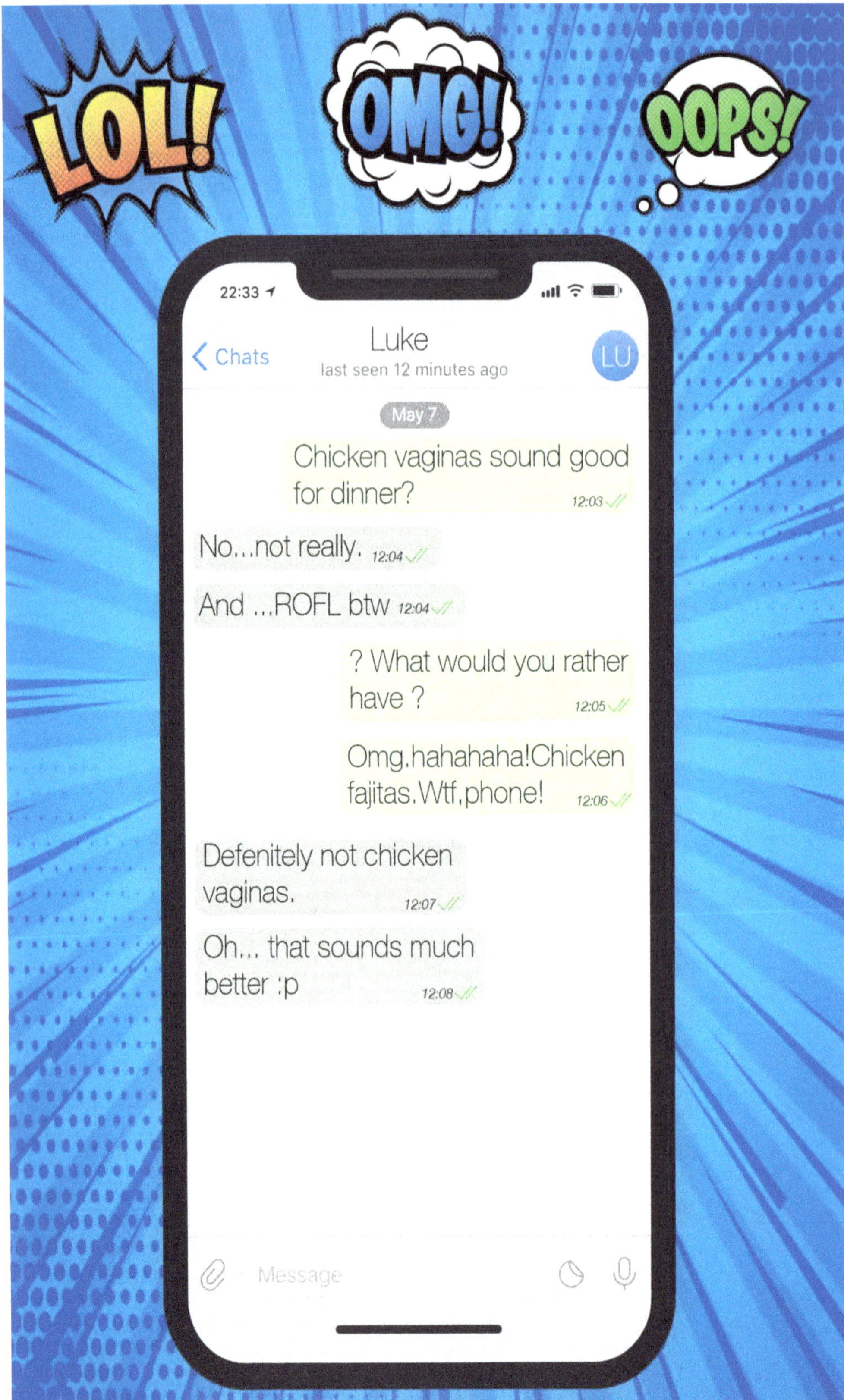
LOL!
OMG!
OOPS!
22:33
Chats
Luke
last seen 12 minutes ago
LU
May 7
Chicken vaginas sound good for dinner? 12:03
No...not really. 12:04
And ...ROFL btw 12:04
? What would you rather have ? 12:05
Omg.hahahaha!Chicken fajitas.Wtf,phone! 12:06
Defenitely not chicken vaginas. 12:07
Oh... that sounds much better :p 12:08
Message

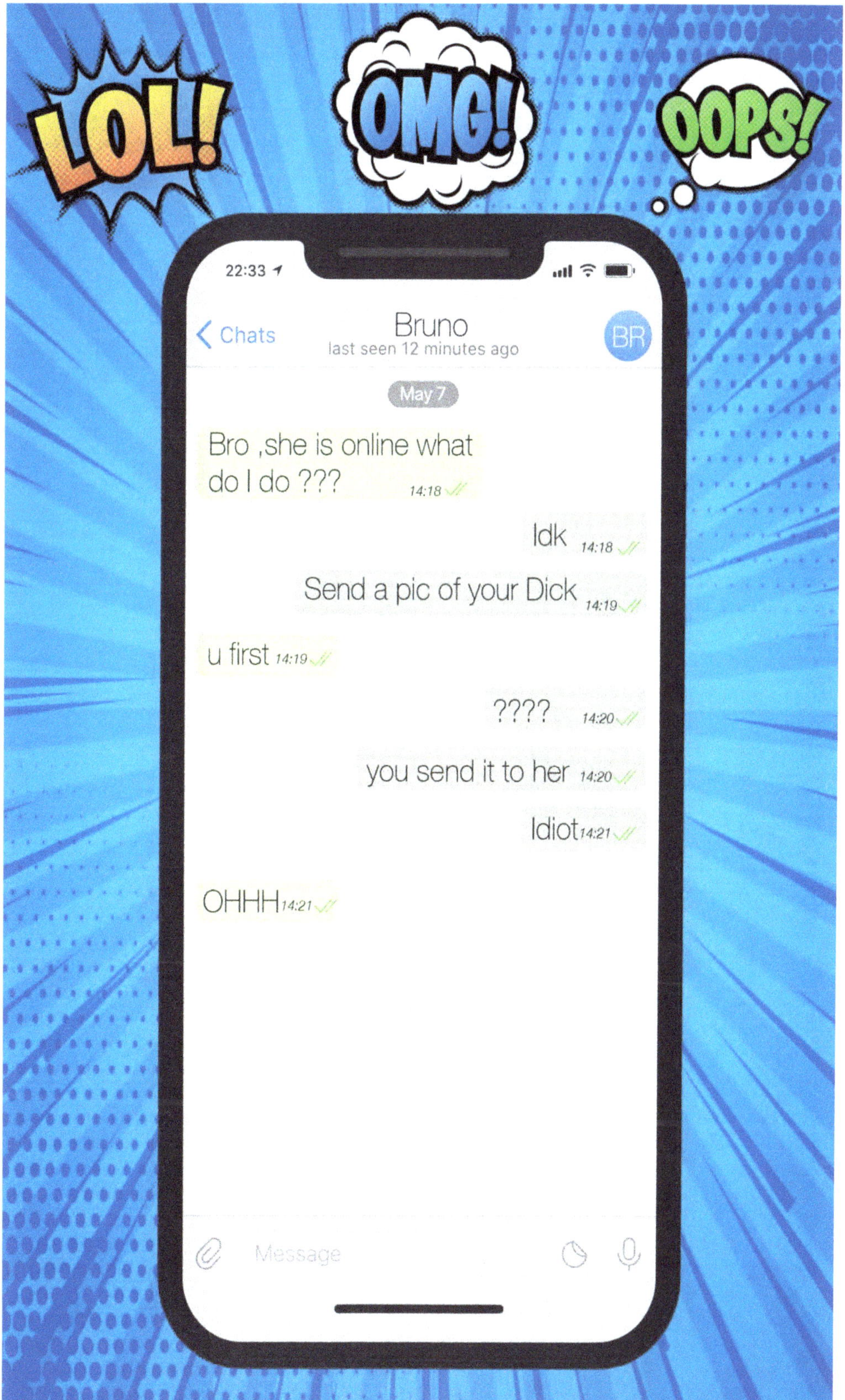
LOL!
OMG!
OOPS!
22:33
Chats
Bruno
last seen 12 minutes ago
BR
May 7
Bro ,she is online what do I do ??? 14:18
Idk 14:18
Send a pic of your Dick 14:19
u first 14:19
???? 14:20
you send it to her 14:20
Idiot 14:21
OHHH 14:21
Message

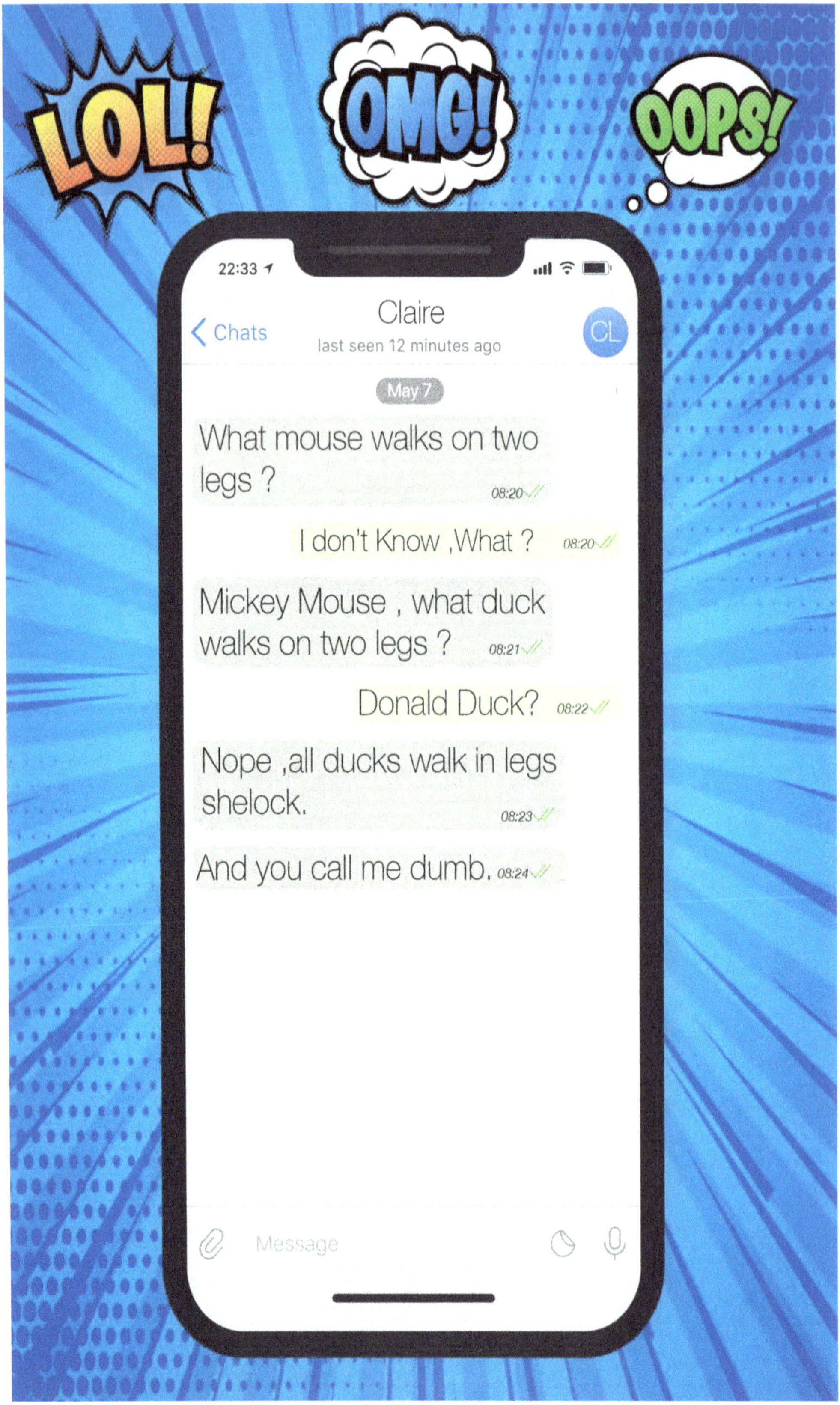
LOL!
OMG!
OOPS!
22:33
Chats
Claire
last seen 12 minutes ago
CL
May 7
What mouse walks on two legs ? 08:20
I don't Know ,What ? 08:20
Mickey Mouse , what duck walks on two legs ? 08:21
Donald Duck? 08:22
Nope ,all ducks walk in legs shelock. 08:23
And you call me dumb. 08:24
Message

LOL!
OMG!
OOPS!
22:33
Chats
Charlie
last seen 12 minutes ago
CH
May 7
Aww i miss you too 11:32
don't think i'm weird but i am sleeping with that shit you left in the bathroom :) 11:33
WHAT?? 11:34
yeah it smells like you and it makes me feel better when you're not here ? 11:34
If you're trying to be cute or funny it's not working 11:35
ohhhhhh myyyyy godddddddd 11:35
********* SHIRTS 11:35
Message

LOL!
OMG!
OOPS!
22:33
Chats
Anna
last seen 12 minutes ago
AN
May 7
How could you ??
I trusted you and you
cheated on me !!
10:12
Oh,sorry Dad.That was
meant for jim
10:12
Oh.
10:13
On a completely unrelated
topic, have you sen my
shotgun anywhere?
10:14
Message

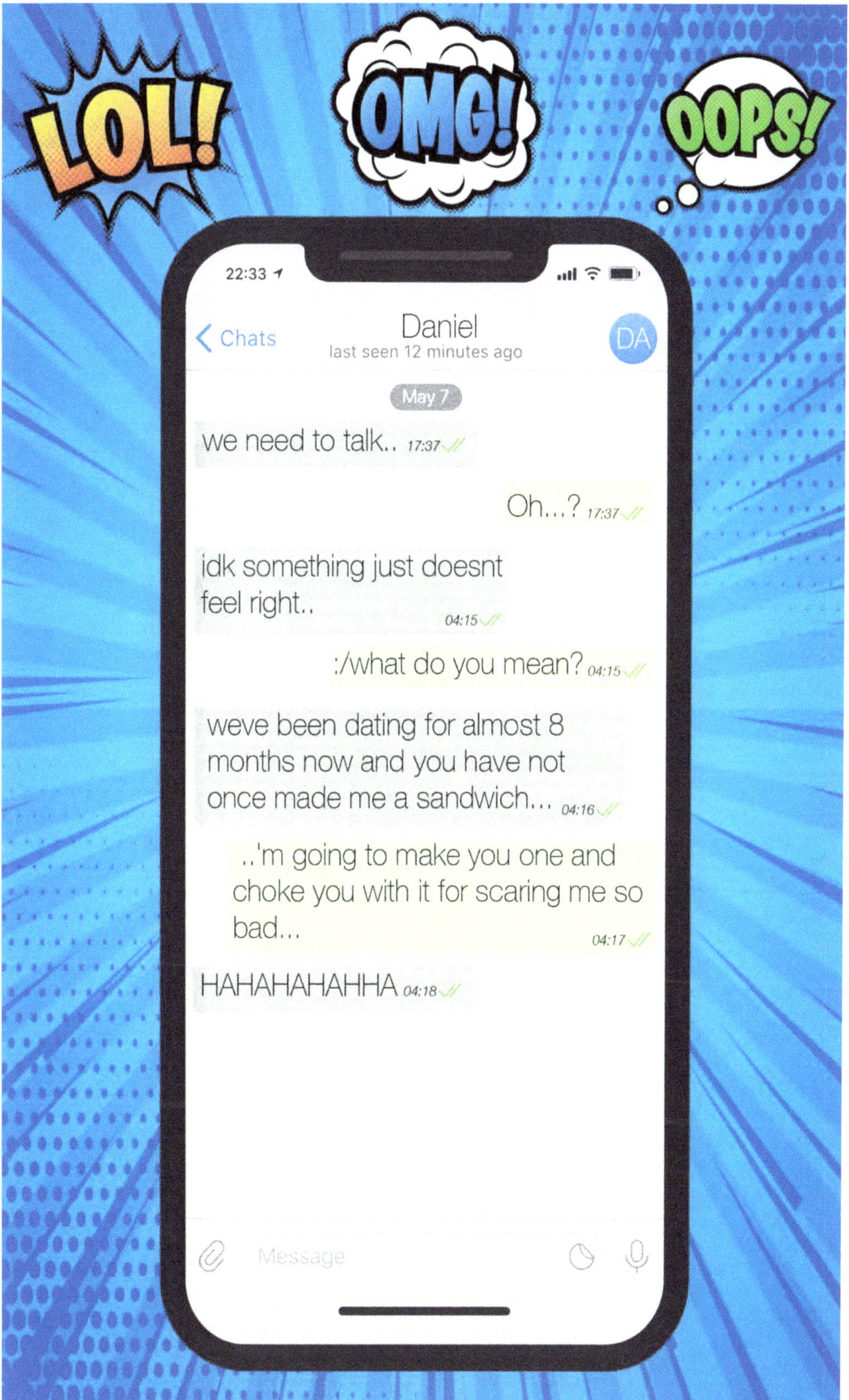
LOL!
OMG!
OOPS!
22:33
Chats
Daniel
last seen 12 minutes ago
DA
May 7
we need to talk.. 17:37
Oh...? 17:37
idk something just doesnt feel right.. 04:15
:/what do you mean? 04:15
weve been dating for almost 8 months now and you have not once made me a sandwich... 04:16
..'m going to make you one and choke you with it for scaring me so bad... 04:17
HAHAHAHAHHA 04:18
Message

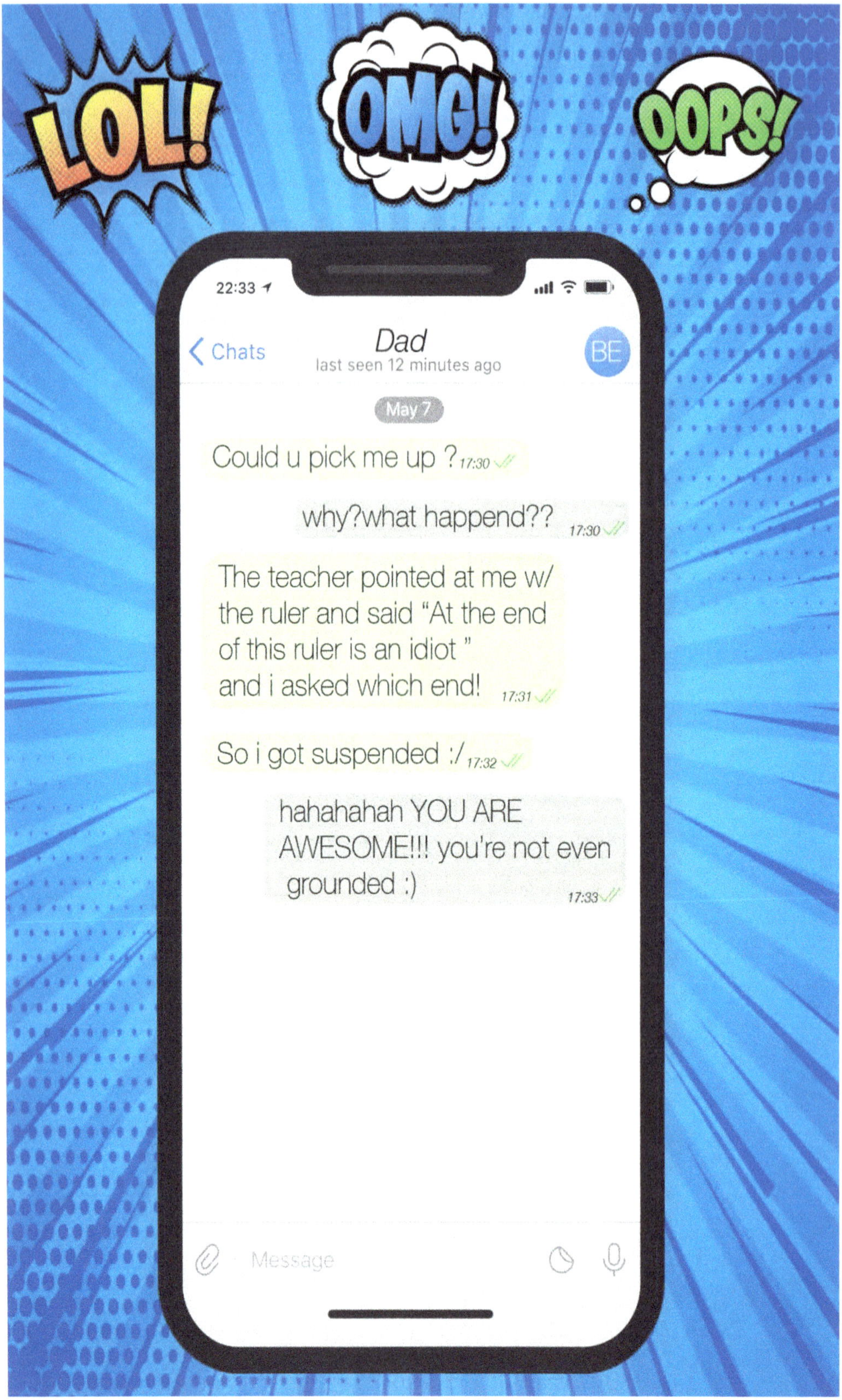
LOL!
OMG!
OOPS!
22:33
Chats
Dad
last seen 12 minutes ago
BE
May 7
Could u pick me up ? 17:30
why?what happend?? 17:30
The teacher pointed at me w/ the ruler and said "At the end of this ruler is an idiot " and i asked which end! 17:31
So i got suspended :/ 17:32
hahahahah YOU ARE AWESOME!!! you're not even grounded :) 17:33
Message

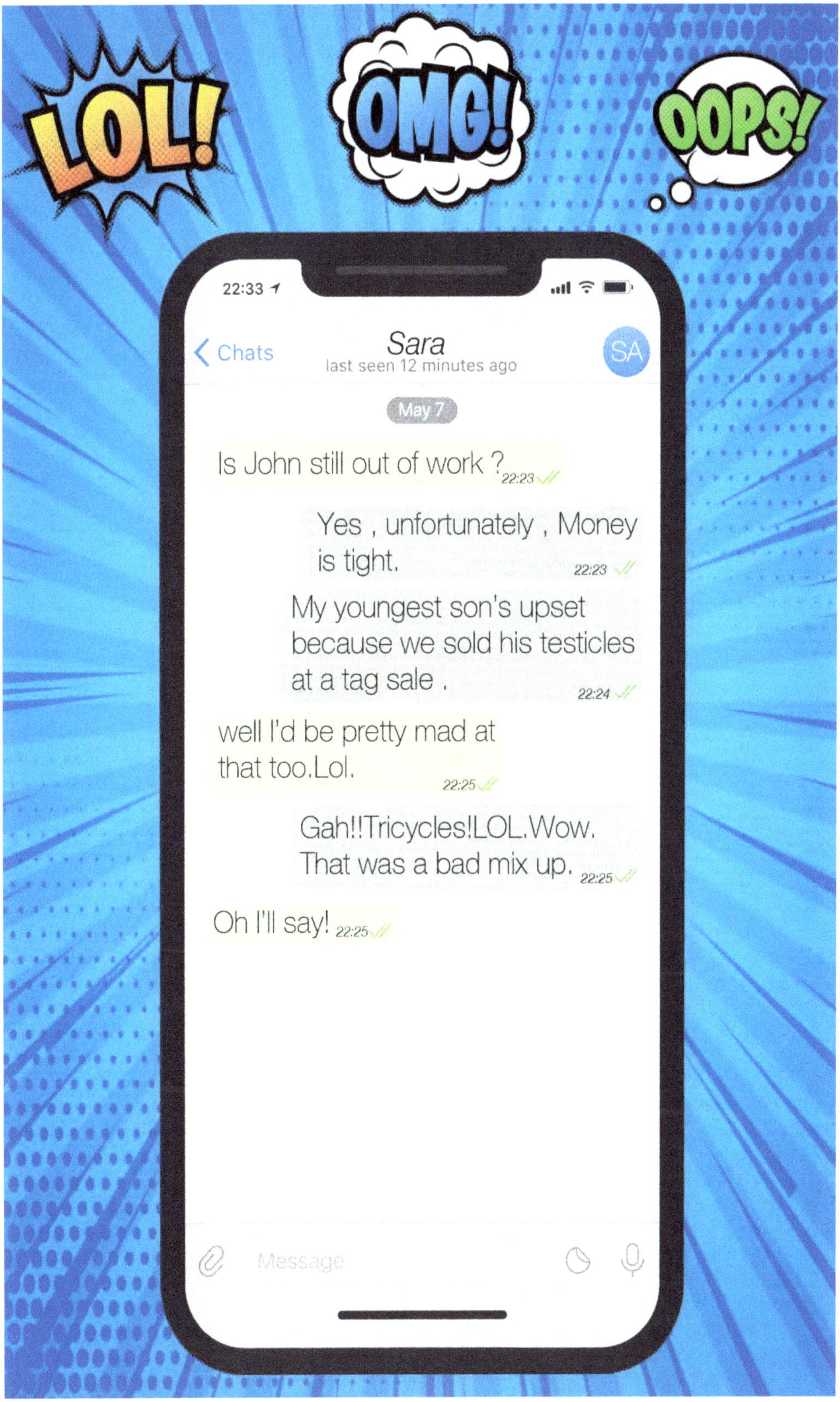
LOL!
OMG!
OOPS!
22:33
Chats
Sara
last seen 12 minutes ago
SA
May 7
Is John still out of work ? 22:23
Yes , unfortunately , Money is tight. 22:23
My youngest son's upset because we sold his testicles at a tag sale . 22:24
well I'd be pretty mad at that too.Lol. 22:25
Gah!!Tricycles!LOL.Wow. That was a bad mix up. 22:25
Oh I'll say! 22:25
Message

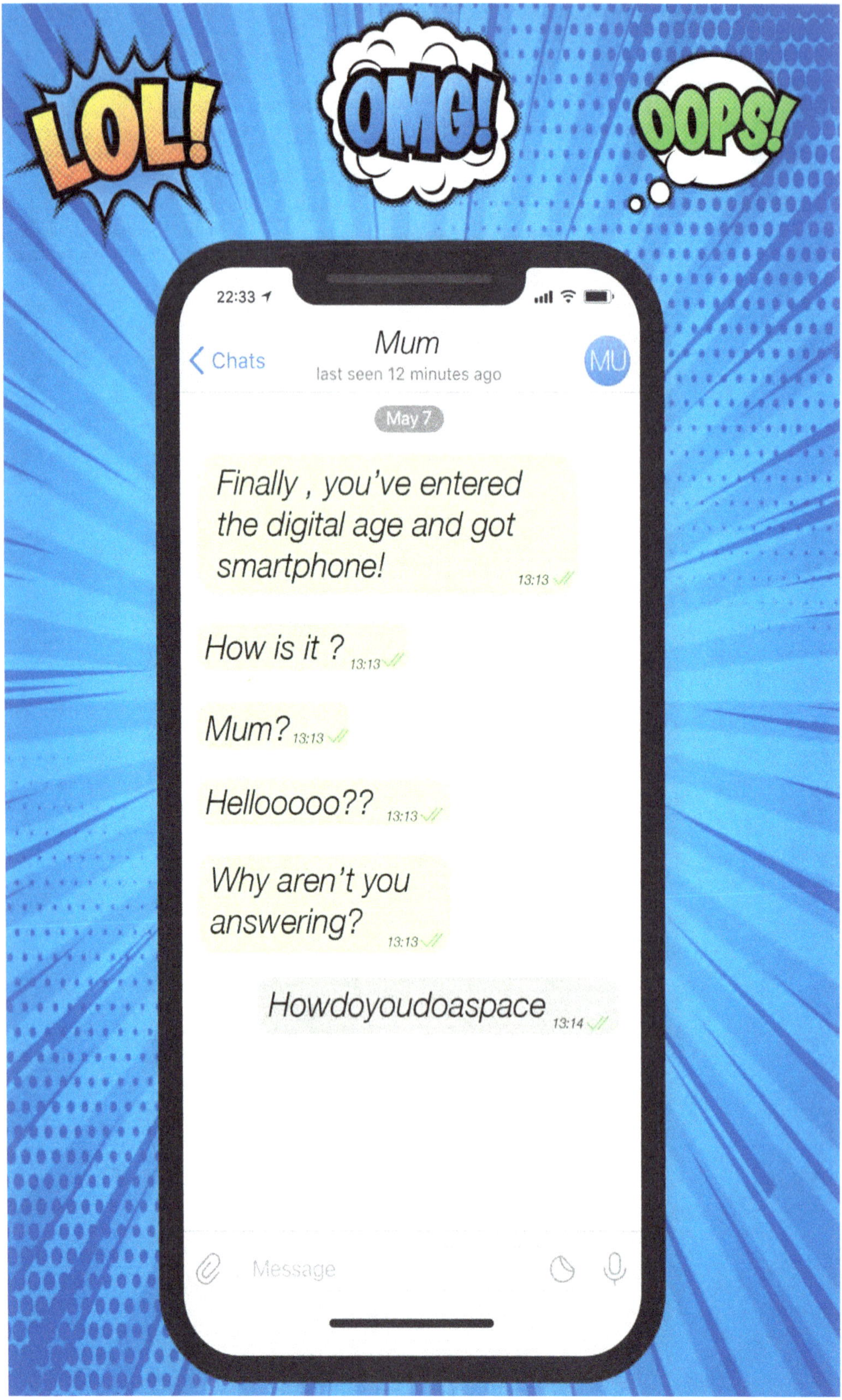
LOL!
OMG!
OOPS!
22:33
Chats
Mum
last seen 12 minutes ago
MU
May 7
Finally , you've entered the digital age and got smartphone! 13:13
How is it ? 13:13
Mum? 13:13
Hellooooo?? 13:13
Why aren't you answering? 13:13
Howdoyoudoaspace 13:14
Message

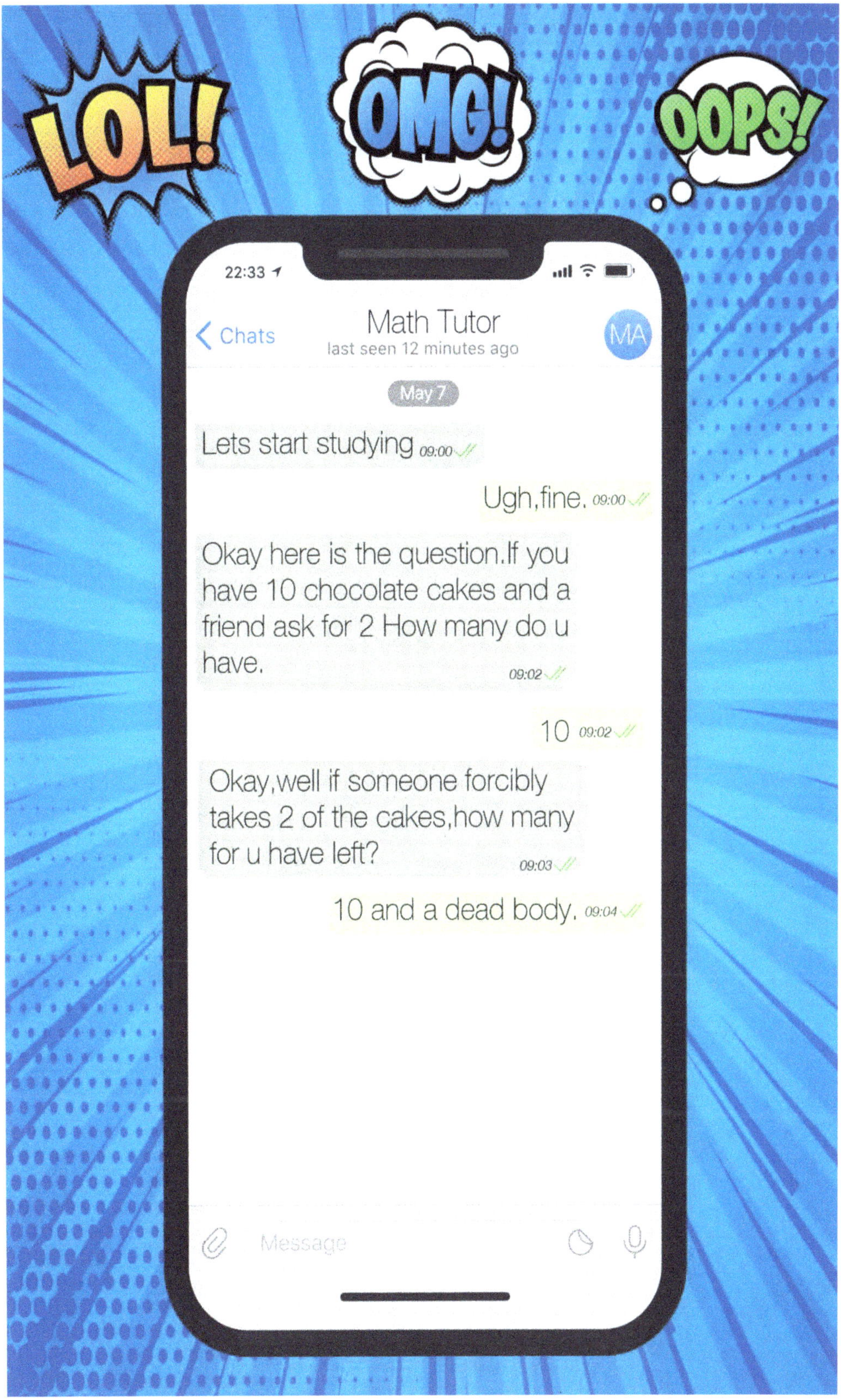
LOL!
OMG!
OOPS!
22:33
Chats
Math Tutor
last seen 12 minutes ago
MA
May 7
Lets start studying 09:00
Ugh,fine. 09:00
Okay here is the question.If you have 10 chocolate cakes and a friend ask for 2 How many do u have. 09:02
10 09:02
Okay,well if someone forcibly takes 2 of the cakes,how many for u have left? 09:03
10 and a dead body. 09:04
Message

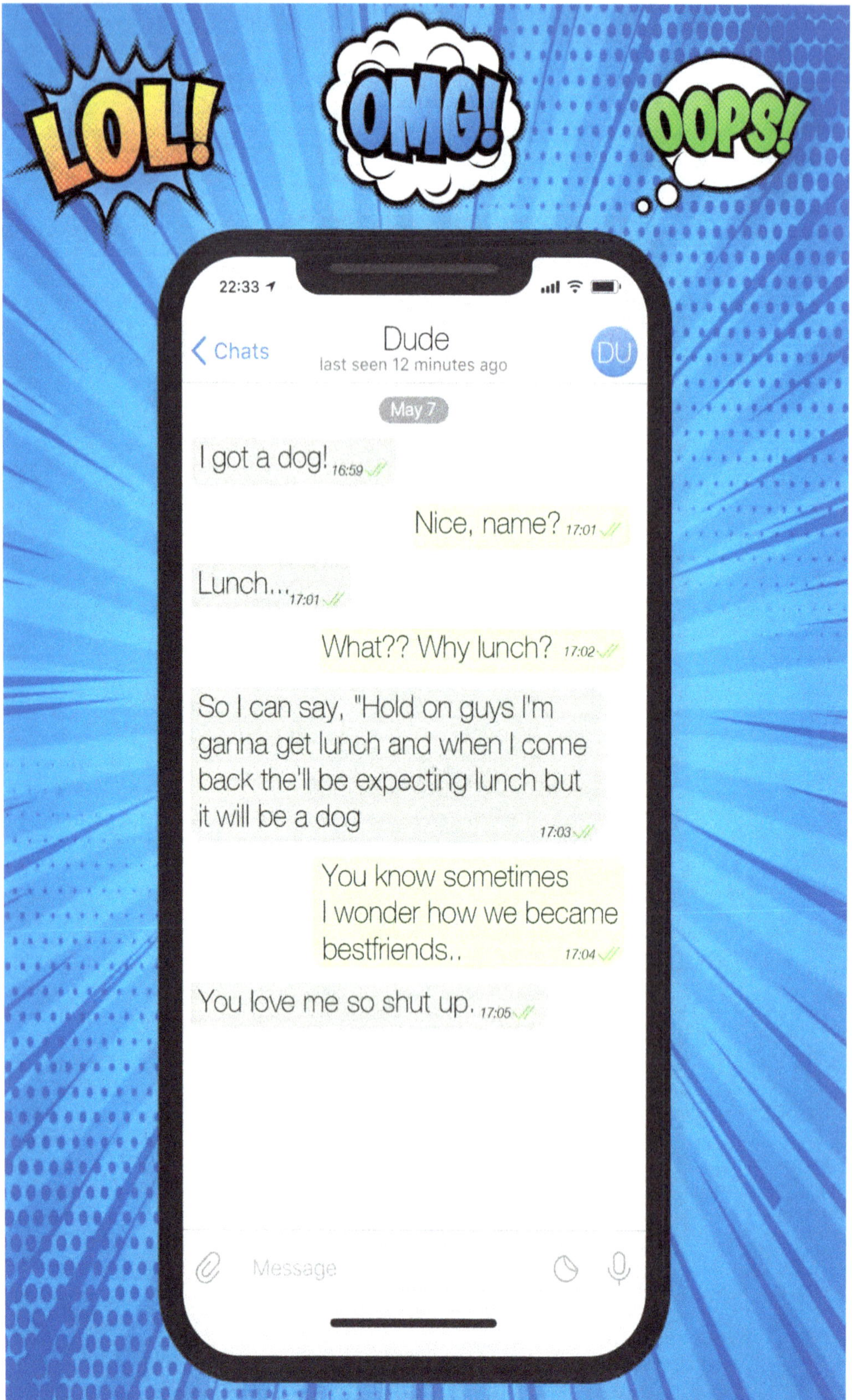
LOL!
OMG!
OOPS!
22:33
Chats
Dude
last seen 12 minutes ago
DU
May 7
I got a dog! 16:59
Nice, name? 17:01
Lunch... 17:01
What?? Why lunch? 17:02
So I can say, "Hold on guys I'm ganna get lunch and when I come back the'll be expecting lunch but it will be a dog 17:03
You know sometimes I wonder how we became bestfriends.. 17:04
You love me so shut up. 17:05
Message

LOL!
OMG!
OOPS!
22:33
Chats
David
last seen 12 minutes ago
DA
May 7
Hey what are you up to ? 02:57
Just finished Masturbating .
it makes me feel so relaxing so
i can go to sleep easier. 02:57
Awkward. 02:58
Shit , I meant menstruating 02:58
Not any less awkward 02:59
OMFG I meant meditating !
What is wrong with us phone. 02:59
Message

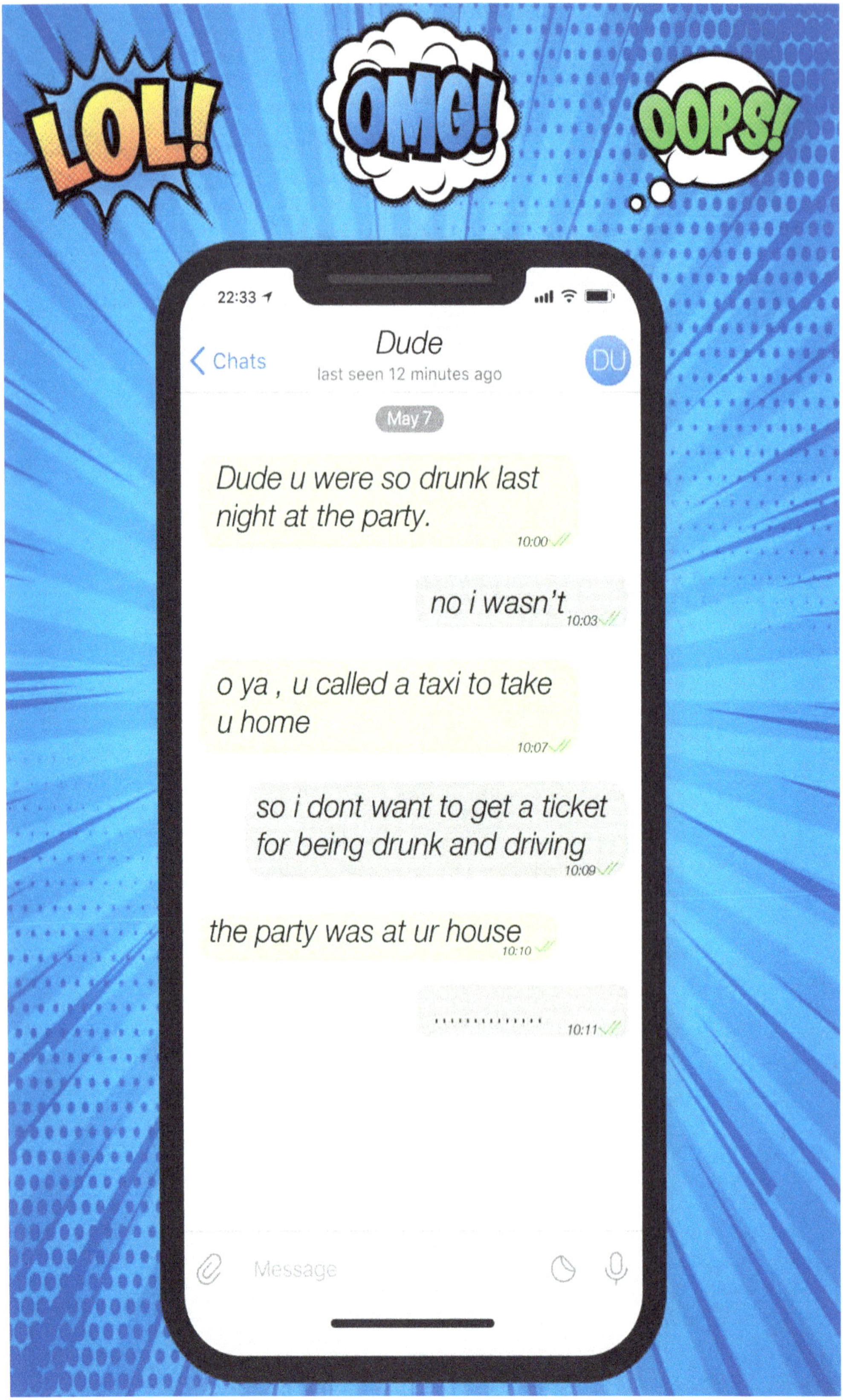
LOL!
OMG!
OOPS!
22:33
Chats
Dude
last seen 12 minutes ago
DU
May 7
Dude u were so drunk last night at the party.
10:00
no i wasn't
10:03
o ya , u called a taxi to take u home
10:07
so i dont want to get a ticket for being drunk and driving
10:09
the party was at ur house
10:10
....
10:11
Message

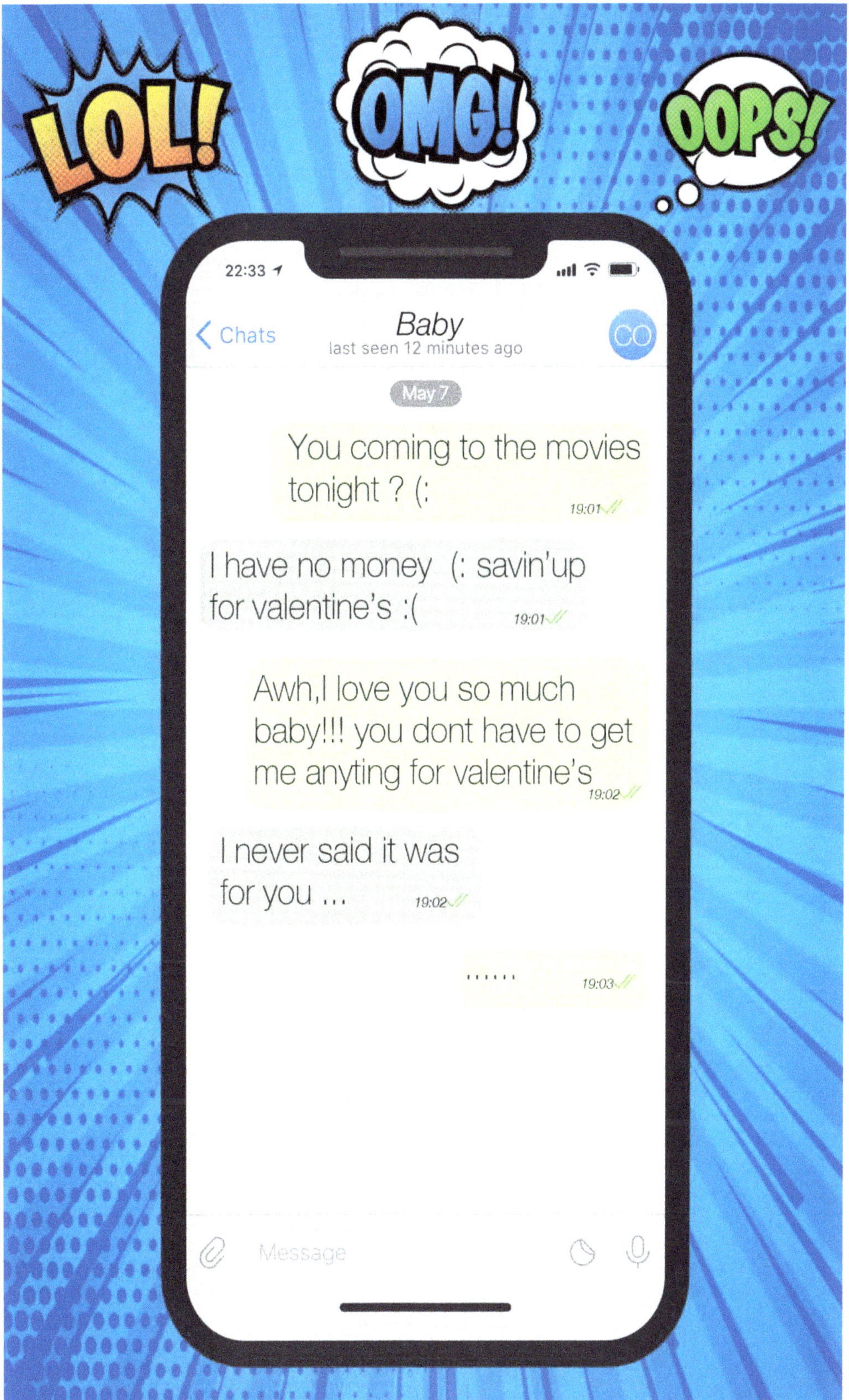

LOL!
OMG!
OOPS!
22:33
Chats
Baby
last seen 12 minutes ago
CO
May 7
You coming to the movies tonight ? (:
19:01
I have no money (: savin'up for valentine's :(
19:01
Awh,I love you so much baby!!! you dont have to get me anyting for valentine's
19:02
I never said it was for you ...
19:02
......
19:03
Message

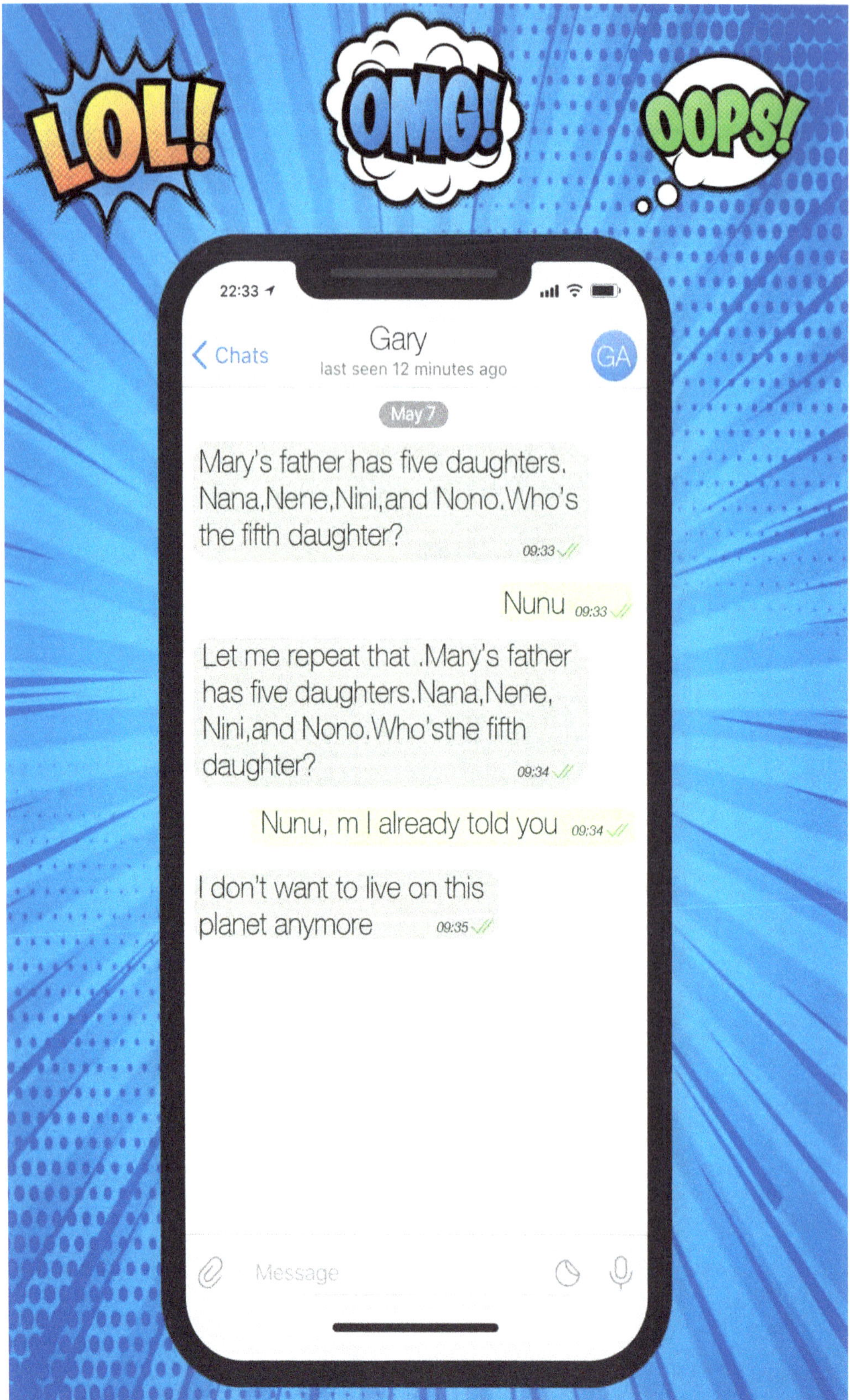
LOL!
OMG!
OOPS!
22:33
Chats
Gary
last seen 12 minutes ago
GA
May 7
Mary's father has five daughters. Nana,Nene,Nini,and Nono.Who's the fifth daughter? 09:33
Nunu 09:33
Let me repeat that .Mary's father has five daughters.Nana,Nene, Nini,and Nono.Who'sthe fifth daughter? 09:34
Nunu, m I already told you 09:34
I don't want to live on this planet anymore 09:35
Message

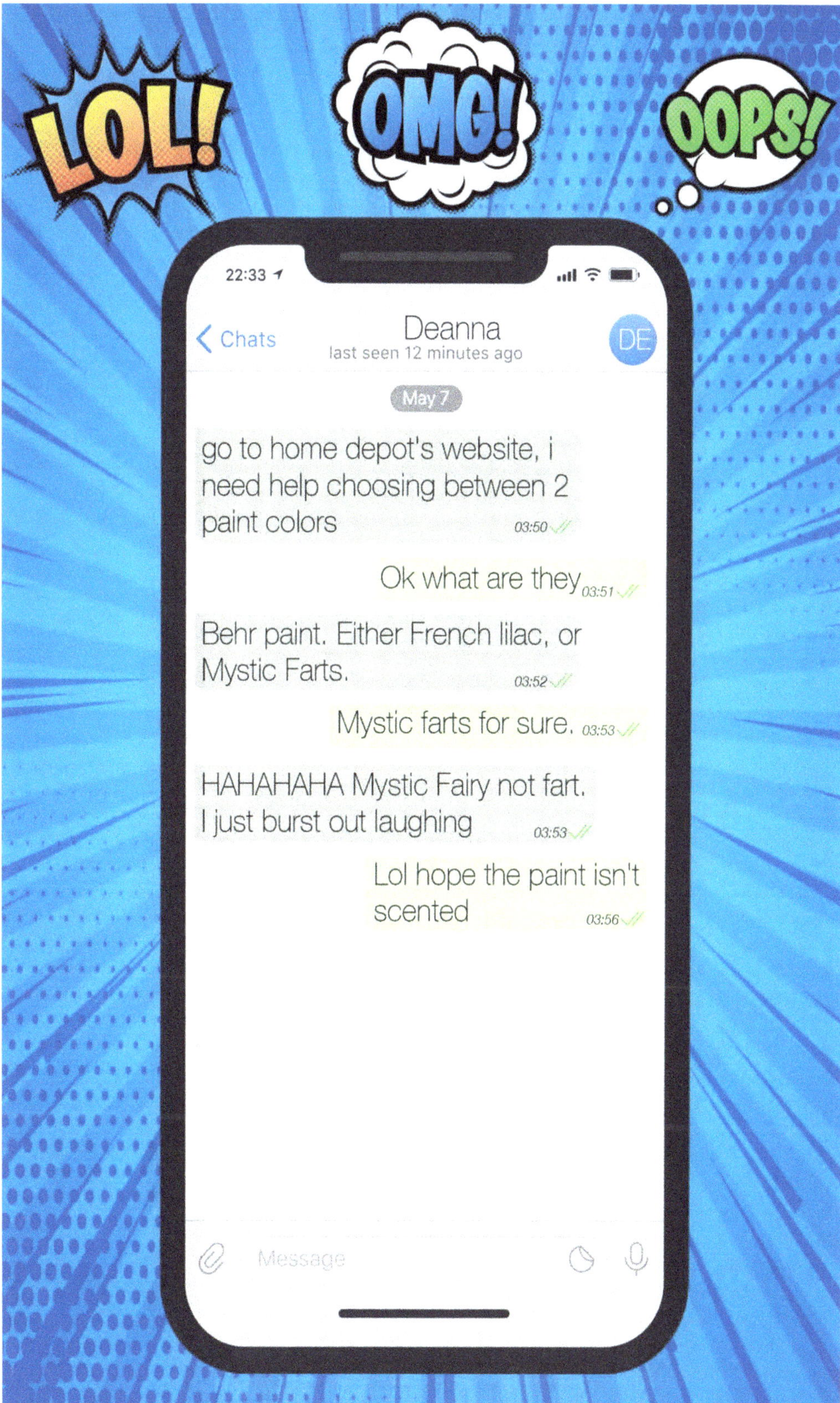
LOL!
OMG!
OOPS!
22:33
Chats
Deanna
last seen 12 minutes ago
DE
May 7
go to home depot's website, i need help choosing between 2 paint colors 03:50
Ok what are they 03:51
Behr paint. Either French lilac, or Mystic Farts. 03:52
Mystic farts for sure. 03:53
HAHAHAHA Mystic Fairy not fart. I just burst out laughing 03:53
Lol hope the paint isn't scented 03:56
Message

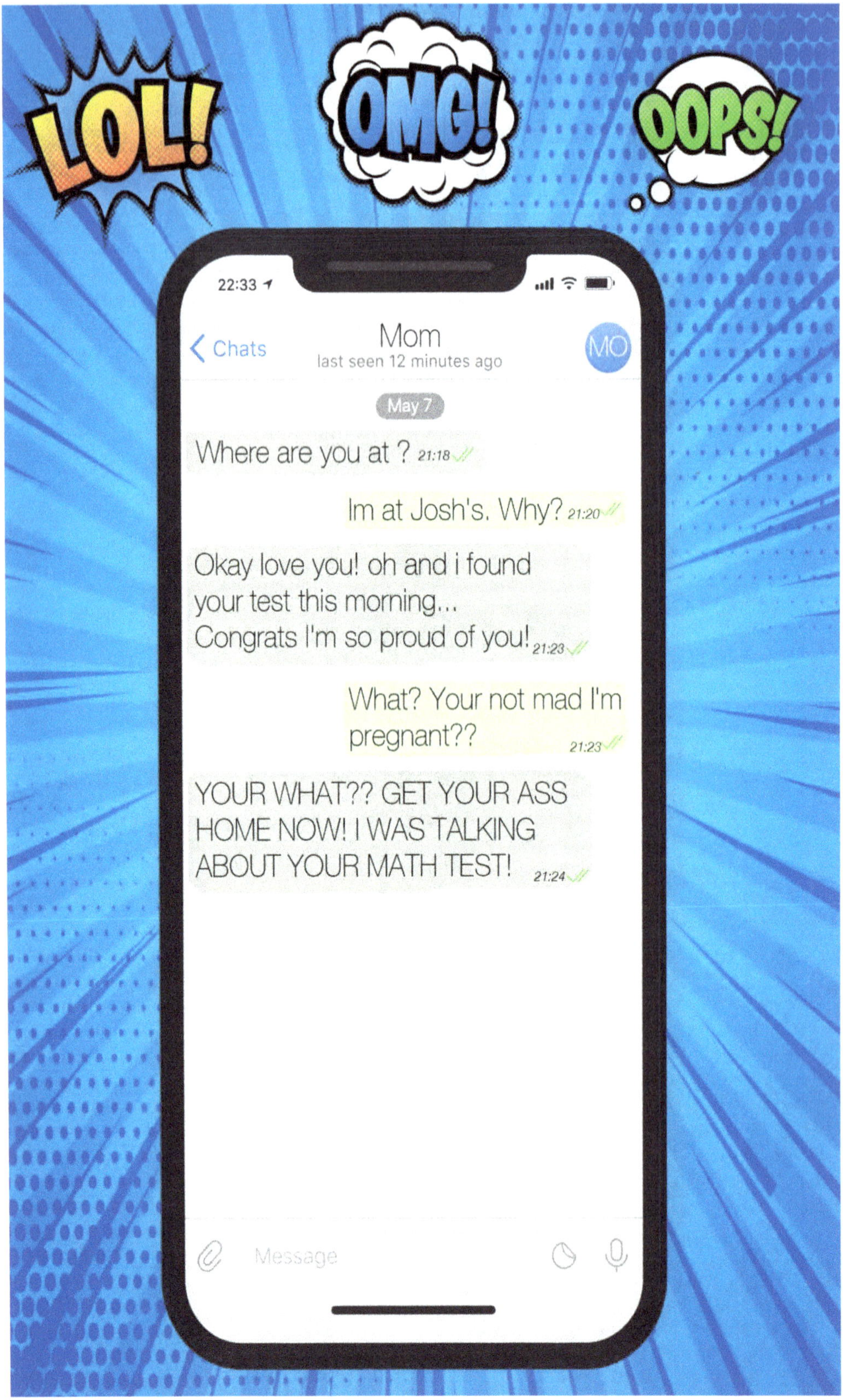
LOL!
OMG!
OOPS!
22:33
Chats
Mom
last seen 12 minutes ago
MO
May 7
Where are you at ? 21:18
Im at Josh's. Why? 21:20
Okay love you! oh and i found your test this morning... Congrats I'm so proud of you! 21:23
What? Your not mad I'm pregnant?? 21:23
YOUR WHAT?? GET YOUR ASS HOME NOW! I WAS TALKING ABOUT YOUR MATH TEST! 21:24
Message

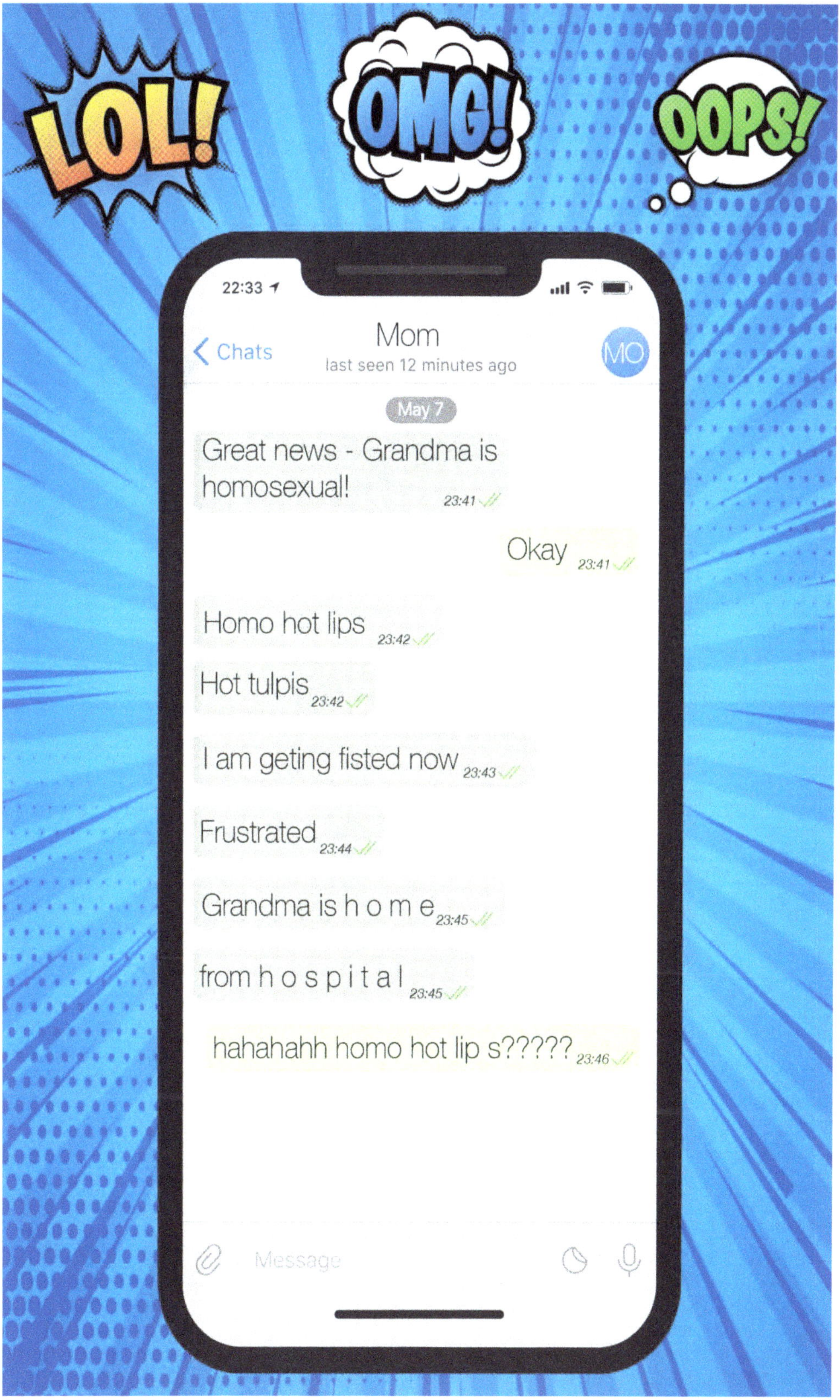
LOL!
OMG!
OOPS!
22:33
Chats
Mom
last seen 12 minutes ago
MO
May 7
Great news - Grandma is homosexual! 23:41
Okay 23:41
Homo hot lips 23:42
Hot tulpis 23:42
I am geting fisted now 23:43
Frustrated 23:44
Grandma is h o m e 23:45
from h o s p i t a l 23:45
hahahahh homo hot lip s????? 23:46
Message

LOL!
OMG!
OOPS!
22:33
Chats
Mom
last seen 12 minutes ago
MO
May 7
Hi Bridget I space space space space how space are space you space doing period capital eye love this new phone exclamation point 20:18
I see youre using voice text. You don't have to say space mom it does it for you 20:20
I cucumber letter pea Ritalin 20:20
What? Mom stop just type 20:21
Message

LOL!
OMG!
OOPS!
22:33
Chats
Disha
last seen 12 minutes ago
DI
May 7
boys are the best 02:55
no girls r best 02:55
they are the toppers in every exam 02:55
Google,Microsoft,Facebook, Apple are owned by boys 02:55
What girls do even after doing top in exams.? 02:56
They gave birth to these legends 02:57
Message

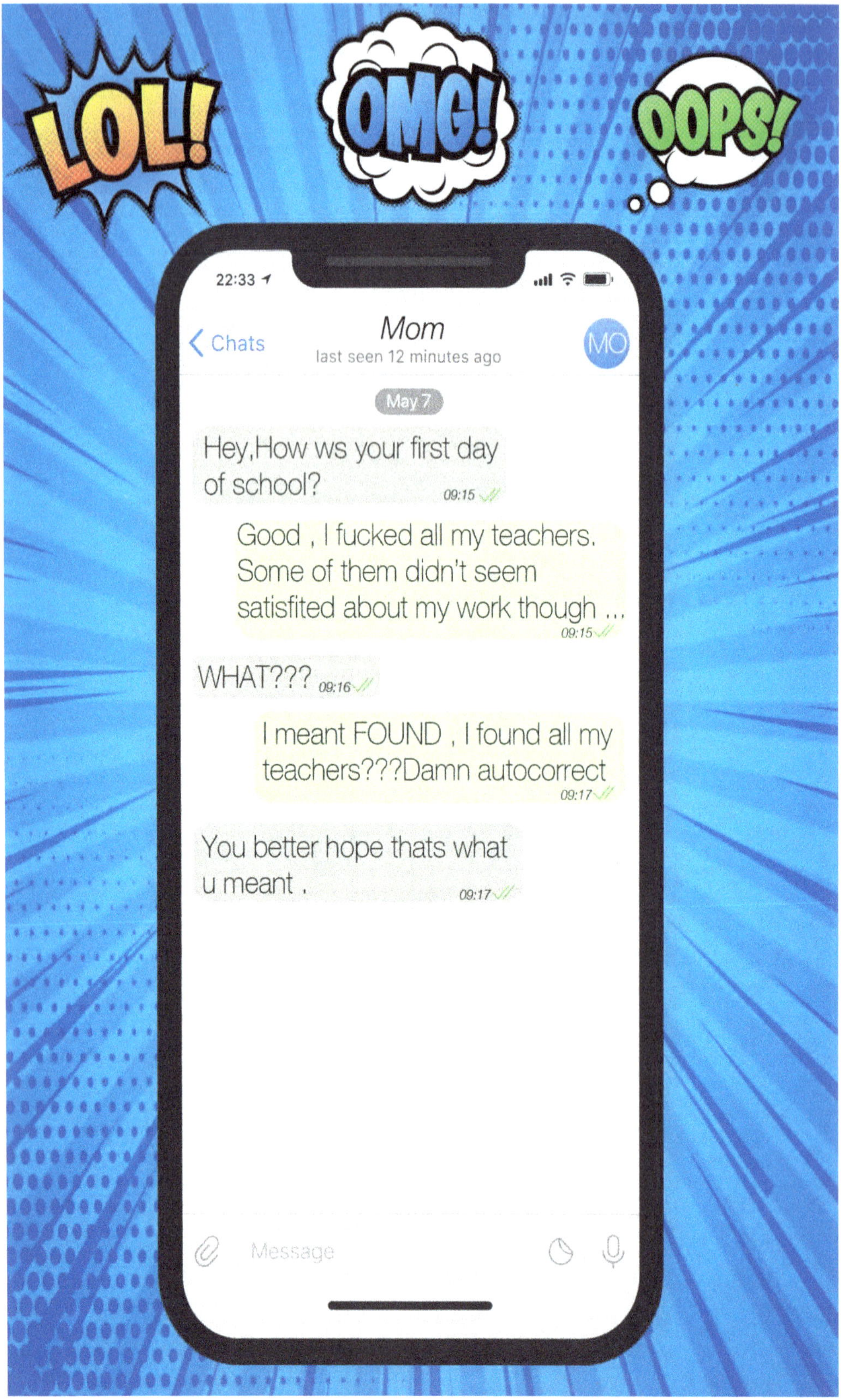
LOL!
OMG!
OOPS!
22:33
Chats
Mom
last seen 12 minutes ago
MO
May 7
Hey,How ws your first day of school? 09:15
Good , I fucked all my teachers. Some of them didn't seem satisfited about my work though ... 09:15
WHAT??? 09:16
I meant FOUND , I found all my teachers???Damn autocorrect 09:17
You better hope thats what u meant . 09:17
Message

LOL!
OMG!
OOPS!
22:33
Chats
Babe
last seen 12 minutes ago
BA
May 7
Hey baby! Sorry for whathappened this morning 14:44
Hi! This is Ashley's dad. You might want to run 14:45
Why? 14:45
Because she just left the house with a baseball bat 14:46
OMG thank you. It was nice knowing you 14:46
No problem. Nice knowing you too son 14:47
Message

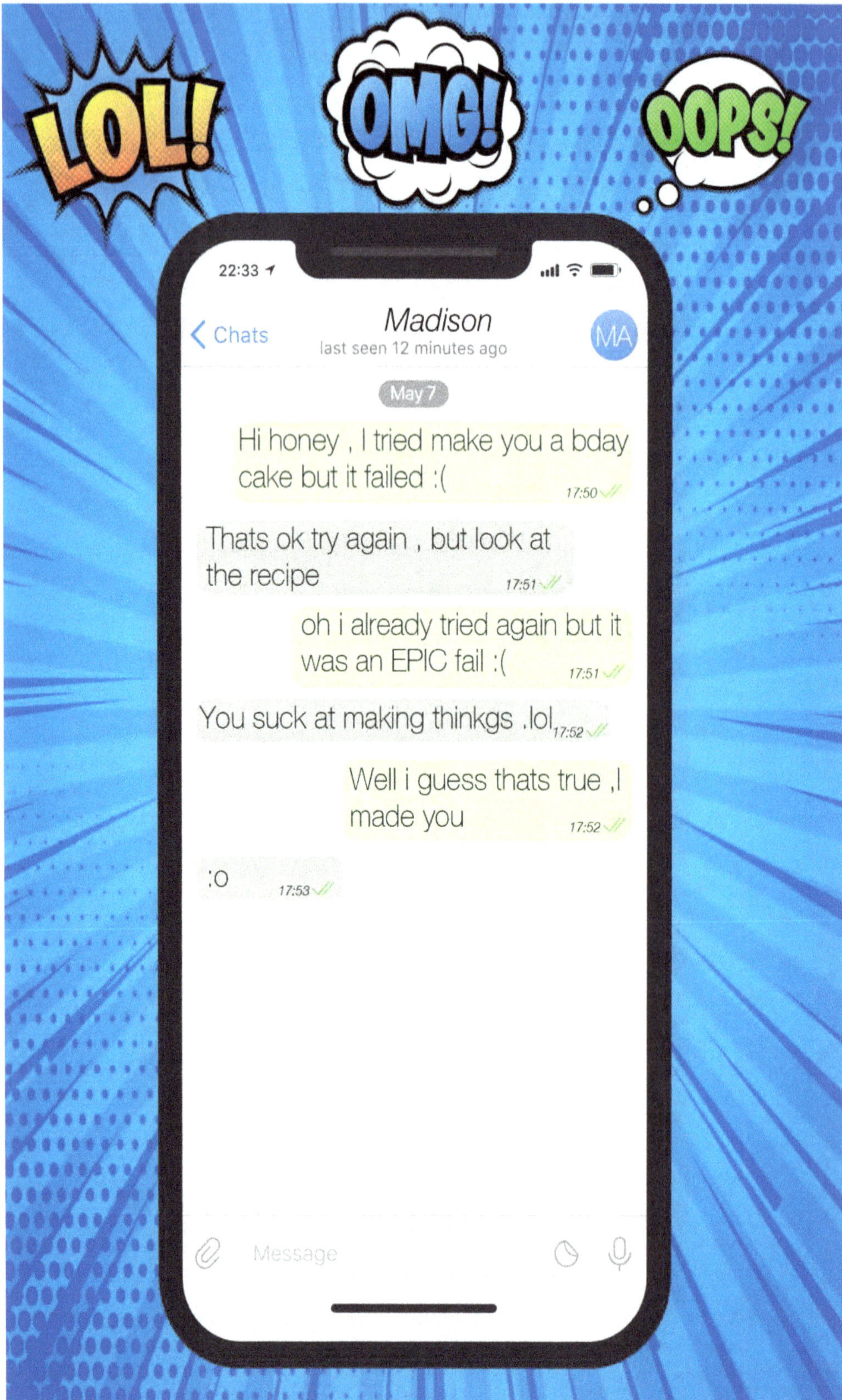
LOL!
OMG!
OOPS!
22:33
Chats
Madison
last seen 12 minutes ago
MA
May 7
Hi honey , I tried make you a bday cake but it failed :(17:50
Thats ok try again , but look at the recipe 17:51
oh i already tried again but it was an EPIC fail :(17:51
You suck at making thinkgs .lol 17:52
Well i guess thats true ,I made you 17:52
:o 17:53
Message

LOL!
OMG!
OOPS!
22:33
Chats
Lauren
last seen 12 minutes ago
LA
May 7
Do you want to bang tonight? 20:12
I meant hang.Duck auto cucumber. 20:13
God donut 20:14
How the duck do I turn this off? 20:15
It's painful watching you struggle man . 20:16
Message

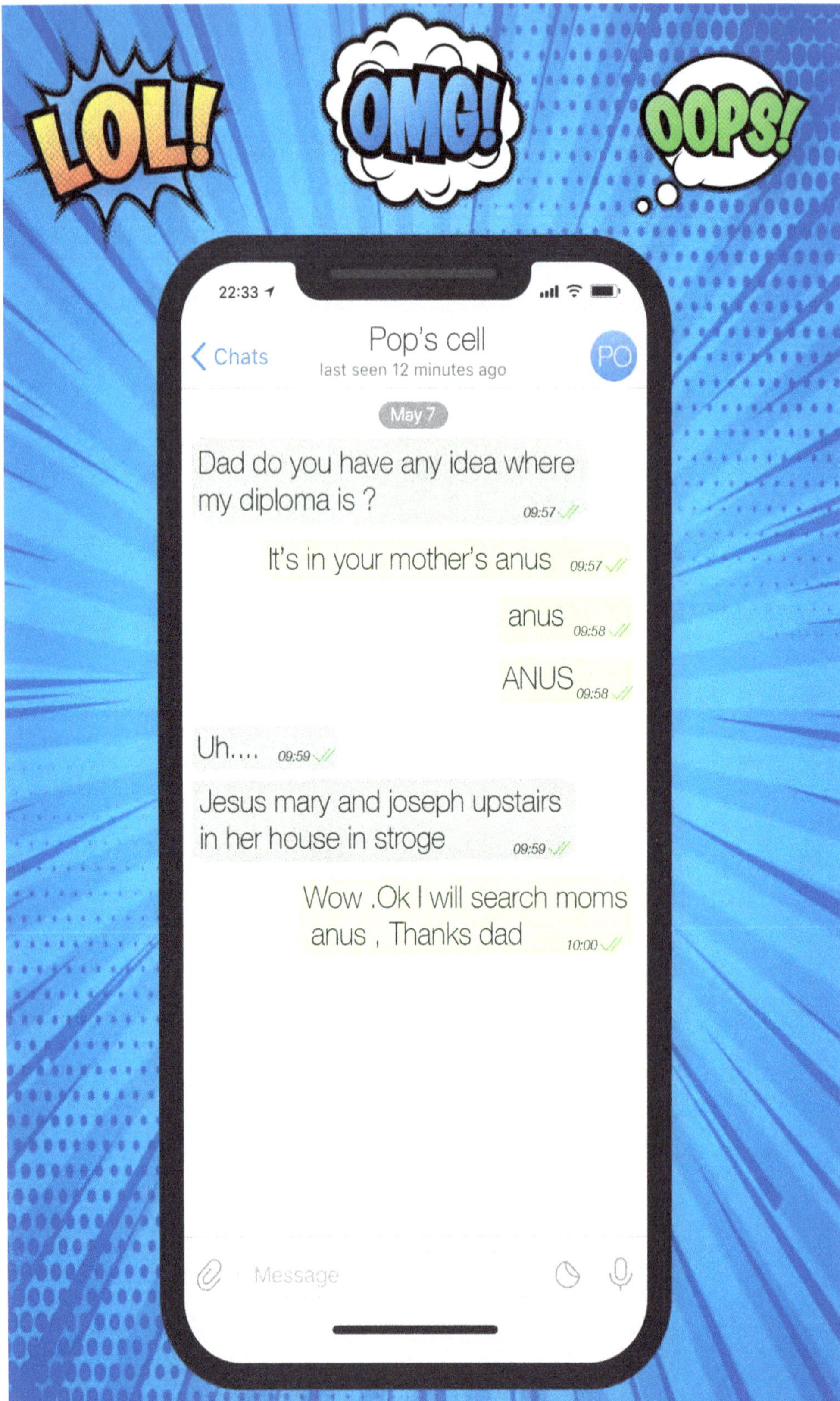
LOL!
OMG!
OOPS!
22:33
Chats
Pop's cell
last seen 12 minutes ago
PO
May 7
Dad do you have any idea where my diploma is ? 09:57
It's in your mother's anus 09:57
anus 09:58
ANUS 09:58
Uh.... 09:59
Jesus mary and joseph upstairs in her house in stroge 09:59
Wow .Ok I will search moms anus , Thanks dad 10:00
Message

LOL!
OMG!
OOPS!
22:33
Chats
Julia
last seen 12 minutes ago
JU
May 7
How did Emily break her finger ? 20:12
Her finger got stuck in my butthole 20:13
WHATTT?! 20:13
Holyshit.My buckle.Belt buckle 20:14
That is the funniest thing I have heard ALL day! 20:15
Message

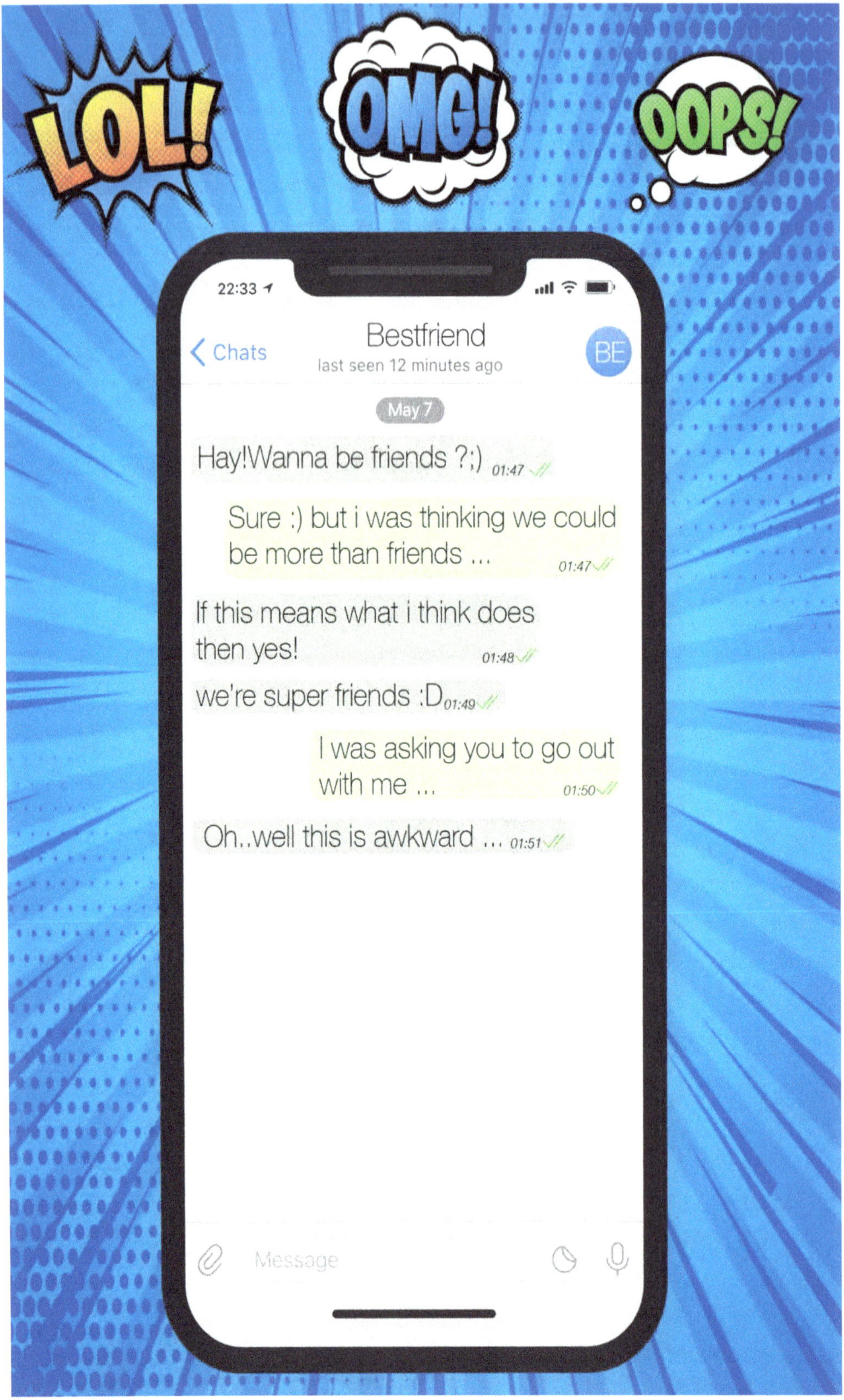
LOL!
OMG!
OOPS!
22:33
Chats
Bestfriend
last seen 12 minutes ago
BE
May 7
Hay!Wanna be friends ?;) 01:47
Sure :) but i was thinking we could be more than friends ... 01:47
If this means what i think does then yes! 01:48
we're super friends :D 01:49
I was asking you to go out with me ... 01:50
Oh..well this is awkward ... 01:51
Message

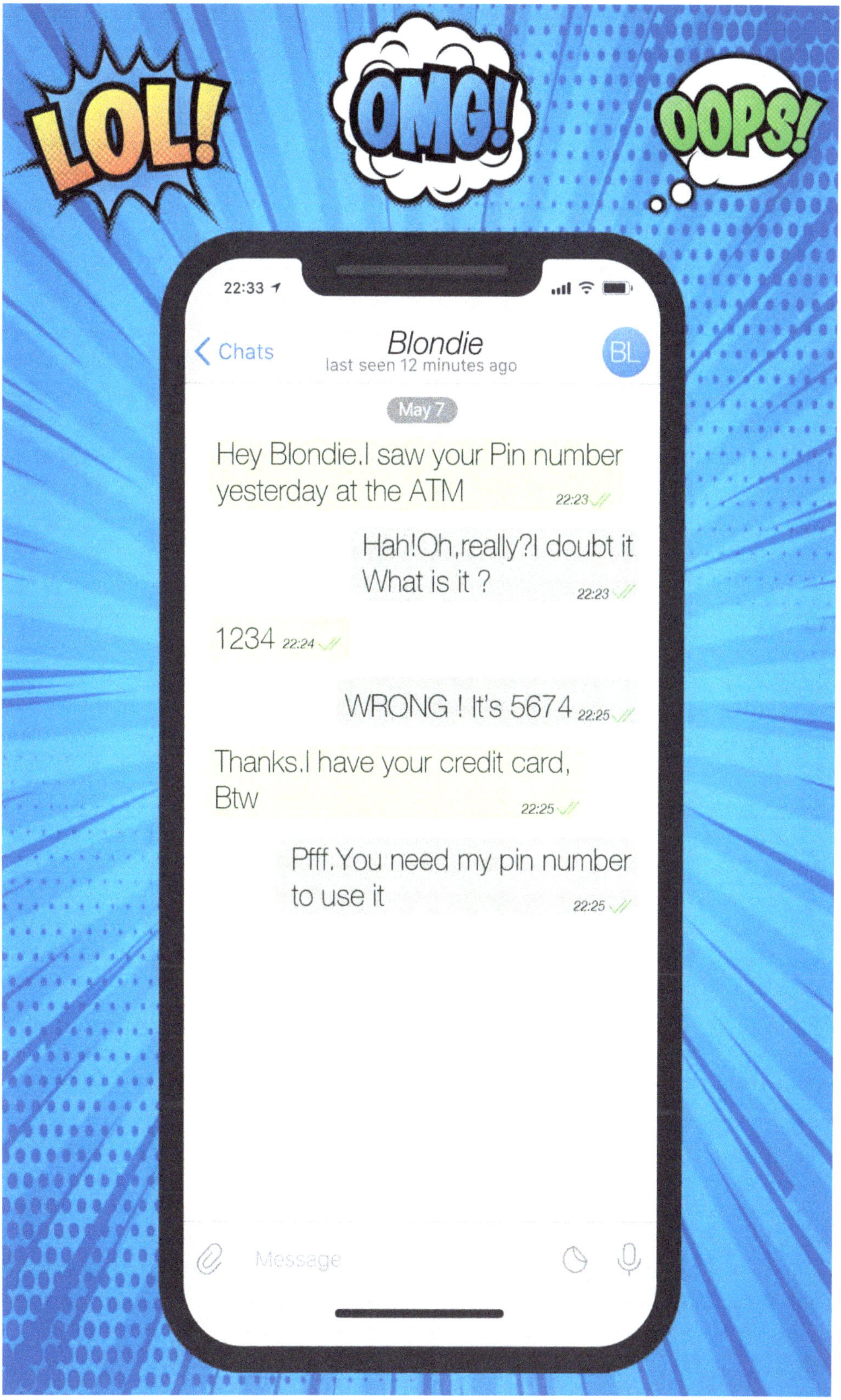
LOL!
OMG!
OOPS!
22:33
Chats
Blondie
last seen 12 minutes ago
BL
May 7
Hey Blondie.I saw your Pin number yesterday at the ATM 22:23
Hah!Oh,really?I doubt it What is it ? 22:23
1234 22:24
WRONG ! It's 5674 22:25
Thanks.I have your credit card, Btw 22:25
Pfff.You need my pin number to use it 22:25
Message

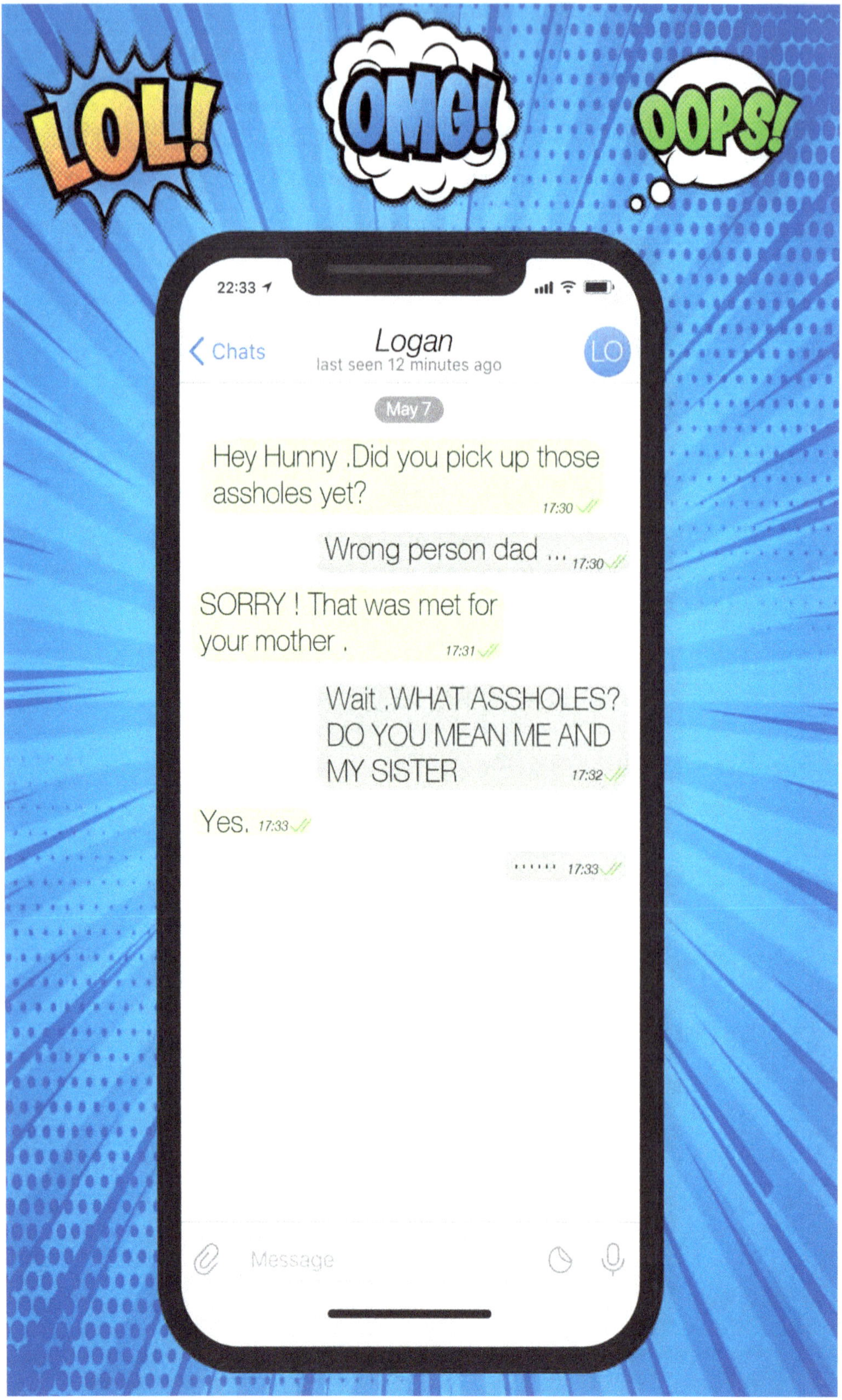

LOL!
OMG!
OOPS!
22:33
Chats
Logan
last seen 12 minutes ago
LO
May 7
Hey Hunny .Did you pick up those assholes yet? 17:30
Wrong person dad ... 17:30
SORRY ! That was met for your mother . 17:31
Wait .WHAT ASSHOLES? DO YOU MEAN ME AND MY SISTER 17:32
Yes. 17:33
.... 17:33
Message

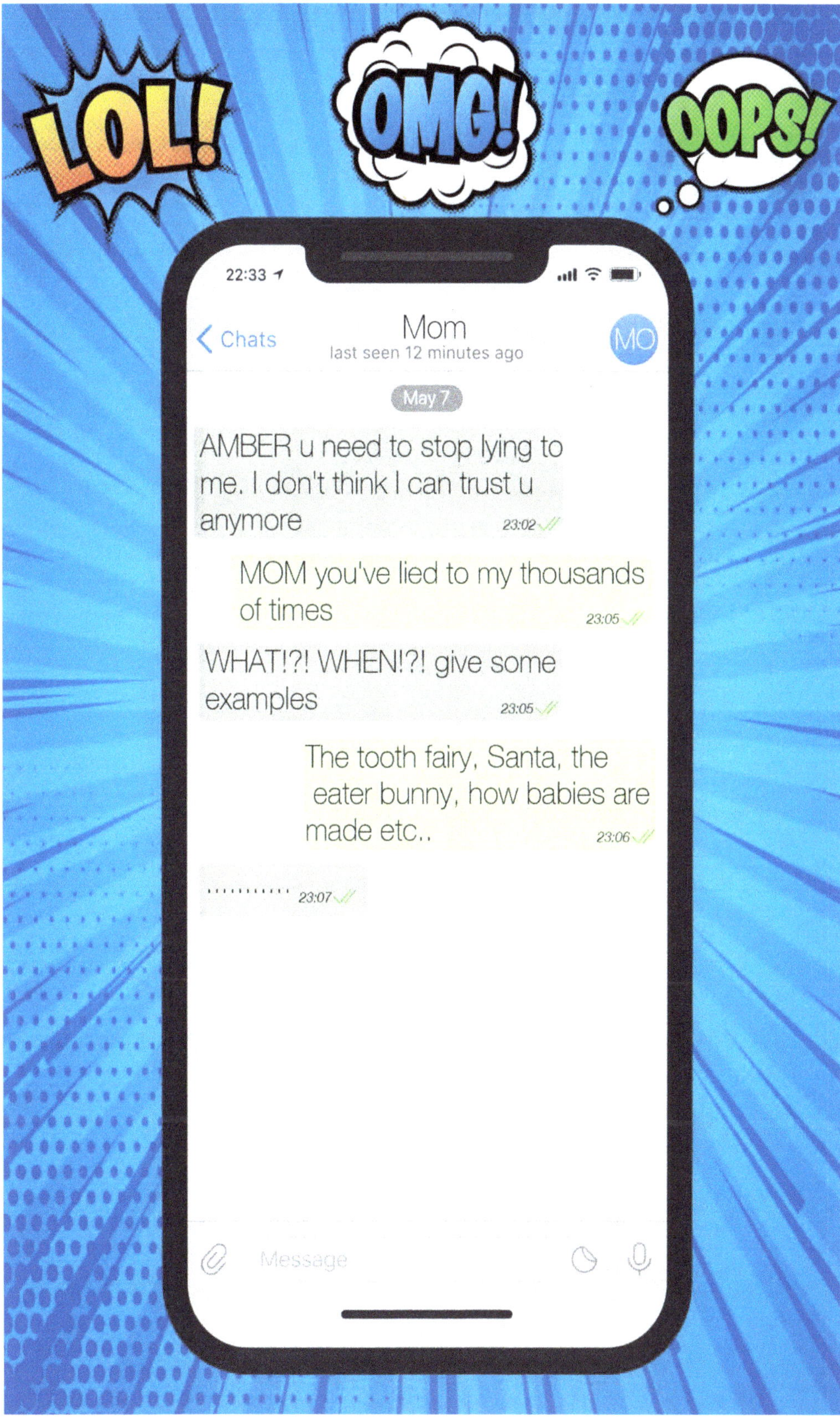
LOL!
OMG!
OOPS!
22:33
Chats
Mom
last seen 12 minutes ago
MO
May 7
AMBER u need to stop lying to me. I don't think I can trust u anymore 23:02
MOM you've lied to my thousands of times 23:05
WHAT!?! WHEN!?! give some examples 23:05
The tooth fairy, Santa, the eater bunny, how babies are made etc.. 23:06
.... 23:07
Message

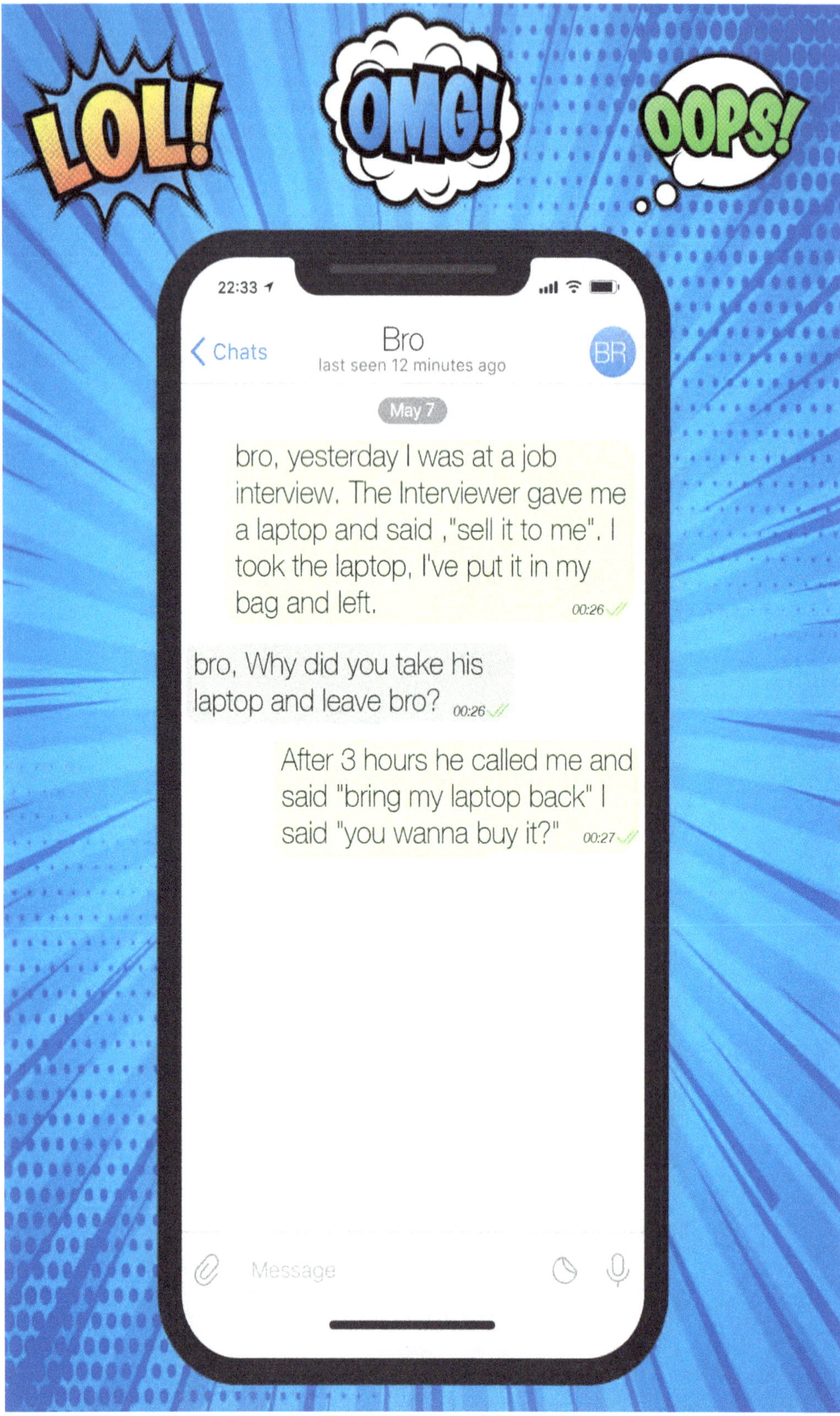

LOL!
OMG!
OOPS!
22:33
Chats
Bro
last seen 12 minutes ago
BR
May 7
bro, yesterday I was at a job interview. The Interviewer gave me a laptop and said ,"sell it to me". I took the laptop, I've put it in my bag and left. 00:26
bro, Why did you take his laptop and leave bro? 00:26
After 3 hours he called me and said "bring my laptop back" I said "you wanna buy it?" 00:27
Message

LOL!
OMG!
OOPS!
22:33
Chats
Benjamin
last seen 12 minutes ago
BE
May 7
Don't come home me and your mon are getting it on tonight 17:30
HAHAH gotta hate autocorrect , right? 17:30
What do you mean 17:31
You made a typo right .... look at your last text. 17:31
No i did not make a typo 17:32
.... 17:33
Message

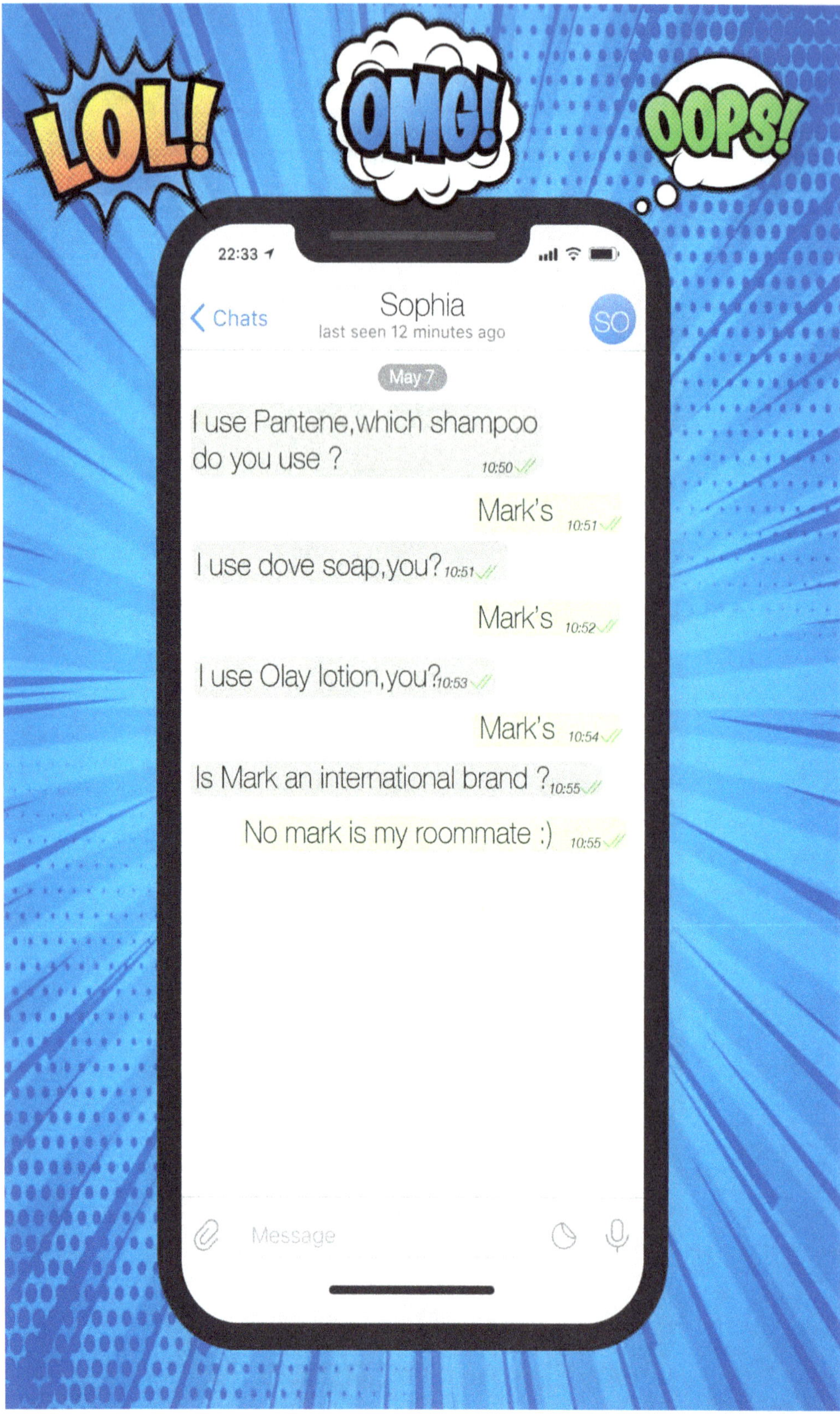
LOL!
OMG!
OOPS!
22:33
Chats
Sophia
last seen 12 minutes ago
SO
May 7
I use Pantene,which shampoo do you use ? 10:50
Mark's 10:51
I use dove soap,you? 10:51
Mark's 10:52
I use Olay lotion,you? 10:53
Mark's 10:54
Is Mark an international brand ? 10:55
No mark is my roommate :) 10:55
Message

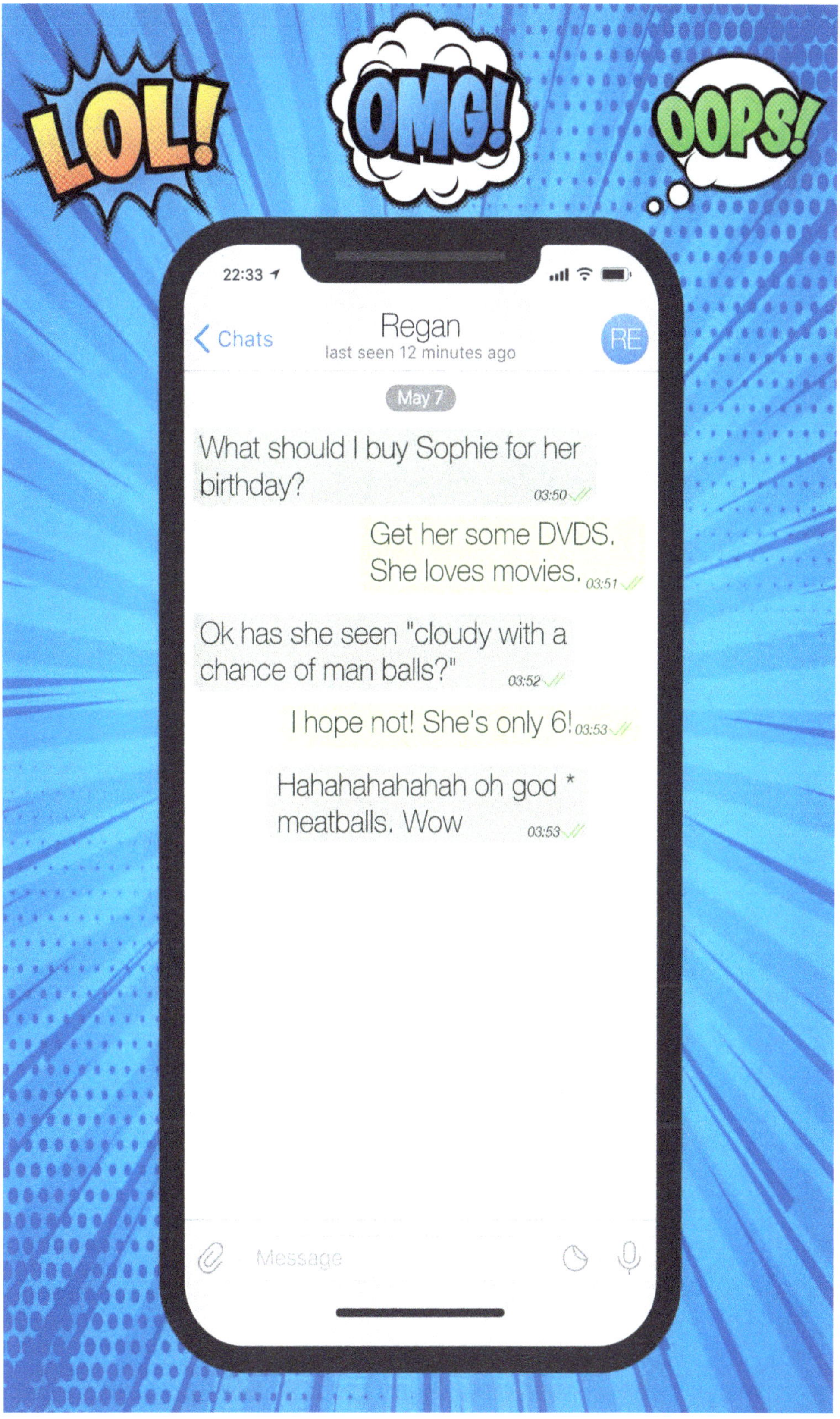
LOL!
OMG!
OOPS!
22:33
Chats
Regan
last seen 12 minutes ago
RE
May 7
What should I buy Sophie for her birthday? 03:50
Get her some DVDS. She loves movies. 03:51
Ok has she seen "cloudy with a chance of man balls?" 03:52
I hope not! She's only 6! 03:53
Hahahahahahah oh god * meatballs. Wow 03:53
Message

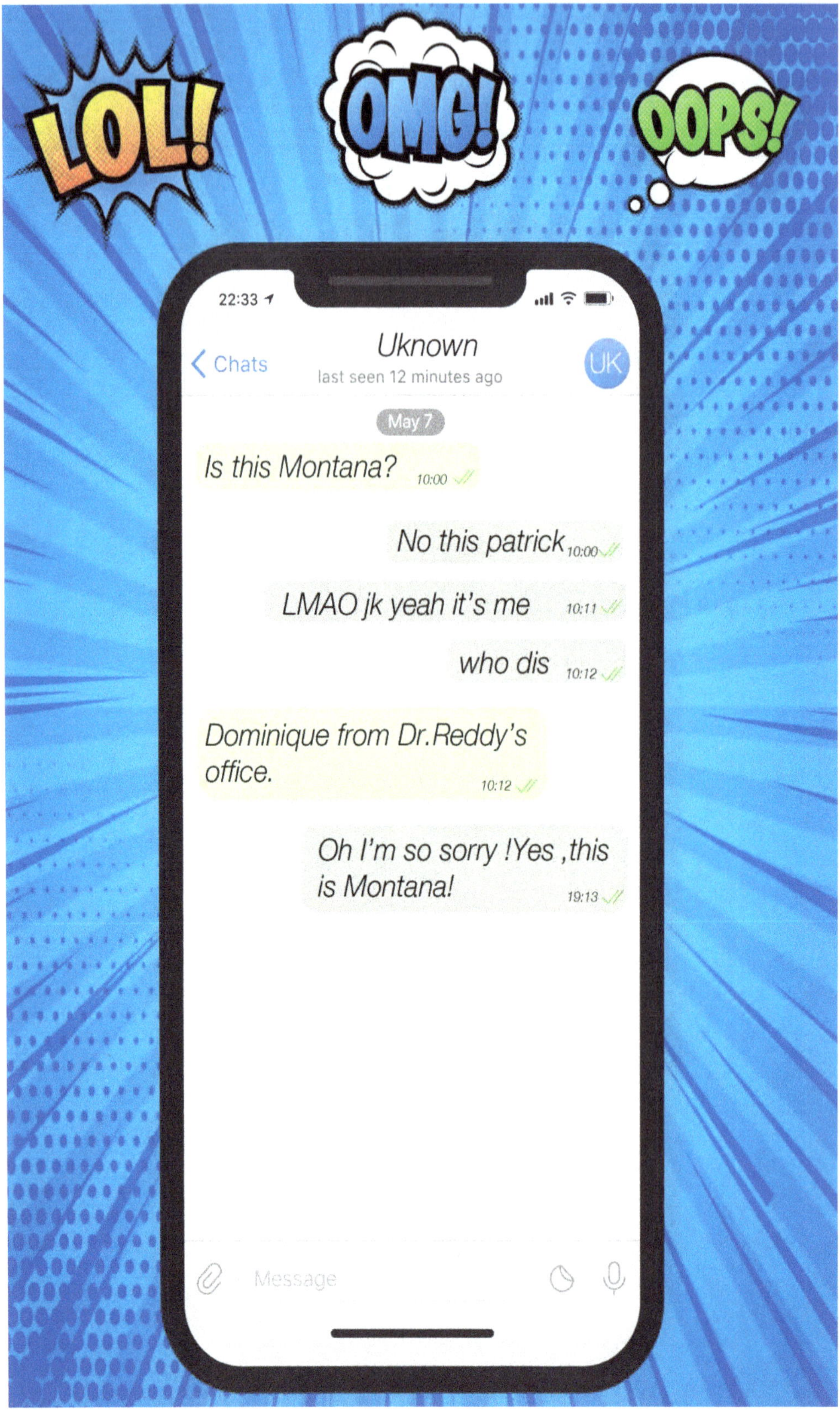

LOL!
OMG!
OOPS!
22:33
Uknown
Chats
last seen 12 minutes ago
UK
May 7
Is this Montana? 10:00
No this patrick 10:00
LMAO jk yeah it's me 10:11
who dis 10:12
Dominique from Dr.Reddy's office. 10:12
Oh I'm so sorry !Yes ,this is Montana! 19:13
Message

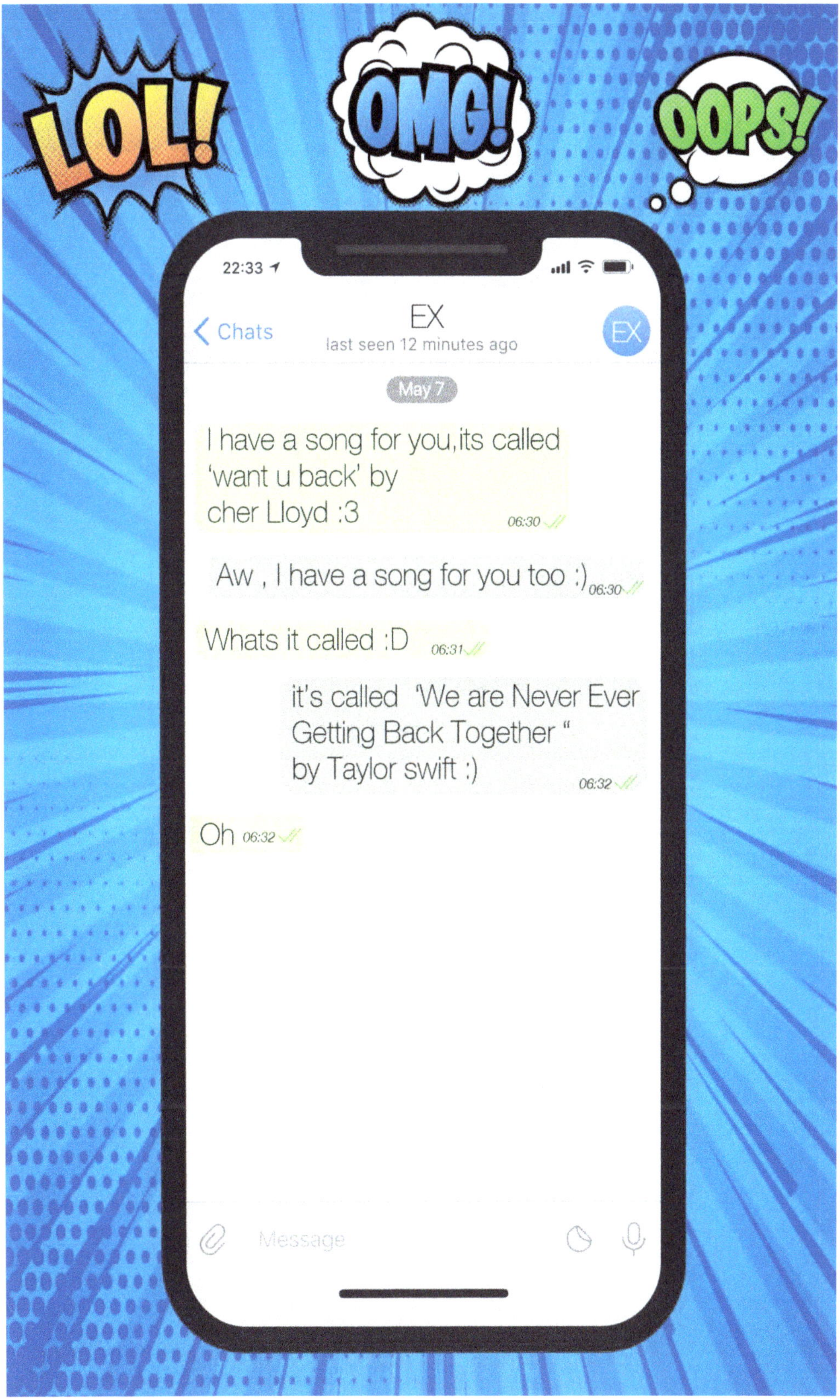
LOL!
OMG!
OOPS!
22:33
Chats
EX
last seen 12 minutes ago
EX
May 7
I have a song for you,its called 'want u back' by cher Lloyd :3 06:30
Aw , I have a song for you too :) 06:30
Whats it called :D 06:31
it's called 'We are Never Ever Getting Back Together " by Taylor swift :) 06:32
Oh 06:32
Message

LOL!
OMG!
OOPS!
22:33
Chats
Daddy
last seen 12 minutes ago
DA
May 7
Daddy you're so smart and amazing and handsome. Can I borrow your car Saturday? ;) 23:25
Oh I knew you wanted something! 23:25
Flatulence will get you nowhere! 23:26
I definitely meant flattery. But flatulence won't get you anywhere either. I know that first hand. 23:26
Message

LOL!
OMG!
OOPS!
22:33
Chats
Noah
last seen 12 minutes ago
NO
May 7
Hi, i know your a teenager, i know your friends smoke weed, i need some. 21:11
SURE!How much you need ? I got some in my room if you pay me. 21:11
Dumbass,that was a test. 21:12
Grounded? 21:13
Get home,now. 21:13
Message

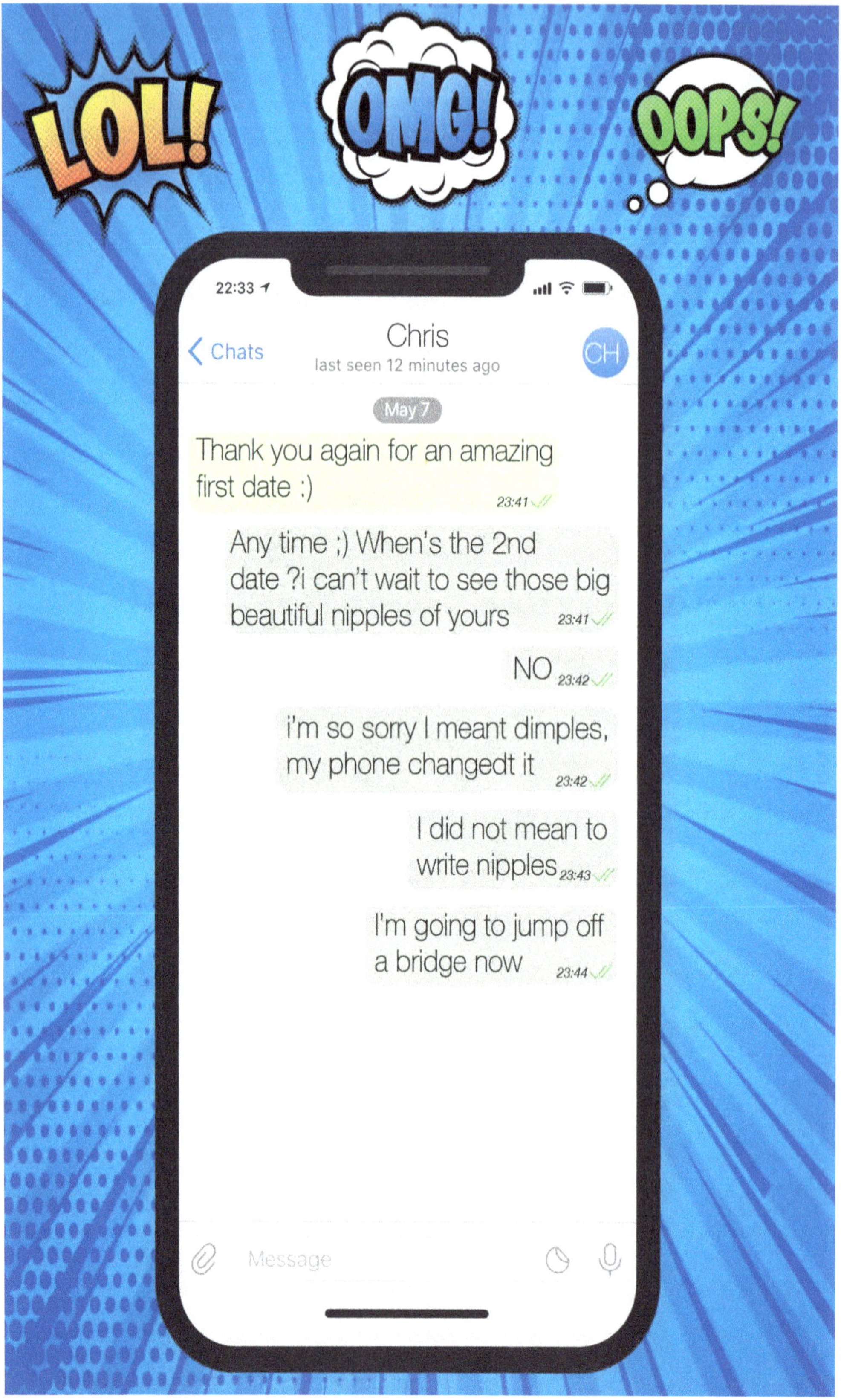
LOL!
OMG!
OOPS!
22:33
Chats
Chris
last seen 12 minutes ago
CH
May 7
Thank you again for an amazing first date :) 23:41
Any time ;) When's the 2nd date ?i can't wait to see those big beautiful nipples of yours 23:41
NO 23:42
i'm so sorry I meant dimples, my phone changedt it 23:42
I did not mean to write nipples 23:43
I'm going to jump off a bridge now 23:44
Message

LOL!
OMG!
OOPS!
22:33
Chats
Mom
last seen 12 minutes ago
MO
May 7
How did dads dr. appointment go? 12:01
Okay. He has heartburn. Doctor prescribed prostitutes. 12:01
2x per day. 12:02
Wow. In that case I have heartburn too. Lol 12:03
Best prescription ever! 12:04
Oh gosh. Not funny. Prilosec. That is my worst auto correct ever! 12:05
Message

LOL!
OMG!
OOPS!
22:33
Chats
Babe
last seen 12 minutes ago
BA
May 7
Hi babe , what are you doing ?
23:00
Nothing much ,I'm really tired.Just going to sleep now babe, And you ?
23:05
In the club standing behind you
23:06
Message

LOL!
OMG!
OOPS!
22:33
Chats
David
last seen 12 minutes ago
DA
May 7
Dad , I'm hungry
09:07
Hi Hungry ! I'm Dad.
09:08
Dad,I'm serious!
09:09
No.you're Hungry!
09:10
Are you joking ?
09:10
No.I'm Dad.
09:11
Message

LOL!
OMG!
OOPS!
22:33
Chats
Uknown
last seen 12 minutes ago
UK
May 7
Hey Tim! I am throwing a Birthday party and you are invited. 11:20
Saturday 8 pm,my place. 11:20
Hey,this is not Tim. 11:21
So sorry,I texted the wrong number. 11:22
Too late to apologize . I got you a gift so text me your adress 11:23
Message

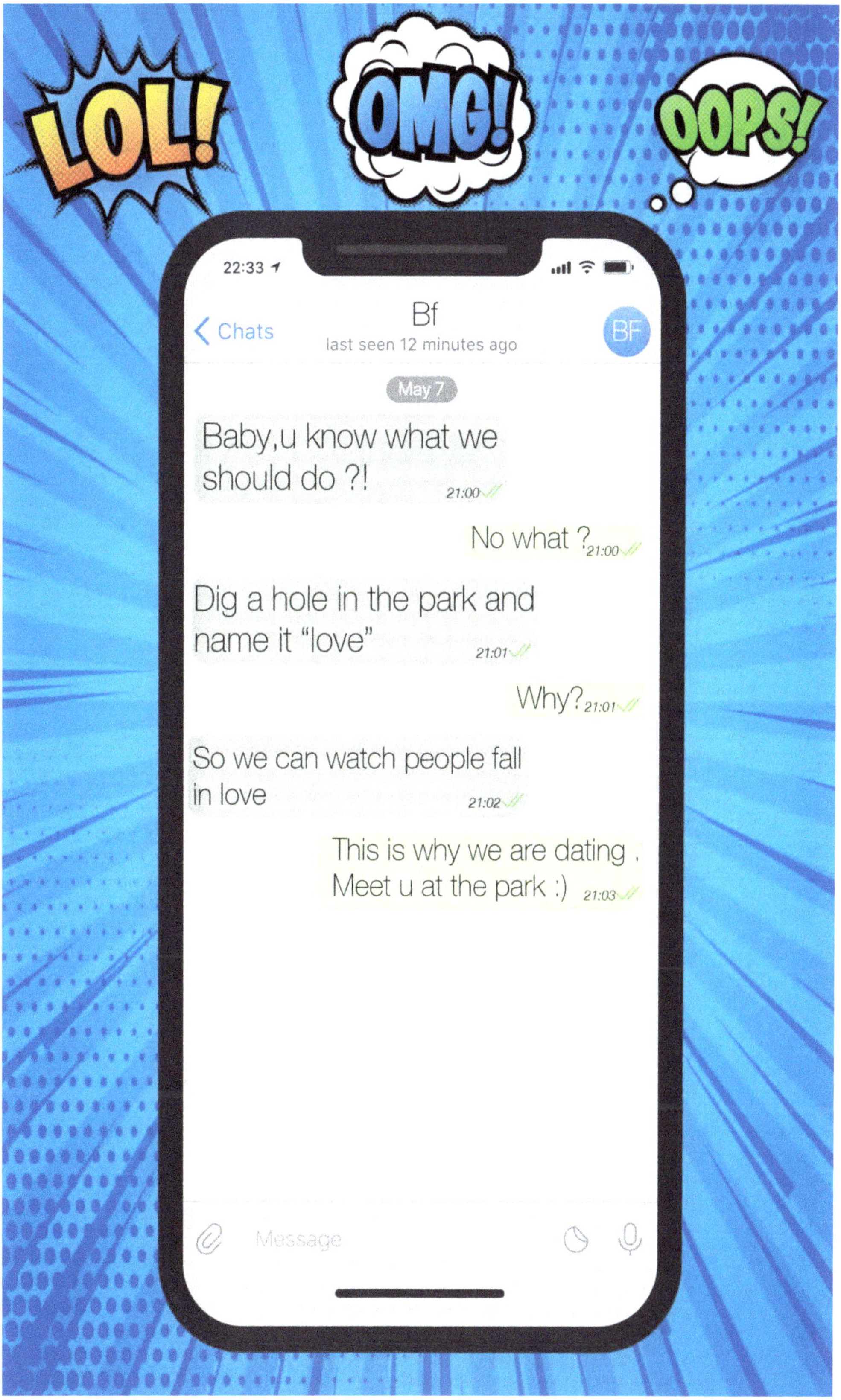
LOL!
OMG!
OOPS!
22:33
Chats
Bf
last seen 12 minutes ago
BF
May 7
Baby,u know what we should do ?! 21:00
No what ? 21:00
Dig a hole in the park and name it "love" 21:01
Why? 21:01
So we can watch people fall in love 21:02
This is why we are dating . Meet u at the park :) 21:03
Message

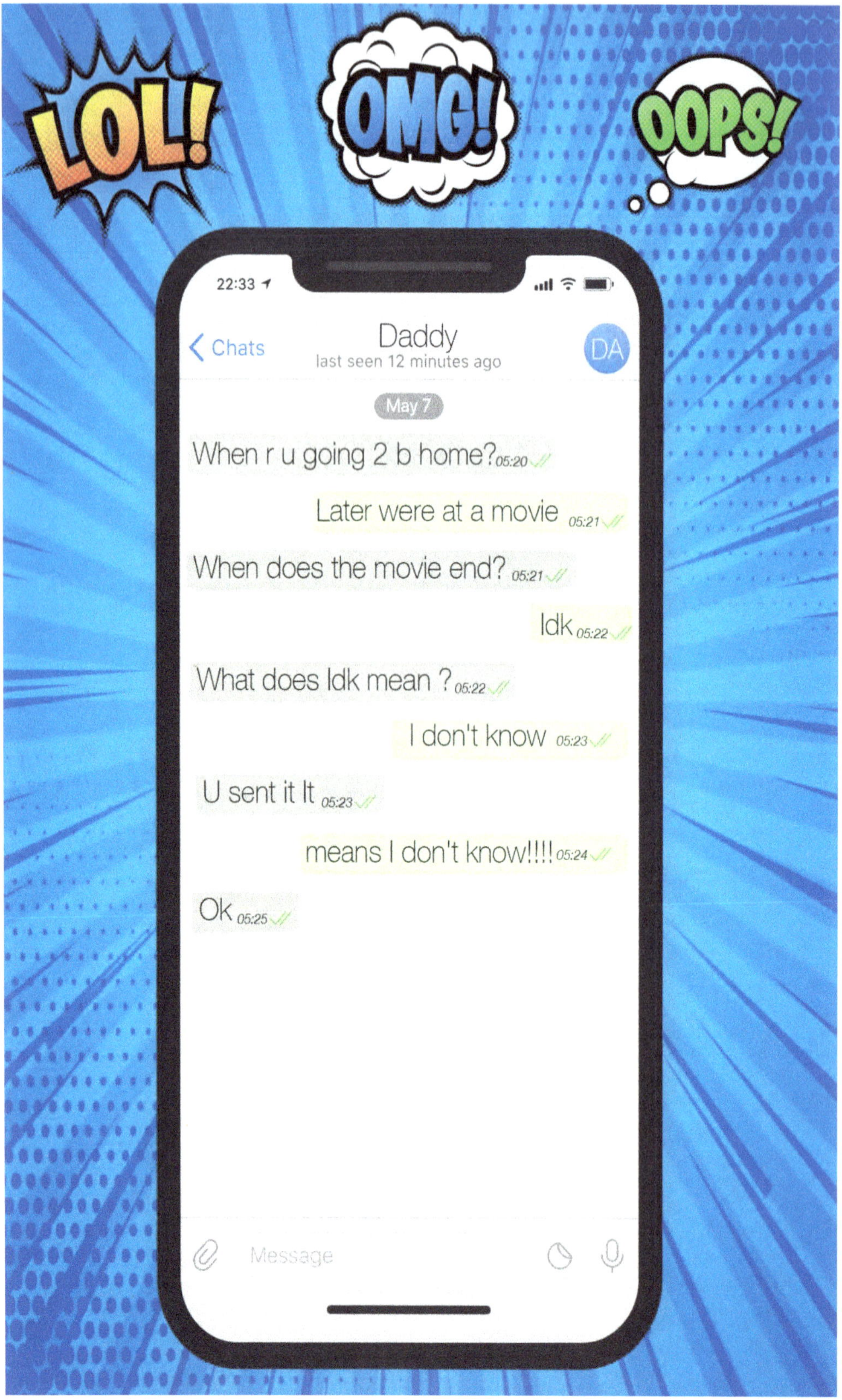
LOL!
OMG!
OOPS!
22:33
Chats
Daddy
last seen 12 minutes ago
DA
May 7
When r u going 2 b home? 05:20
Later were at a movie 05:21
When does the movie end? 05:21
Idk 05:22
What does Idk mean ? 05:22
I don't know 05:23
U sent it It 05:23
means I don't know!!!! 05:24
Ok 05:25
Message

LOL!
OMG!
OOPS!
22:33
Chats
Cameron
last seen 12 minutes ago
CA
May 7
You were so drunk last night ! 17:01
No I wasn't 17:03
Dude, you went into my fish tank grabbed my clownfish, put it into a plastic bag filled with water and then called the police and started shouting I FOUND NEMO 17:04
Ok maybe I was drunk 17:04
Message

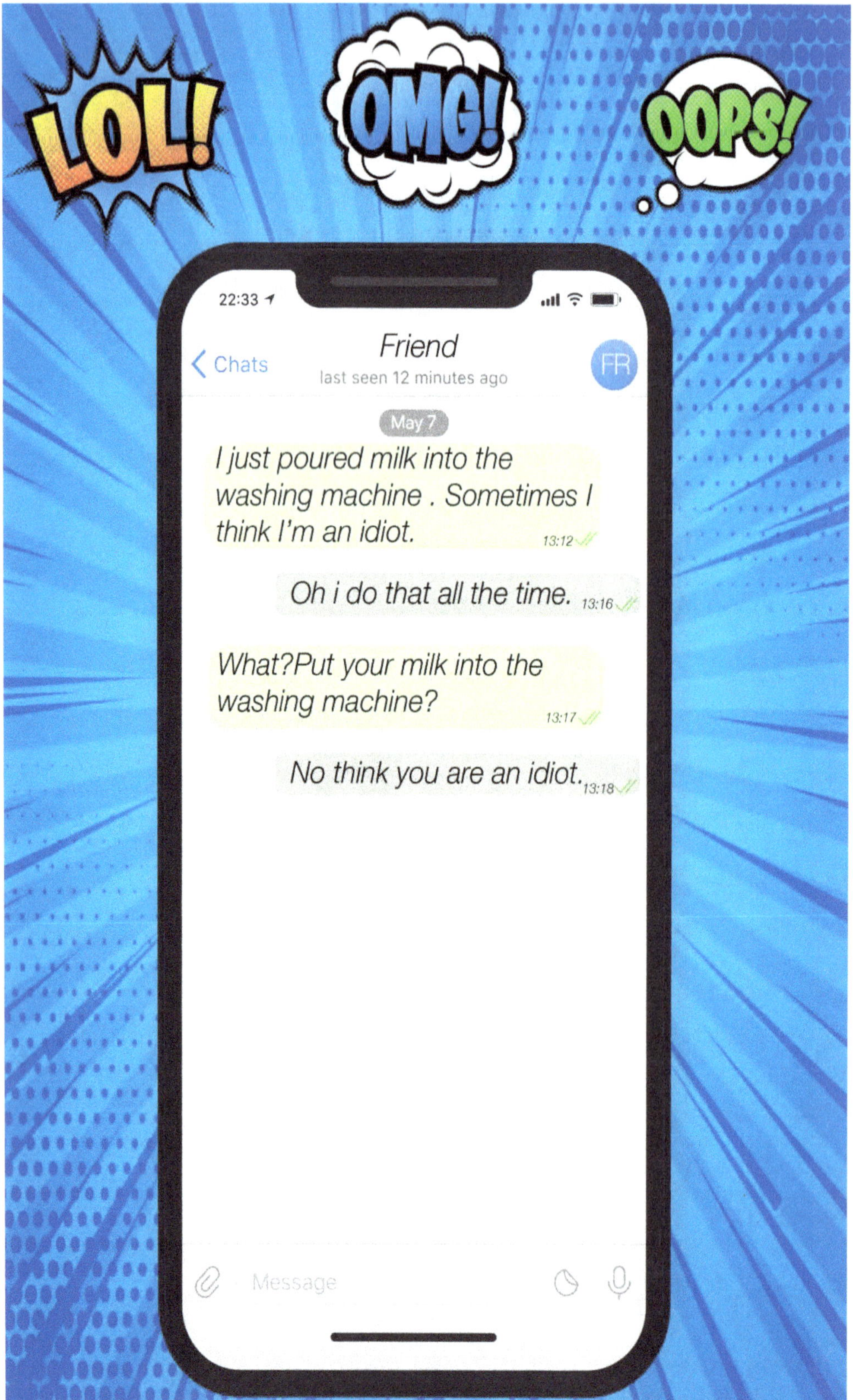

LOL!
OMG!
OOPS!
22:33
Chats
Friend
last seen 12 minutes ago
FR
May 7
I just poured milk into the washing machine . Sometimes I think I'm an idiot.
13:12
Oh i do that all the time.
13:16
What?Put your milk into the washing machine?
13:17
No think you are an idiot.
13:18
Message

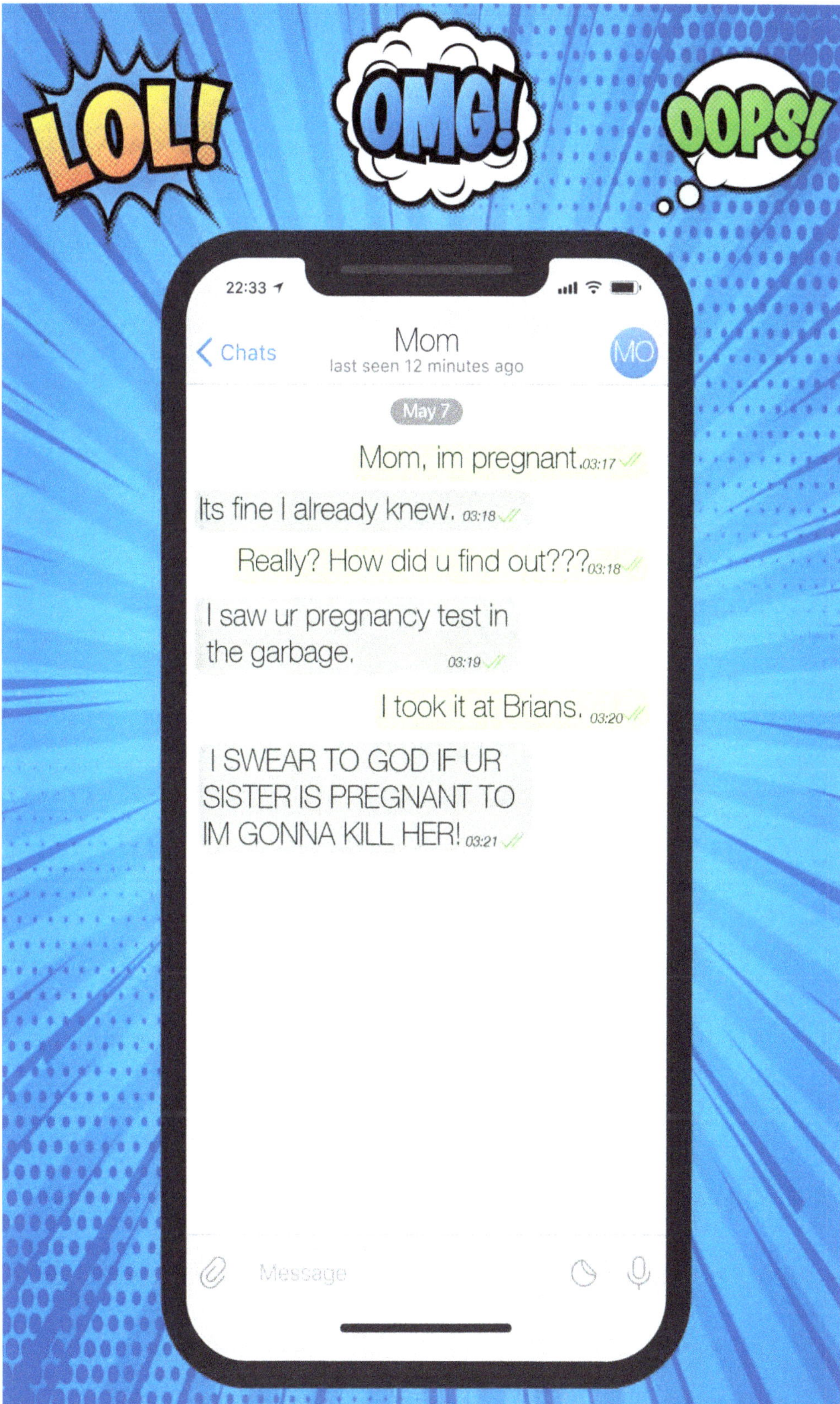
LOL!
OMG!
OOPS!
22:33
Chats
Mom
last seen 12 minutes ago
MO
May 7
Mom, im pregnant. 03:17
Its fine I already knew. 03:18
Really? How did u find out??? 03:18
I saw ur pregnancy test in the garbage. 03:19
I took it at Brians. 03:20
I SWEAR TO GOD IF UR SISTER IS PREGNANT TO IM GONNA KILL HER! 03:21
Message

LOL!
OMG!
OOPS!
22:33
Chats
Mom
last seen 12 minutes ago
MO
May 7
How do I delete a voice mail off the home phone?? 06:24
Press 06:25
GRASSY ASS! 06:25
What?I don't get it 06:26
It means "thank you" in spanish right? 06:27
Mom u mean gracias !lol 06:27
Message

LOL!
OMG!
OOPS!
22:33
Chats
Mom
last seen 12 minutes ago
MO
May 7
Watcha doing?? 02:05
Been playing call of duty for three hours. Wbu? 02:05
So you finished your reading assignment? 02:06
What? I can't hear you... we're .. u.. I think I'm .. a tunnel. 02:06
Sarah.... 02:07
The number you have dialed is currently unavailable.
Please again later. 02:08
Message

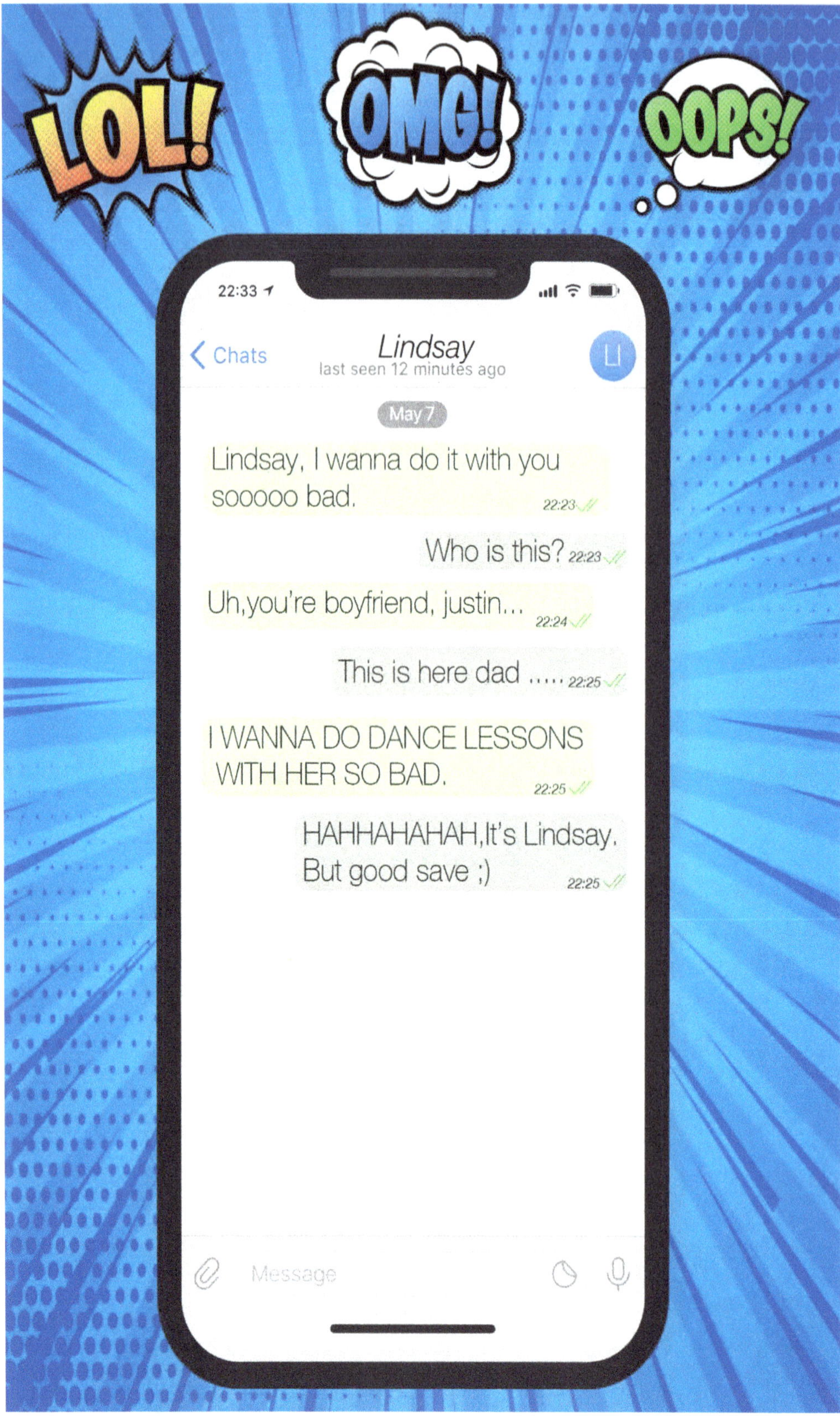
LOL!
OMG!
OOPS!
22:33
Chats
Lindsay
last seen 12 minutes ago
LI
May 7
Lindsay, I wanna do it with you sooooo bad. 22:23
Who is this? 22:23
Uh,you're boyfriend, justin... 22:24
This is here dad 22:25
I WANNA DO DANCE LESSONS WITH HER SO BAD. 22:25
HAHHAHAHAH,It's Lindsay. But good save ;) 22:25
Message

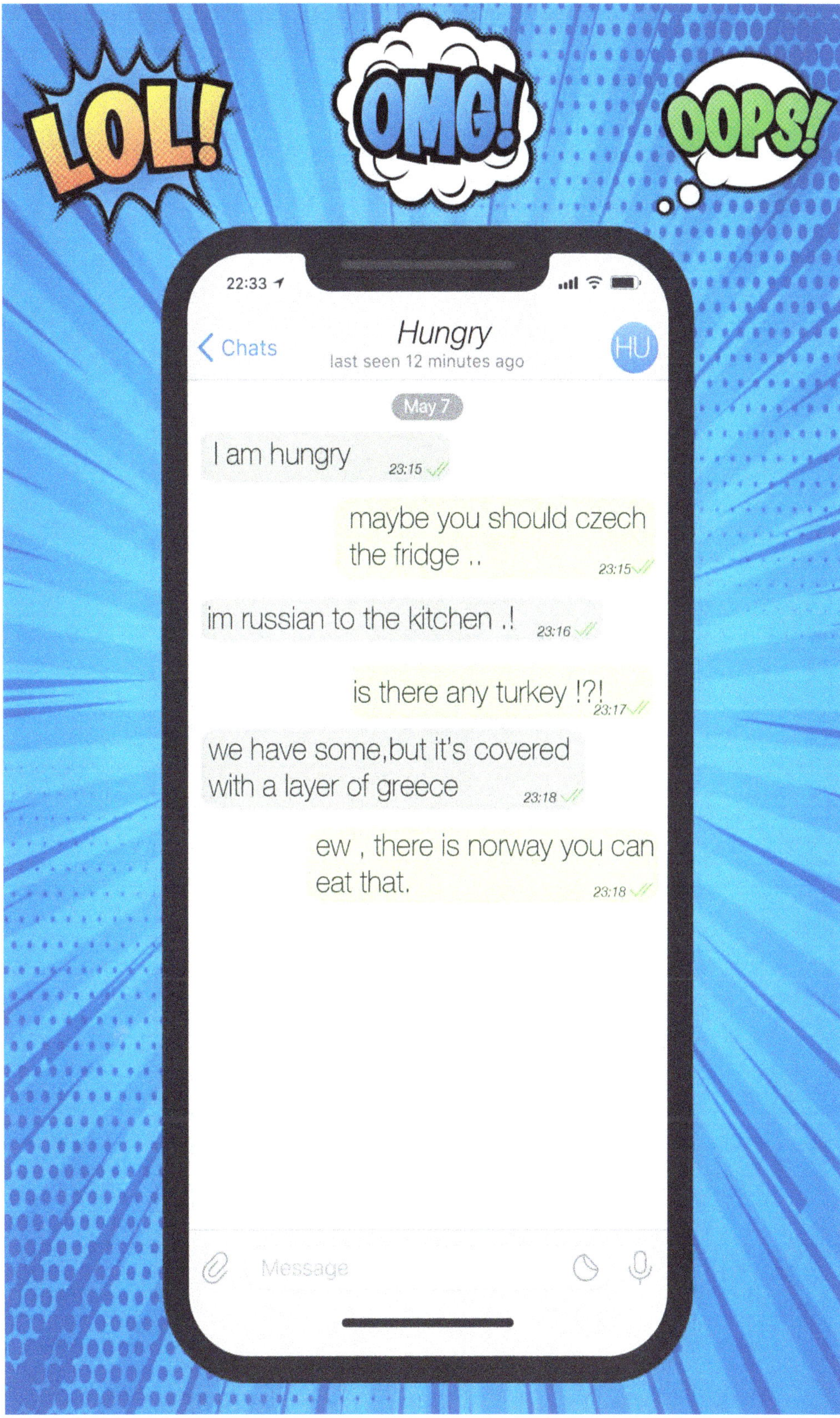
LOL!
OMG!
OOPS!
22:33
Chats
Hungry
last seen 12 minutes ago
HU
May 7
I am hungry 23:15
maybe you should czech the fridge .. 23:15
im russian to the kitchen .! 23:16
is there any turkey !?! 23:17
we have some,but it's covered with a layer of greece 23:18
ew , there is norway you can eat that. 23:18
Message

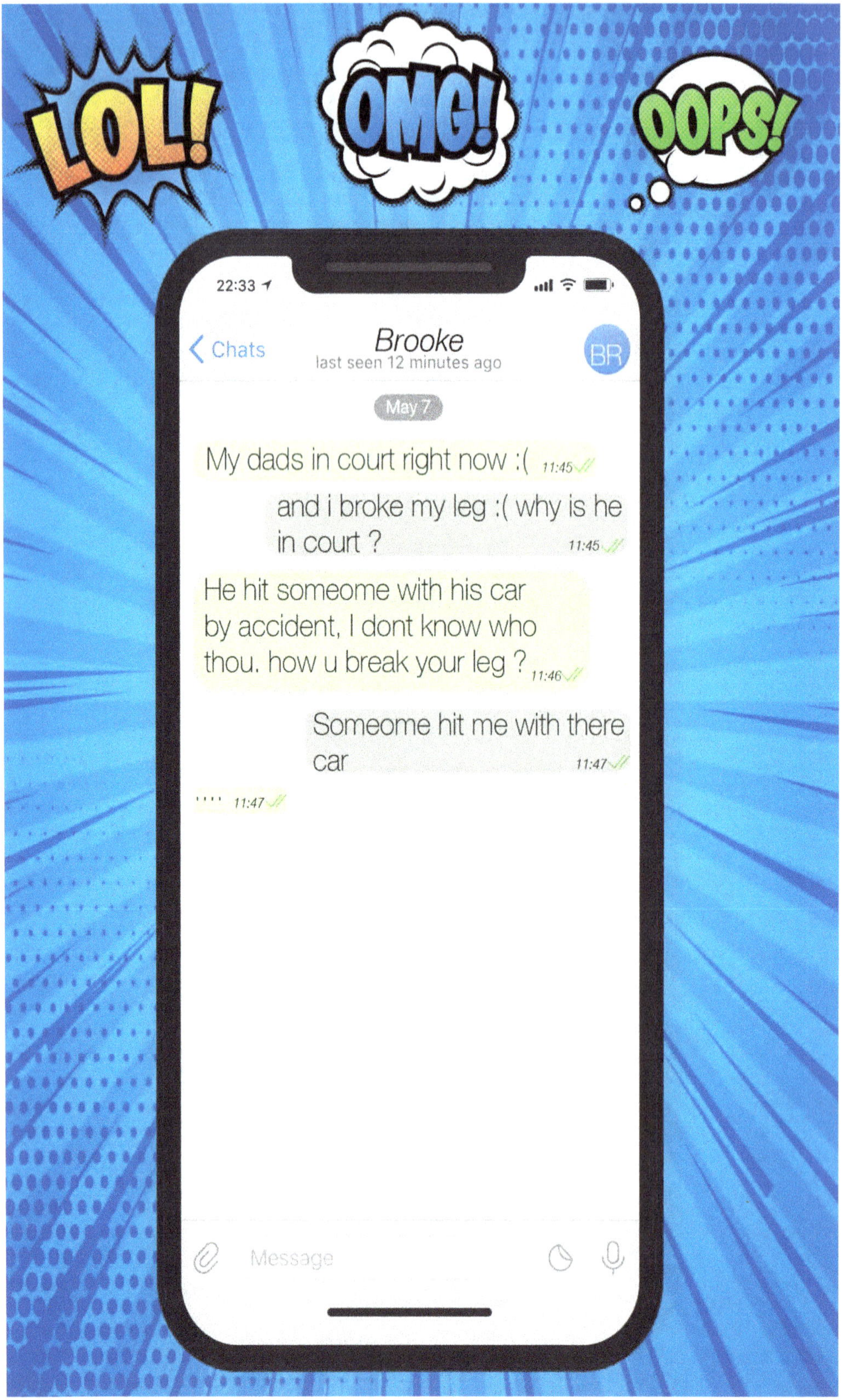
LOL!
OMG!
OOPS!
22:33
Chats
Brooke
last seen 12 minutes ago
BR
May 7
My dads in court right now :(11:45
and i broke my leg :(why is he in court ? 11:45
He hit someome with his car by accident, I dont know who thou. how u break your leg ? 11:46
Someome hit me with there car 11:47
.... 11:47
Message

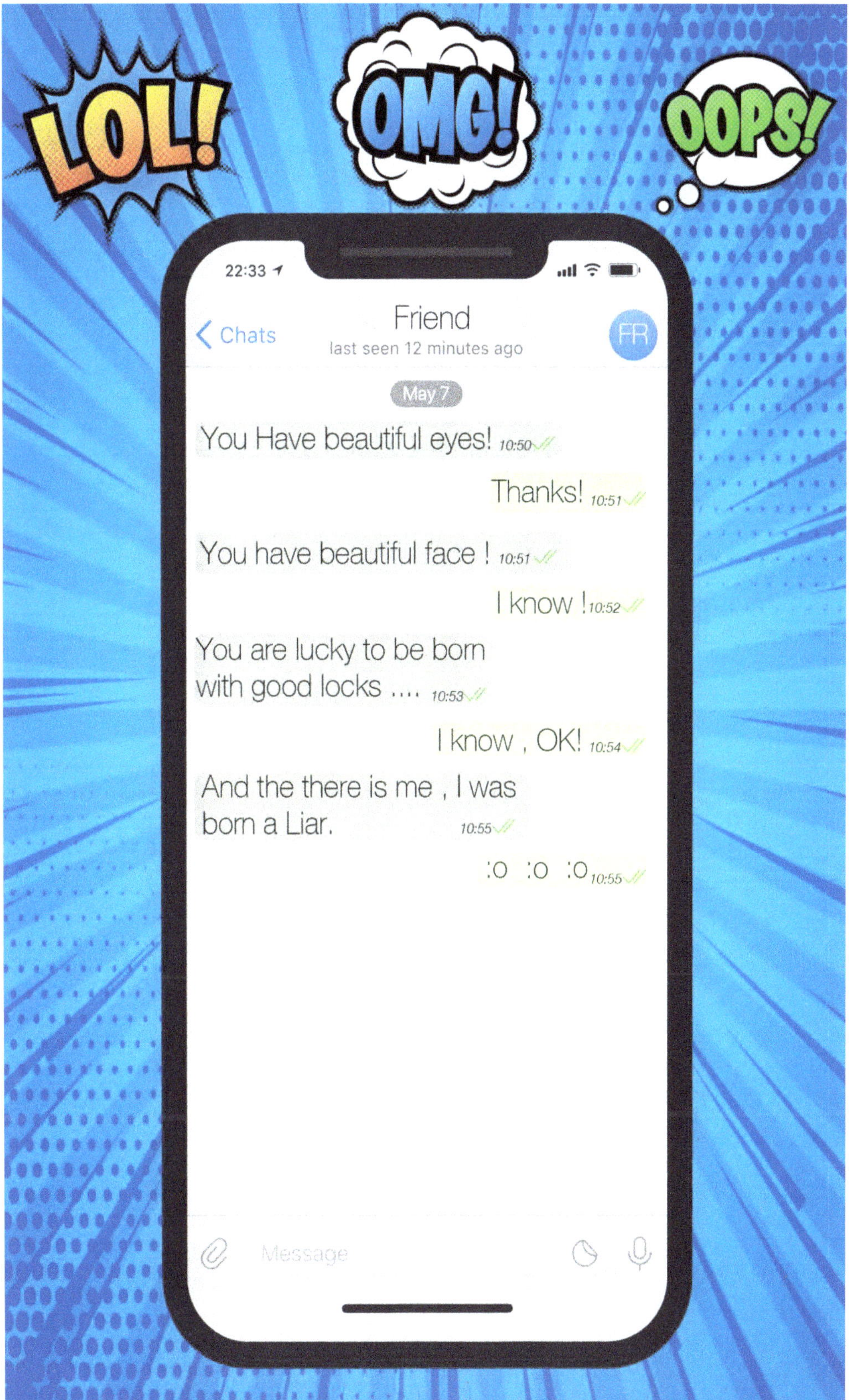
LOL!
OMG!
OOPS!
22:33
Chats
Friend
last seen 12 minutes ago
FR
May 7
You Have beautiful eyes! 10:50
Thanks! 10:51
You have beautiful face ! 10:51
I know !10:52
You are lucky to be born with good locks 10:53
I know , OK! 10:54
And the there is me , I was born a Liar. 10:55
:O :O :O 10:55
Message

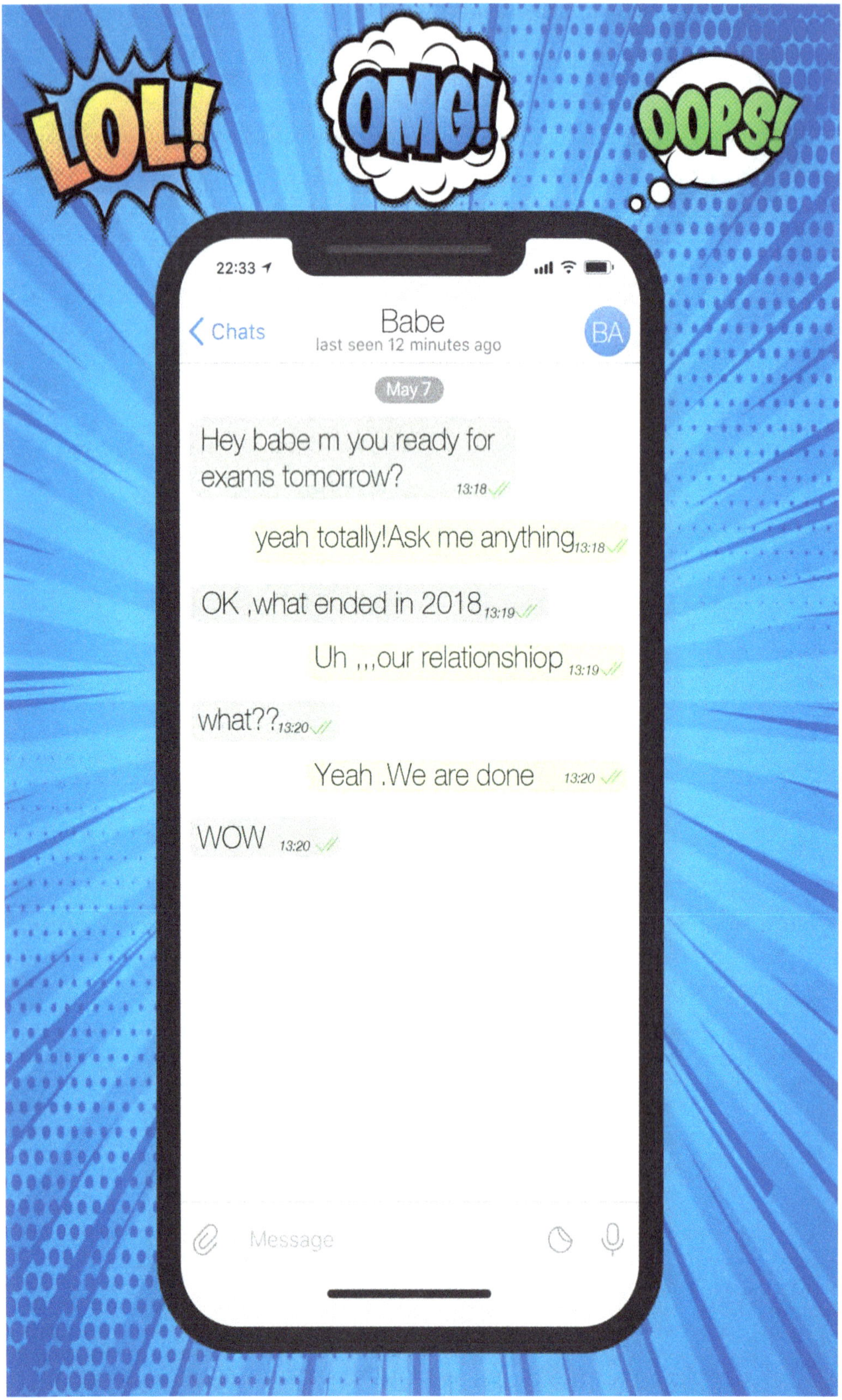

LOL!
OMG!
OOPS!
22:33
Chats
Babe
last seen 12 minutes ago
BA
May 7
Hey babe m you ready for exams tomorrow? 13:18
yeah totally!Ask me anything 13:18
OK ,what ended in 2018 13:19
Uh ,,,our relationshiop 13:19
what?? 13:20
Yeah .We are done 13:20
WOW 13:20
Message

LOL!
OMG!
OOPS!
22:33
Chats
EX
last seen 12 minutes ago
EX
May 7
Hey my friend changed all my contact names can u tell me who you can
19:24
what does it say
19:25
Bitch
19:25
Oh wow ... and btw its carlonie, your ex
19:25
Oh I guess he didn't change this one
19:26
Message

LOL!
OMG!
OOPS!
22:33
Chats
Maddy
last seen 12 minutes ago
MA
May 7
Im so proud of My Boyfriend 09:59
Why?? 09:59
Because Last night he was so tired he didnt recognize me!! 10:00
Whats so good about that?? 10:00
So, when I tried to give him a hug he said "Back of, I have a girlfriend!" 10:01
AWwwwwwwww! :):)) 10:01
Message

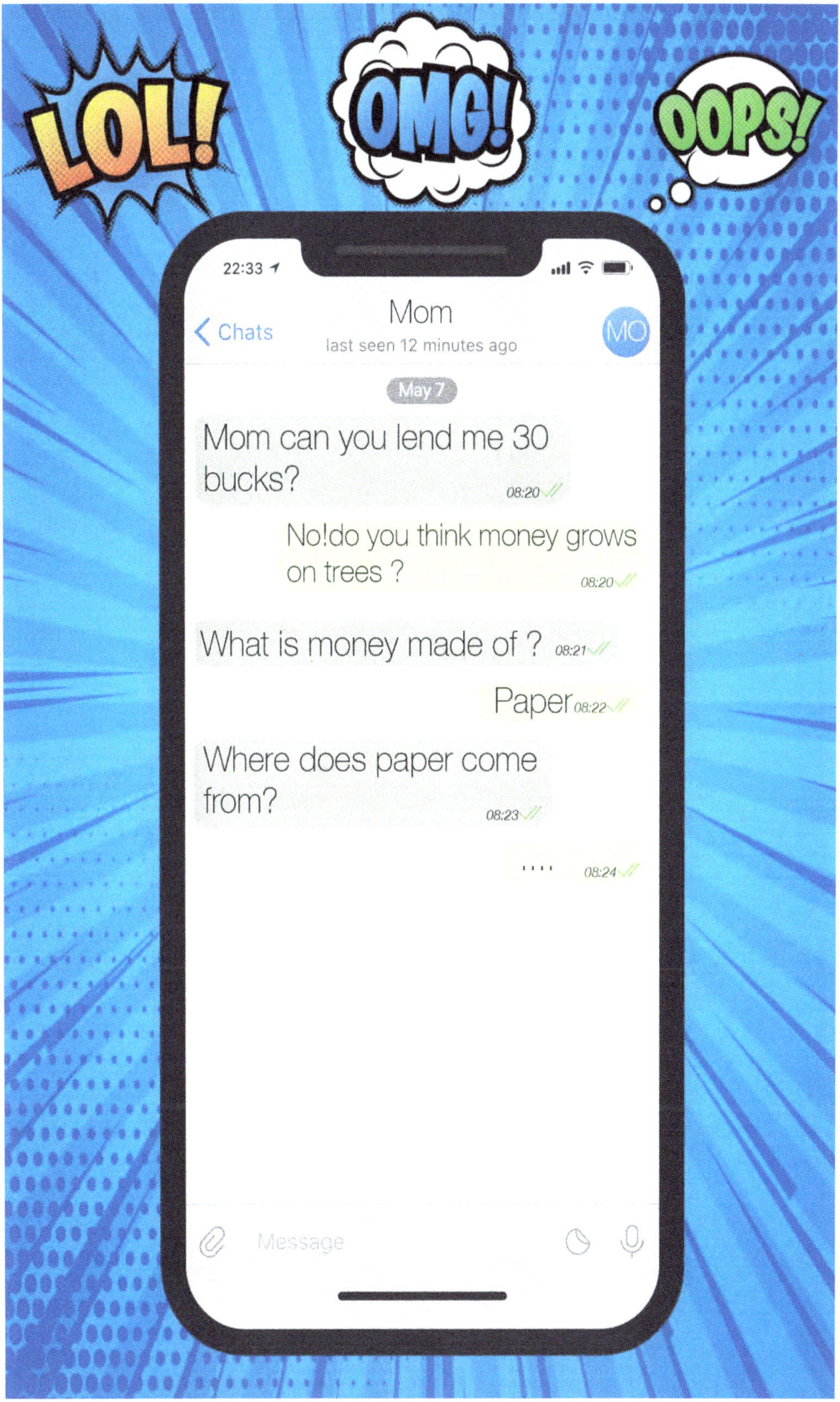
LOL!
OMG!
OOPS!
22:33
Mom
Chats
last seen 12 minutes ago
MO
May 7
Mom can you lend me 30 bucks? 08:20
No!do you think money grows on trees ? 08:20
What is money made of ? 08:21
Paper 08:22
Where does paper come from? 08:23
.... 08:24
Message

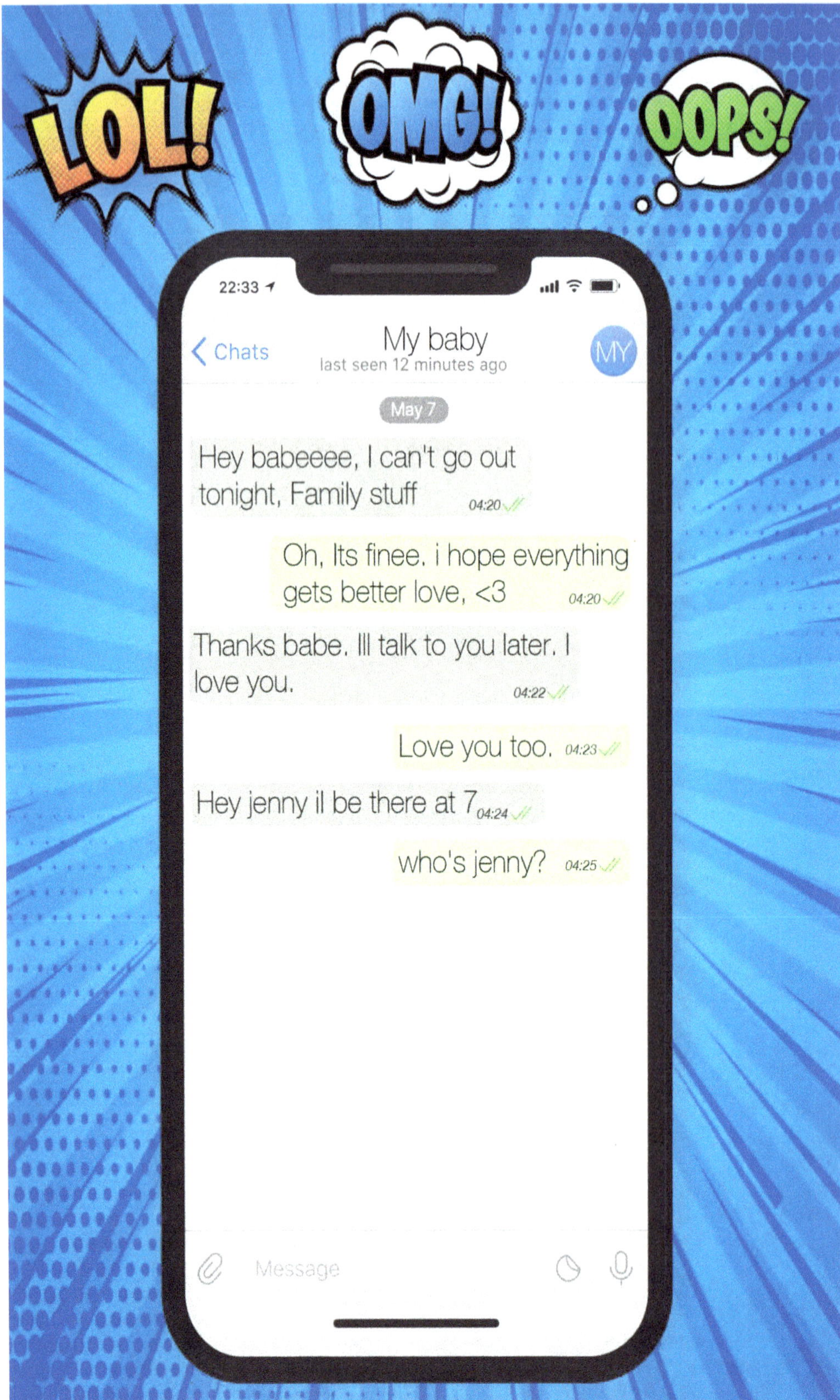
LOL!
OMG!
OOPS!
22:33
Chats
My baby
last seen 12 minutes ago
MY
May 7
Hey babeeee, I can't go out tonight, Family stuff 04:20
Oh, Its finee. i hope everything gets better love, <3 04:20
Thanks babe. Ill talk to you later. I love you. 04:22
Love you too. 04:23
Hey jenny il be there at 7 04:24
who's jenny? 04:25
Message

LOL!
OMG!
OOPS!
22:33
Chats
Mom
last seen 12 minutes ago
MO
May 7
I think there's something wrong with my phone. I don't think my texts are going througt.
20:02
yeah , they're getting through.
20:06
how can you be sure ?
20:07
Message

LOL!
OMG!
OOPS!
22:33
Chats
Jacob
last seen 12 minutes ago
JA
May 7
Hey, Dave!! 11:20
Don't talk to me . 11:20
What ,what did I do ? 11:21
last night you were so drunk you got my iPad and put it in the blender 11:22
Really????? 11:23
Yeah , and you said that you were making apple juice. 11:23
Message

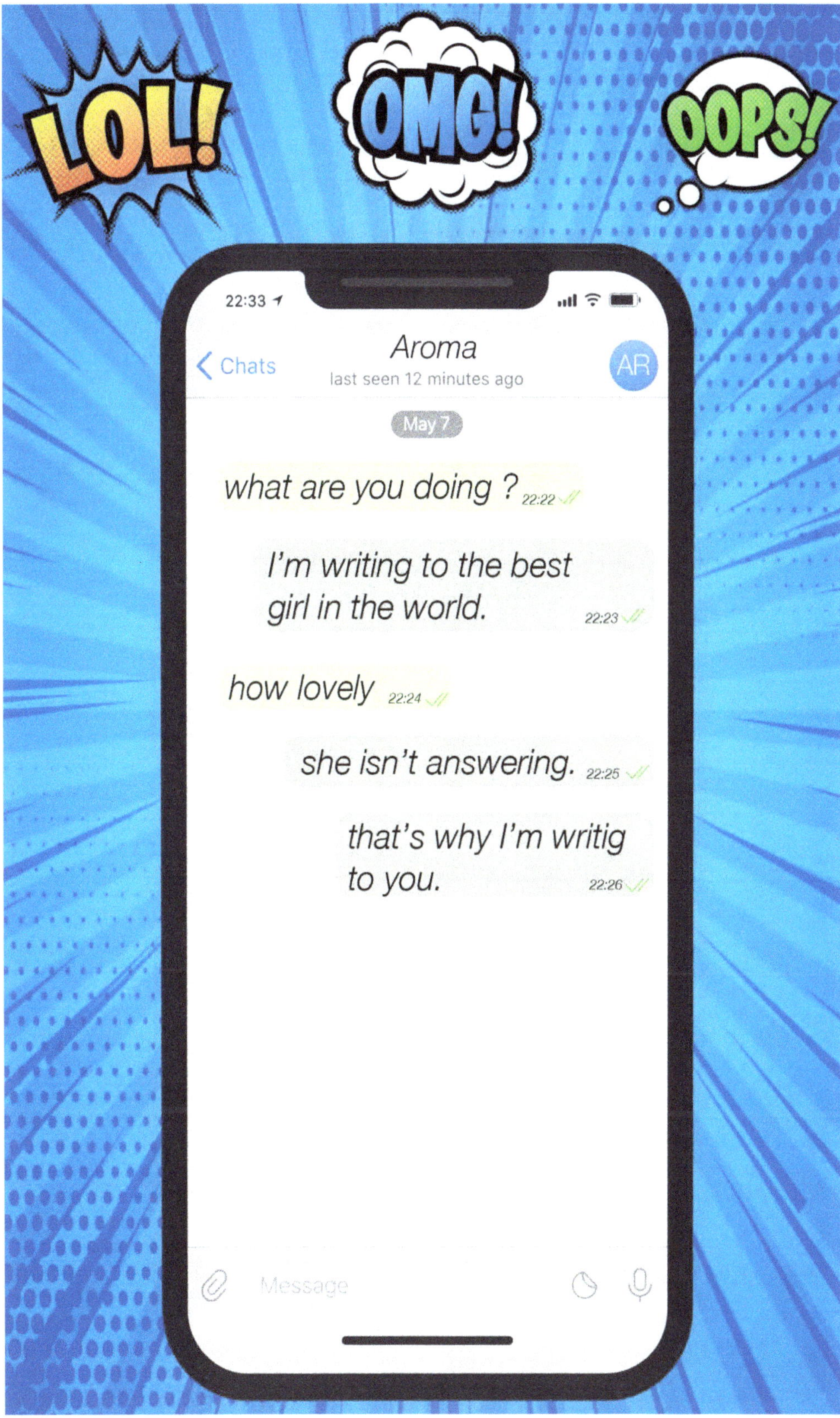
LOL!
OMG!
OOPS!
22:33
Chats
Aroma
last seen 12 minutes ago
AR
May 7
what are you doing ? 22:22
I'm writing to the best girl in the world. 22:23
how lovely 22:24
she isn't answering. 22:25
that's why I'm writig to you. 22:26
Message

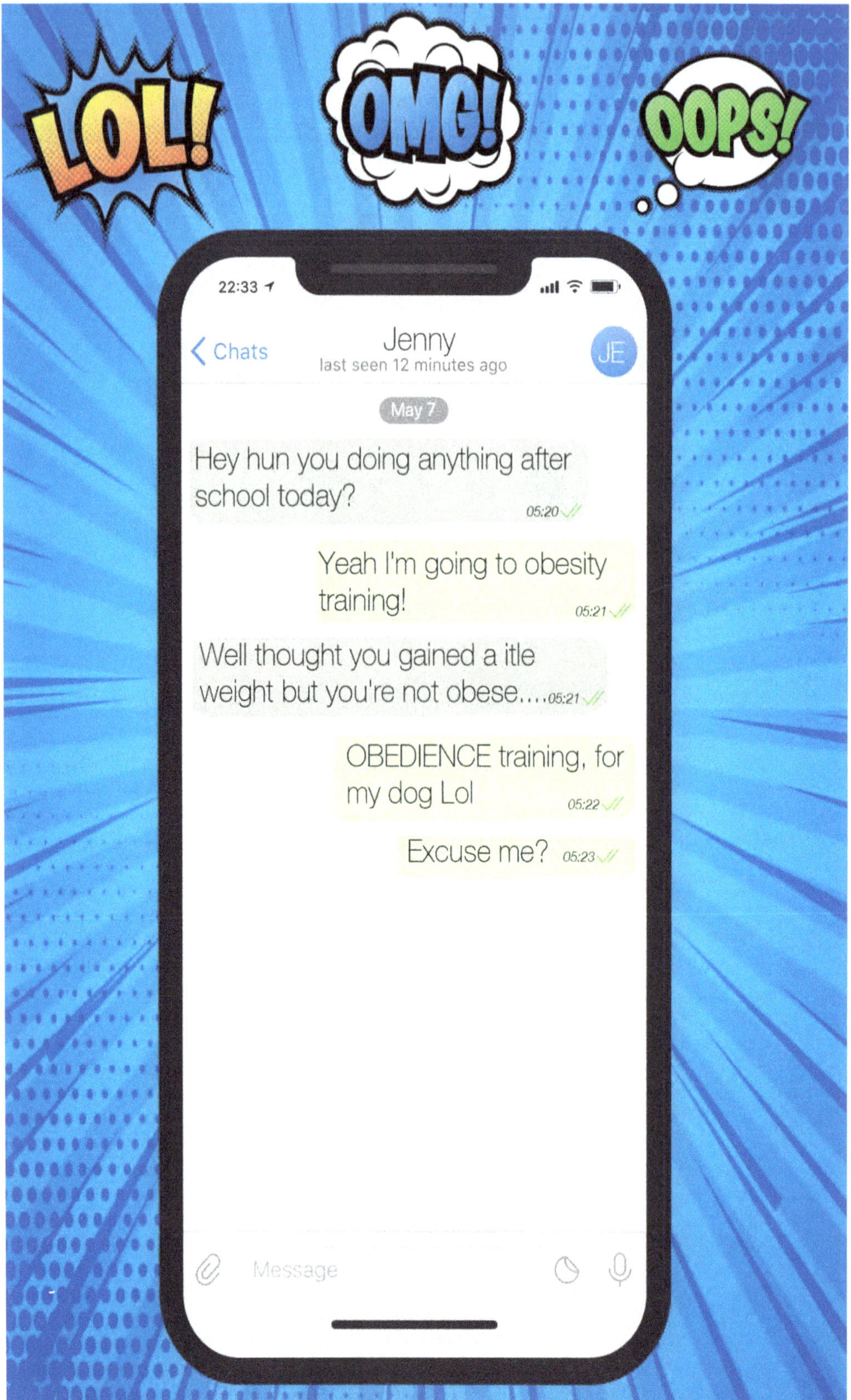
LOL!
OMG!
OOPS!
22:33
Chats
Jenny
last seen 12 minutes ago
JE
May 7
Hey hun you doing anything after school today? 05:20
Yeah I'm going to obesity training! 05:21
Well thought you gained a itle weight but you're not obese.... 05:21
OBEDIENCE training, for my dog Lol 05:22
Excuse me? 05:23
Message

LOL!
OMG!
OOPS!
22:33
Chats
Dad
last seen 12 minutes ago
DA
May 7
Dad,what is better ? to pass or to fail?
09:03
To pass obviously
09:04
OH GOOD YOU'LL BE PROUD OF ME!
09:04
I PASSED MY PREGNANCY TEST
09:05
GET YOUR ASS HOME NOW !!!
09:06
Message

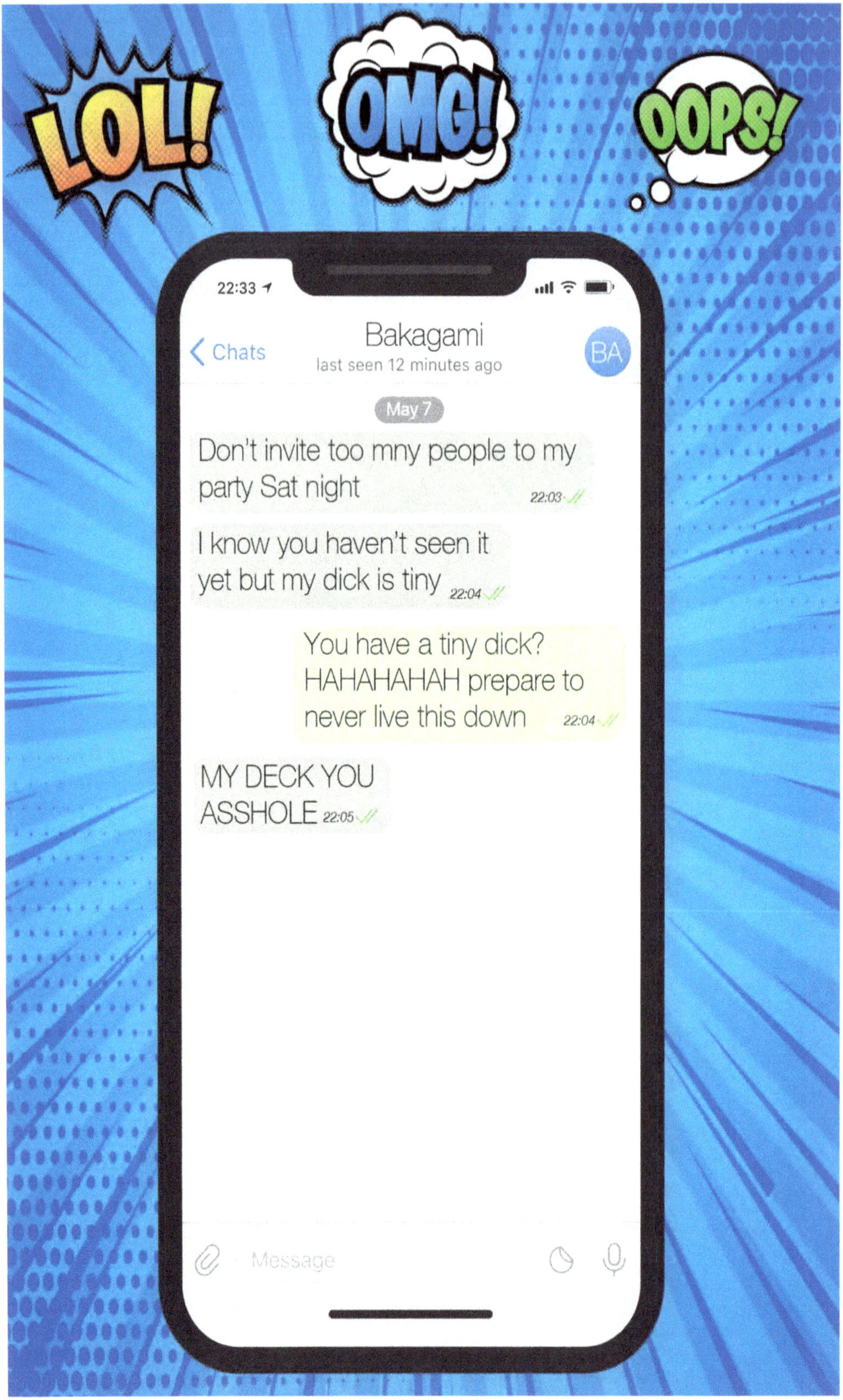

LOL!
OMG!
OOPS!
22:33
Chats
Bakagami
last seen 12 minutes ago
BA
May 7
Don't invite too mny people to my party Sat night 22:03
I know you haven't seen it yet but my dick is tiny 22:04
You have a tiny dick? HAHAHAHAH prepare to never live this down 22:04
MY DECK YOU ASSHOLE 22:05
Message

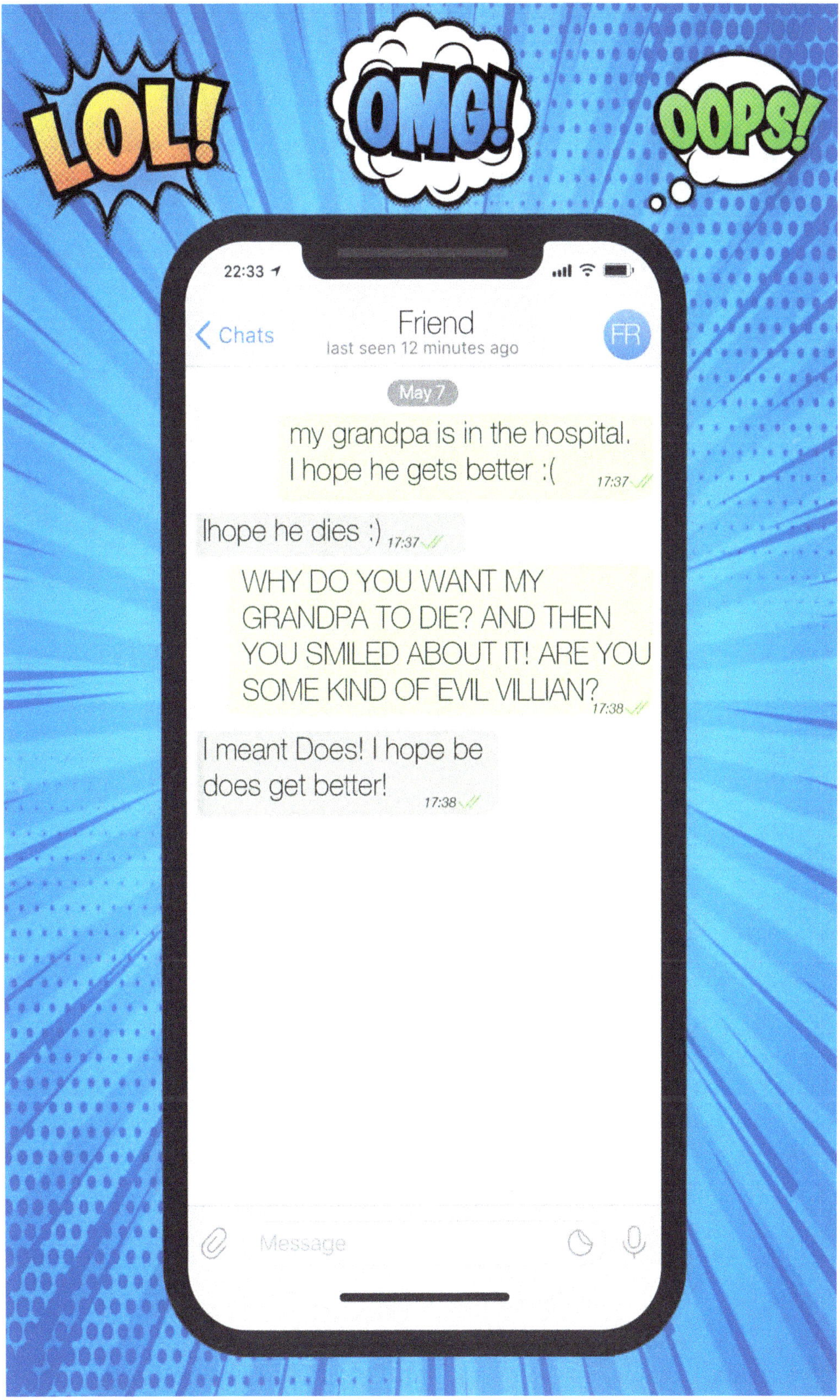
LOL!
OMG!
OOPS!
22:33
Chats
Friend
last seen 12 minutes ago
FR
May 7
my grandpa is in the hospital. I hope he gets better :(17:37
Ihope he dies :) 17:37
WHY DO YOU WANT MY GRANDPA TO DIE? AND THEN YOU SMILED ABOUT IT! ARE YOU SOME KIND OF EVIL VILLIAN? 17:38
I meant Does! I hope be does get better! 17:38
Message

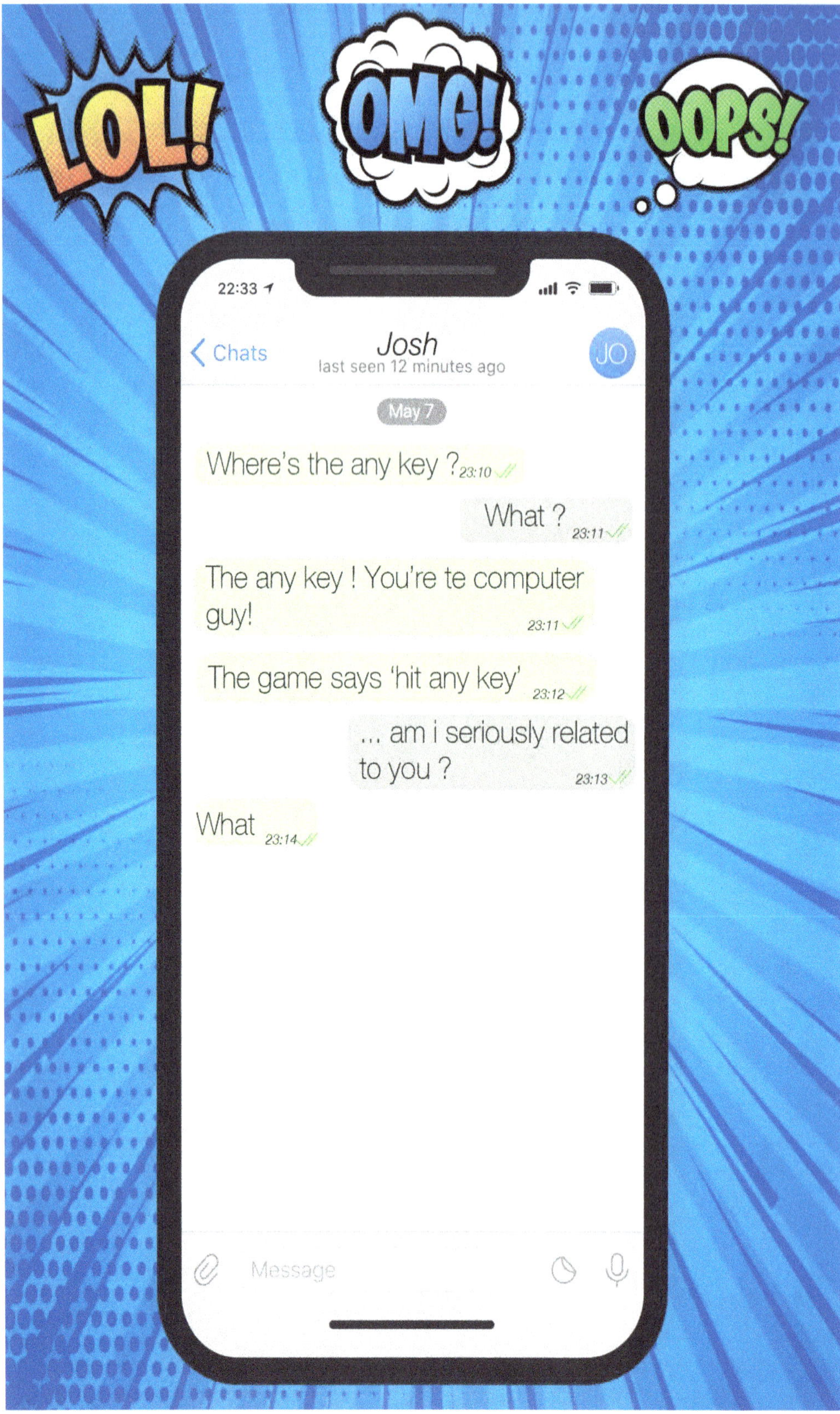
LOL!
OMG!
OOPS!
22:33
Chats
Josh
last seen 12 minutes ago
JO
May 7
Where's the any key ? 23:10
What ? 23:11
The any key ! You're te computer guy! 23:11
The game says 'hit any key' 23:12
... am i seriously related to you ? 23:13
What 23:14
Message

LOL!
OMG!
OOPS!
22:33
Chats
Dude
last seen 12 minutes ago
DU
May 7
Dude you should stop drinking ... 09:03
why? 09:04
Remember last night?? 09:04
Yeah, but i wasn't really drunk 09:05
Dude u almost jump down from 15th floor singing "i believe i can fly" 09:06
Message

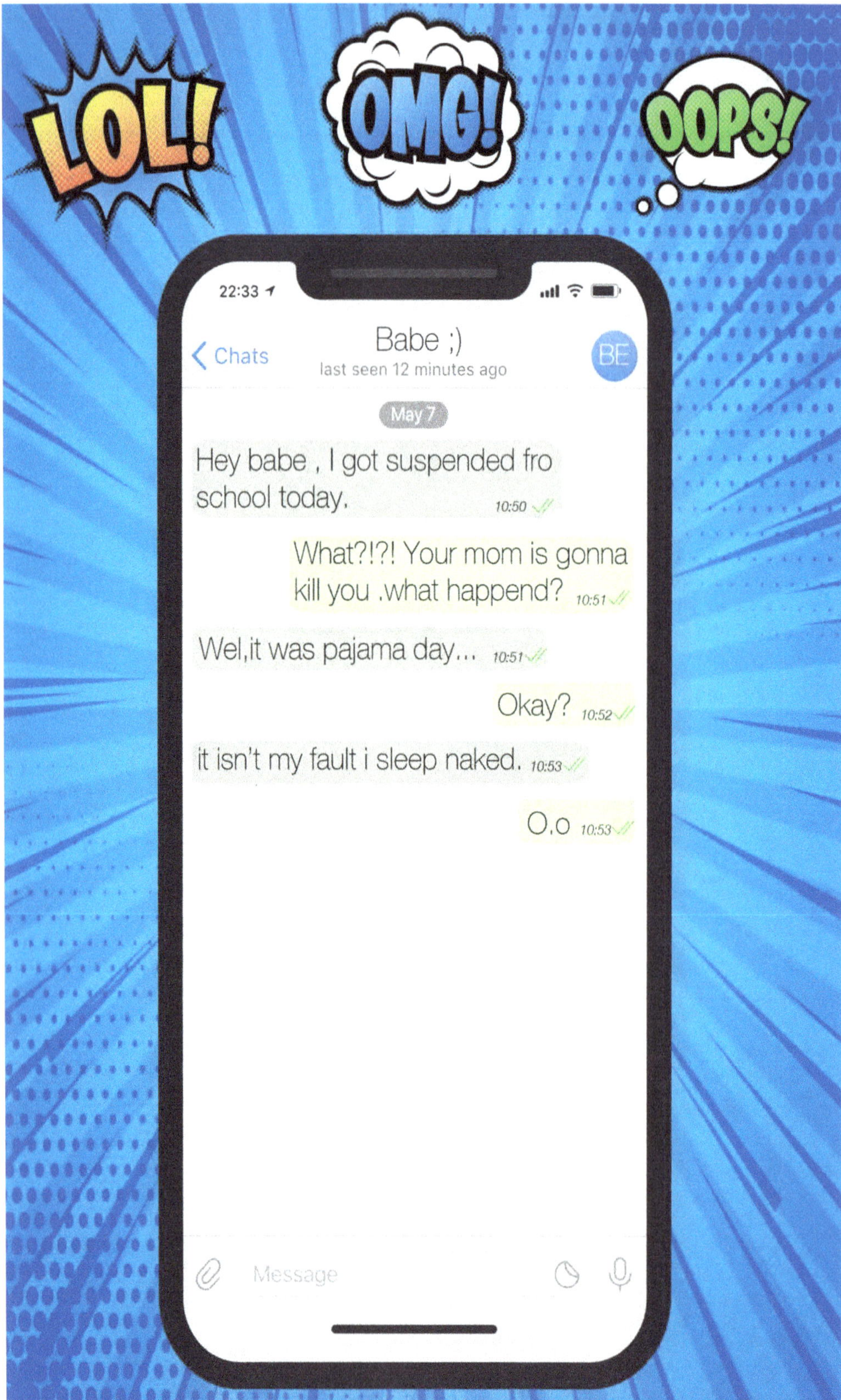
LOL!
OMG!
OOPS!
22:33
Chats
Babe ;)
last seen 12 minutes ago
BE
May 7
Hey babe , I got suspended fro school today. 10:50
What?!?! Your mom is gonna kill you .what happend? 10:51
Wel,it was pajama day... 10:51
Okay? 10:52
it isn't my fault i sleep naked. 10:53
O.o 10:53
Message

LOL!
OMG!
OOPS!
22:33
Chats
John
last seen 12 minutes ago
JO
May 7
Hey john! 06:24
Hey! 06:25
Did you know Microsoft just bought Skype for more than10 millions dollars? 06:25
Really?!? 06:27
Idiots ... they could have downloaded it for free 06:27
Message

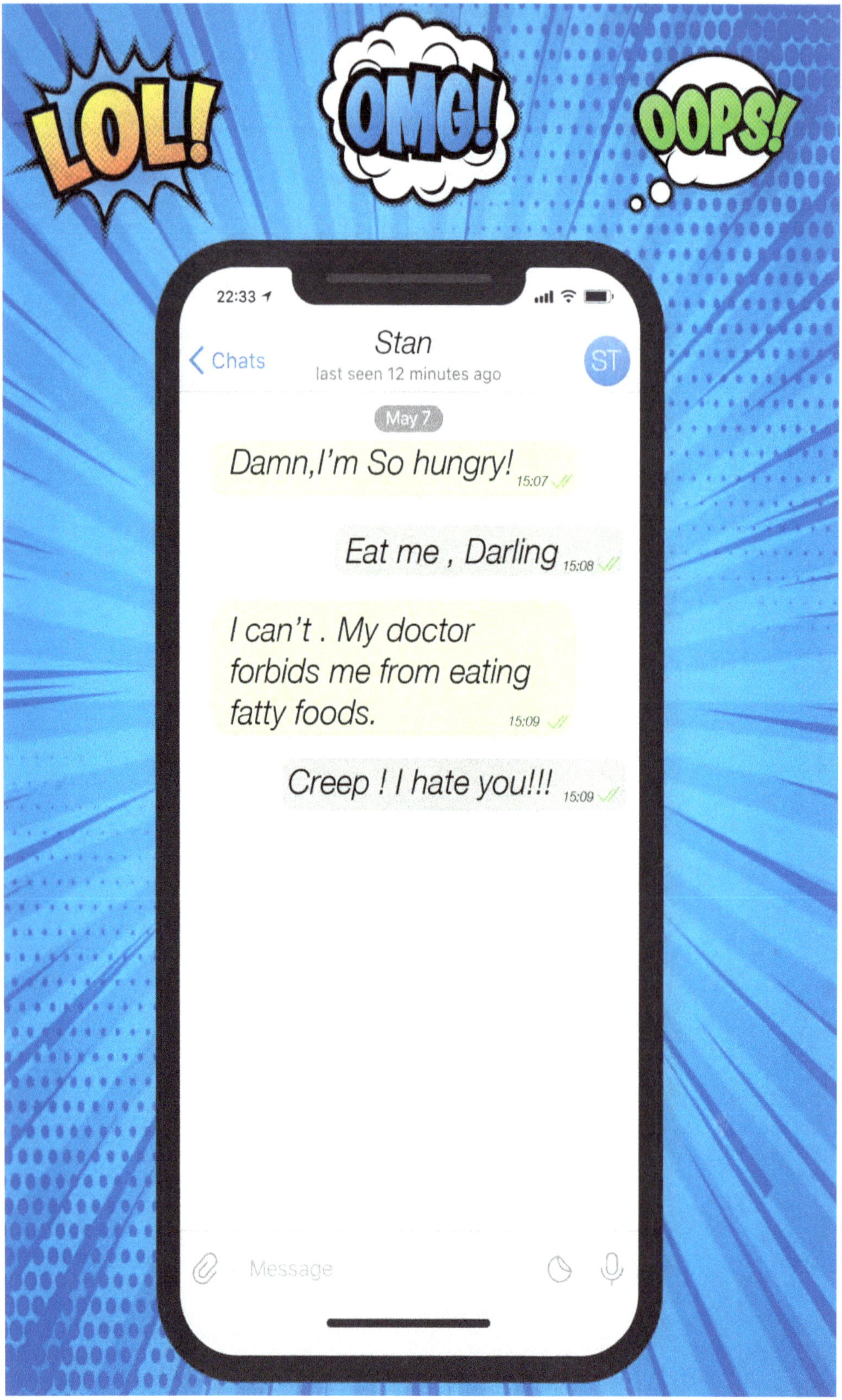
LOL!
OMG!
OOPS!
22:33
Chats
Stan
last seen 12 minutes ago
ST
May 7
Damn,I'm So hungry! 15:07
Eat me , Darling 15:08
I can't . My doctor forbids me from eating fatty foods. 15:09
Creep ! I hate you!!! 15:09
Message

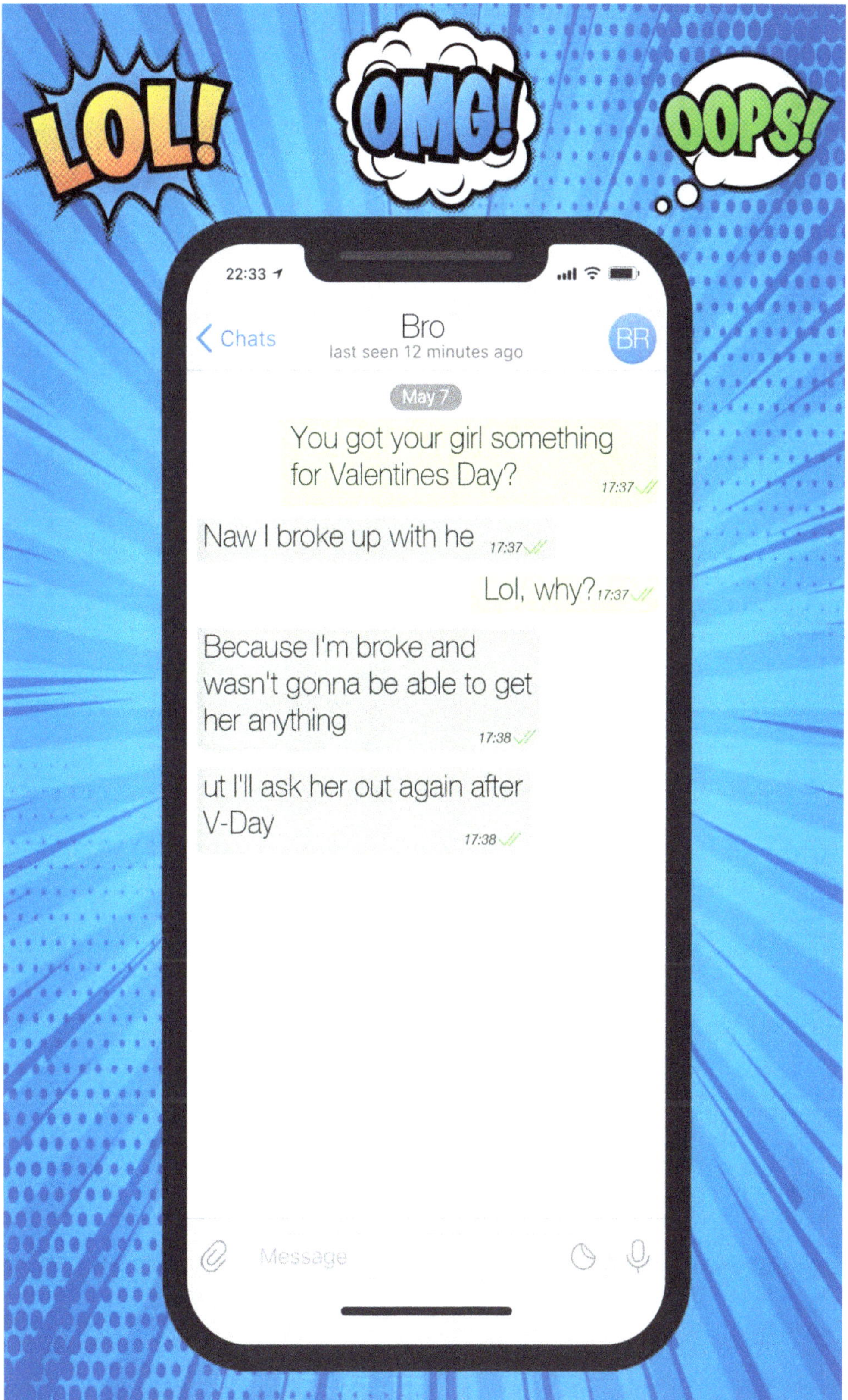
LOL!
OMG!
OOPS!
22:33
Chats
Bro
last seen 12 minutes ago
BR
May 7
You got your girl something for Valentines Day? 17:37
Naw I broke up with he 17:37
Lol, why? 17:37
Because I'm broke and wasn't gonna be able to get her anything 17:38
ut I'll ask her out again after V-Day 17:38
Message

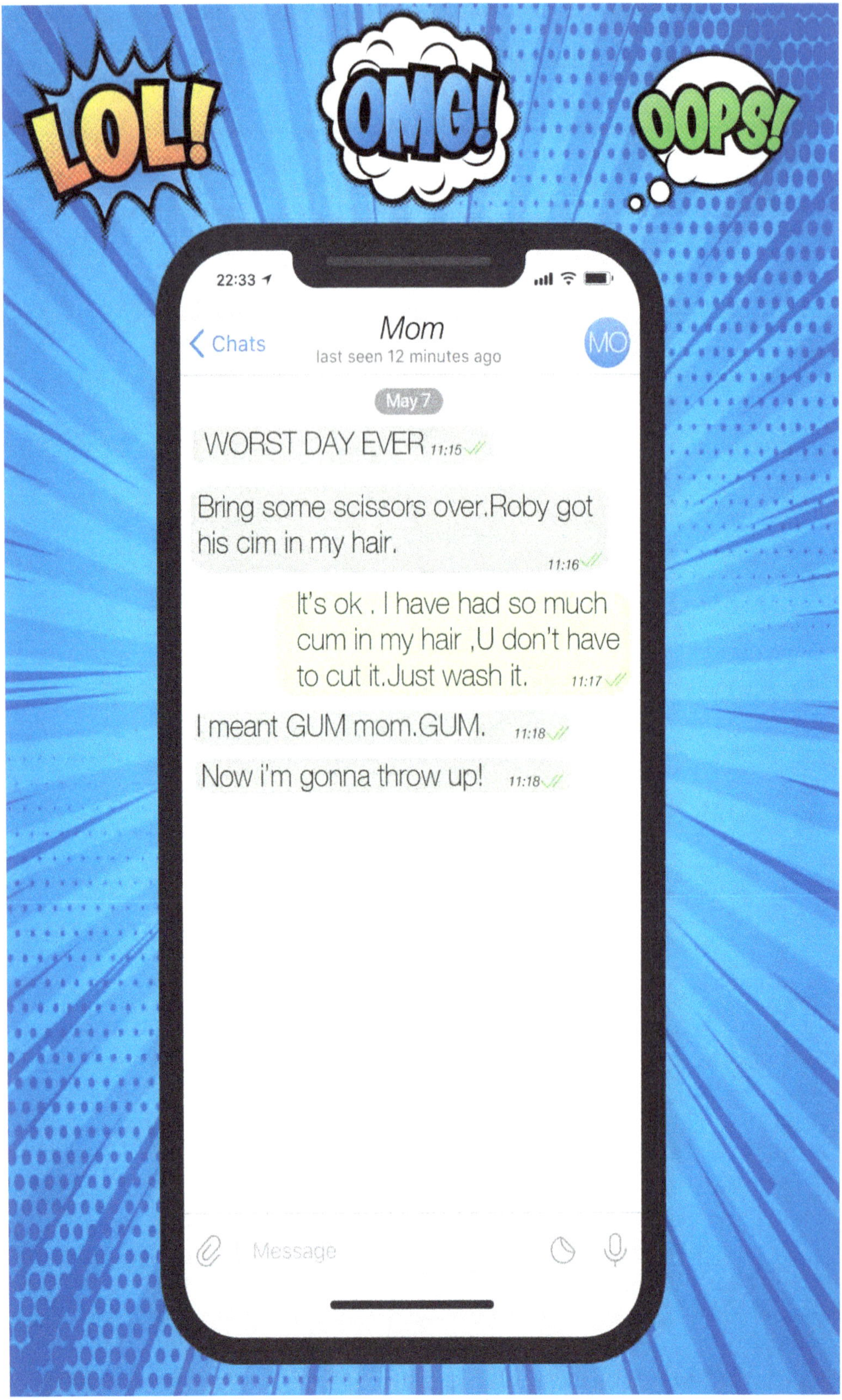
LOL!
OMG!
OOPS!
22:33
Chats
Mom
last seen 12 minutes ago
MO
May 7
WORST DAY EVER 11:15
Bring some scissors over.Roby got his cim in my hair. 11:16
It's ok . I have had so much cum in my hair ,U don't have to cut it.Just wash it. 11:17
I meant GUM mom.GUM. 11:18
Now i'm gonna throw up! 11:18
Message

LOL!
OMG!
OOPS!
22:33
Chats
Dad
last seen 12 minutes ago
DA
May 7
Hi , I am fairky new to Facebook .Mind accepting my friends request ?
09:11
you made a facebok?WTF
09:12
What does "WTF" mean??
09:12
oh it means Welcome to Facebook
09:13
Message

LOL!
OMG!
OOPS!
22:33
Chats
My Love
last seen 12 minutes ago
MY
May 7
So how do I tell this girl that love her? 18:50
Just suck it up and do it. 18:50
Ok love you 18:51
Awww love you too, now go tell her! 18:52
ljust did :) 18:53
How did it go??? did she say it back?!? 18:54
Message

LOL!
OMG!
OOPS!
22:33
Chats
Bf
last seen 12 minutes ago
BF
May 7
Baby, do you promise you'll never love another girl? 23:25
No, I'll love another girl in about nine months. She'll look just like you and call you Mommy. 23:26
Aw, ur so sweet! 23:26
Wait, NINE MONTHS. 23:27
Yeah, the condom broke last night 23:27
Message

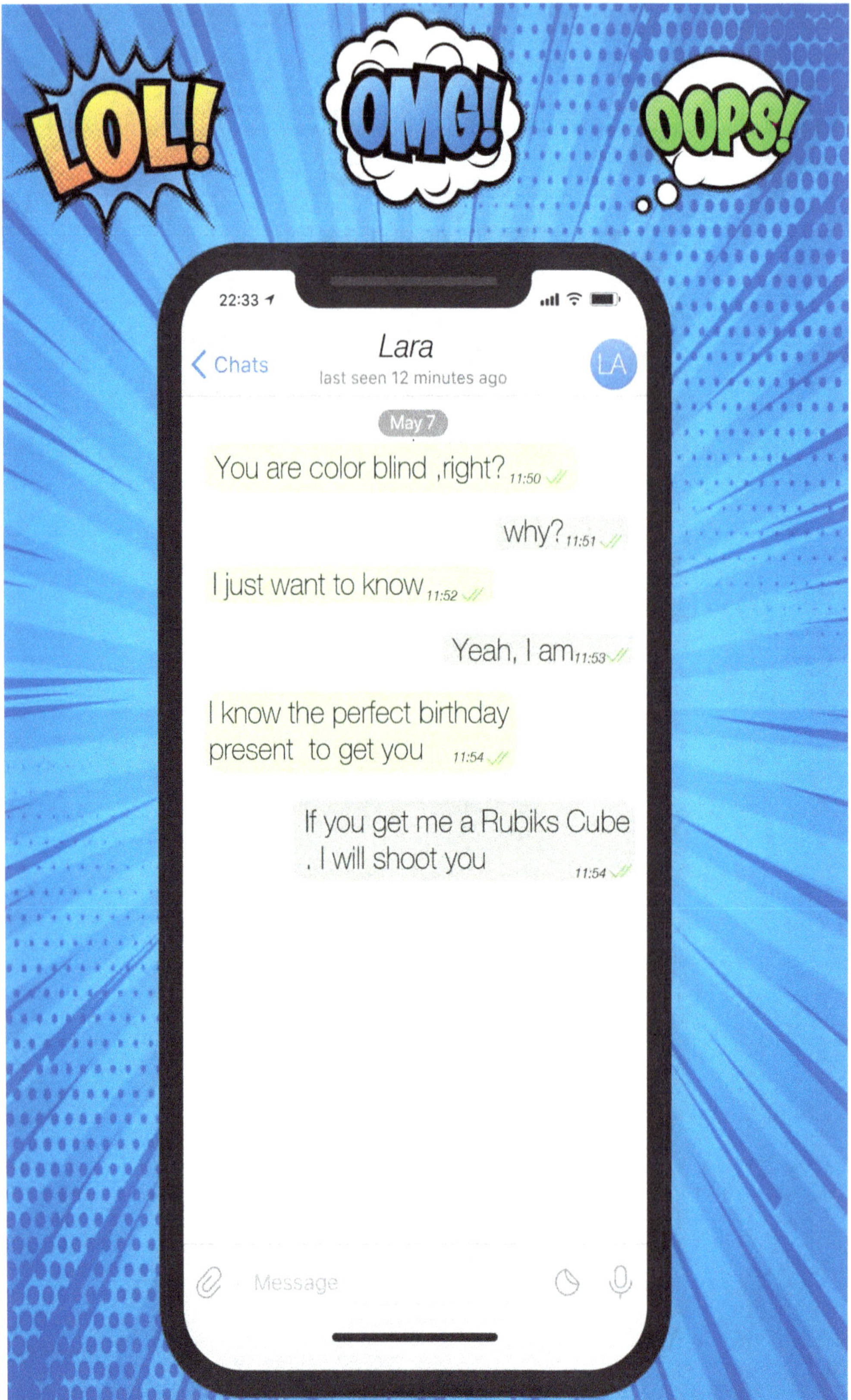
LOL!
OMG!
OOPS!
22:33
Chats
Lara
last seen 12 minutes ago
LA
May 7
You are color blind ,right? 11:50
why? 11:51
I just want to know 11:52
Yeah, I am 11:53
I know the perfect birthday present to get you 11:54
If you get me a Rubiks Cube . I will shoot you 11:54
Message

LOL!
OMG!
OOPS!
22:33
Chats
Dexter
last seen 12 minutes ago
DE
May 7
Hey dude,I bet ten bucks i can make you math so hard. 22:00
OMG IMEANT BATH 22:00
WTF I MEANT LAUGH 22:01
hahahha lol you just made my day dude 22:02
you owe me ten bucks 22:02
Message

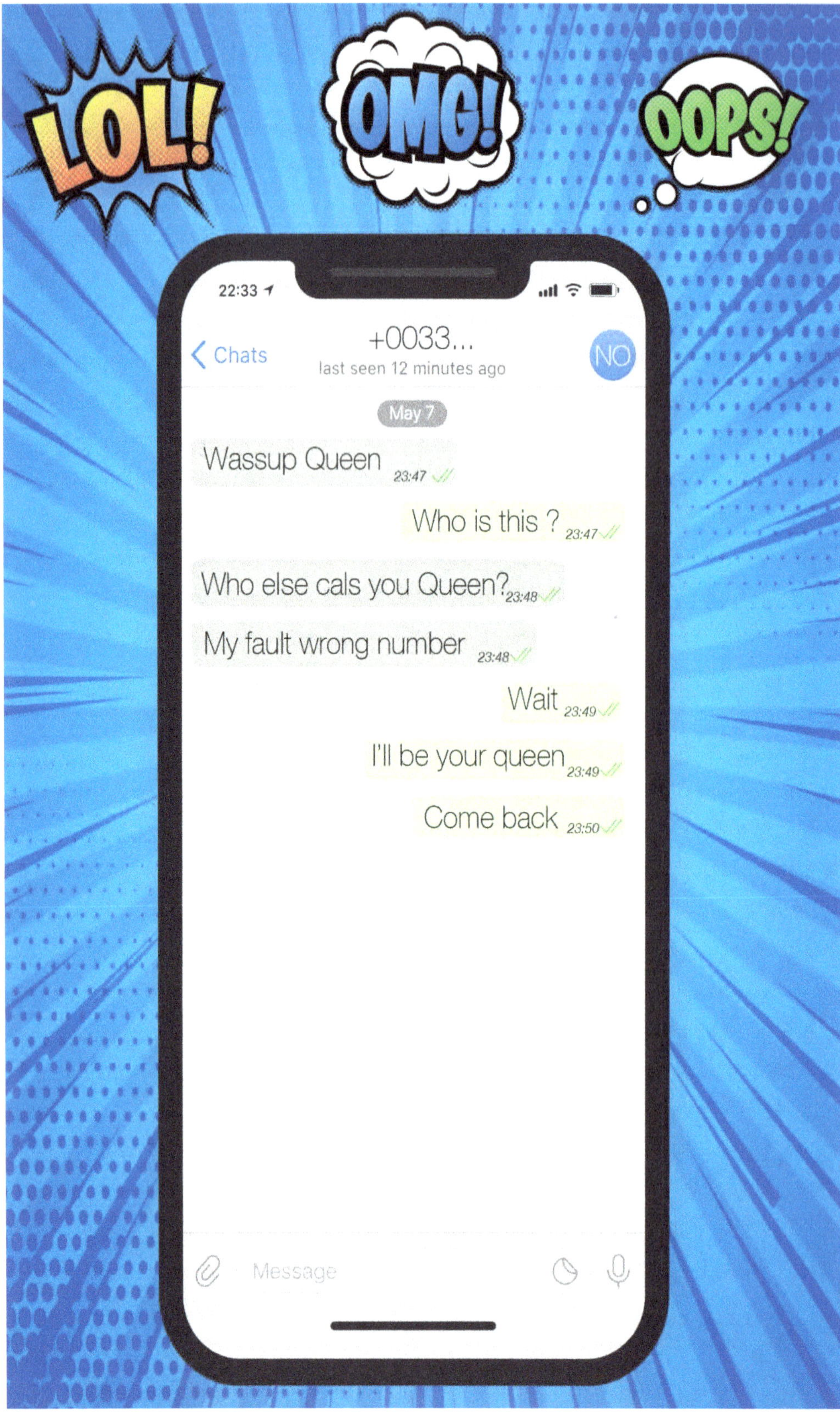

LOL!
OMG!
OOPS!
22:33
Chats
+0033...
last seen 12 minutes ago
NO
May 7
Wassup Queen 23:47
Who is this ? 23:47
Who else cals you Queen? 23:48
My fault wrong number 23:48
Wait 23:49
I'll be your queen 23:49
Come back 23:50
Message

LOL!
OMG!
OOPS!
22:33
Chats
Friend
last seen 12 minutes ago
FR
May 7
Your such a jerk! 01:40
You're 01:40
OMG your so annoying! 01:41
You're 01:42
Stop doingg that Your making me mad! 01:43
You're 01:44
Fine! I'm gonna slap you're face! 01:44
Your* 01:45
Message

LOL!
OMG!
OOPS!
22:33
Chats
Crush
last seen 12 minutes ago
CR
May 7
Hi Bro 09:50
Hi baby 09:51
What baby? 09:51
What bro ? 09:51
Hello...I have a boyfriend don't try to be one be in your limit 09:51
Oh hello madam.I have a sister ..don't try to make me your brother 09:52
Message

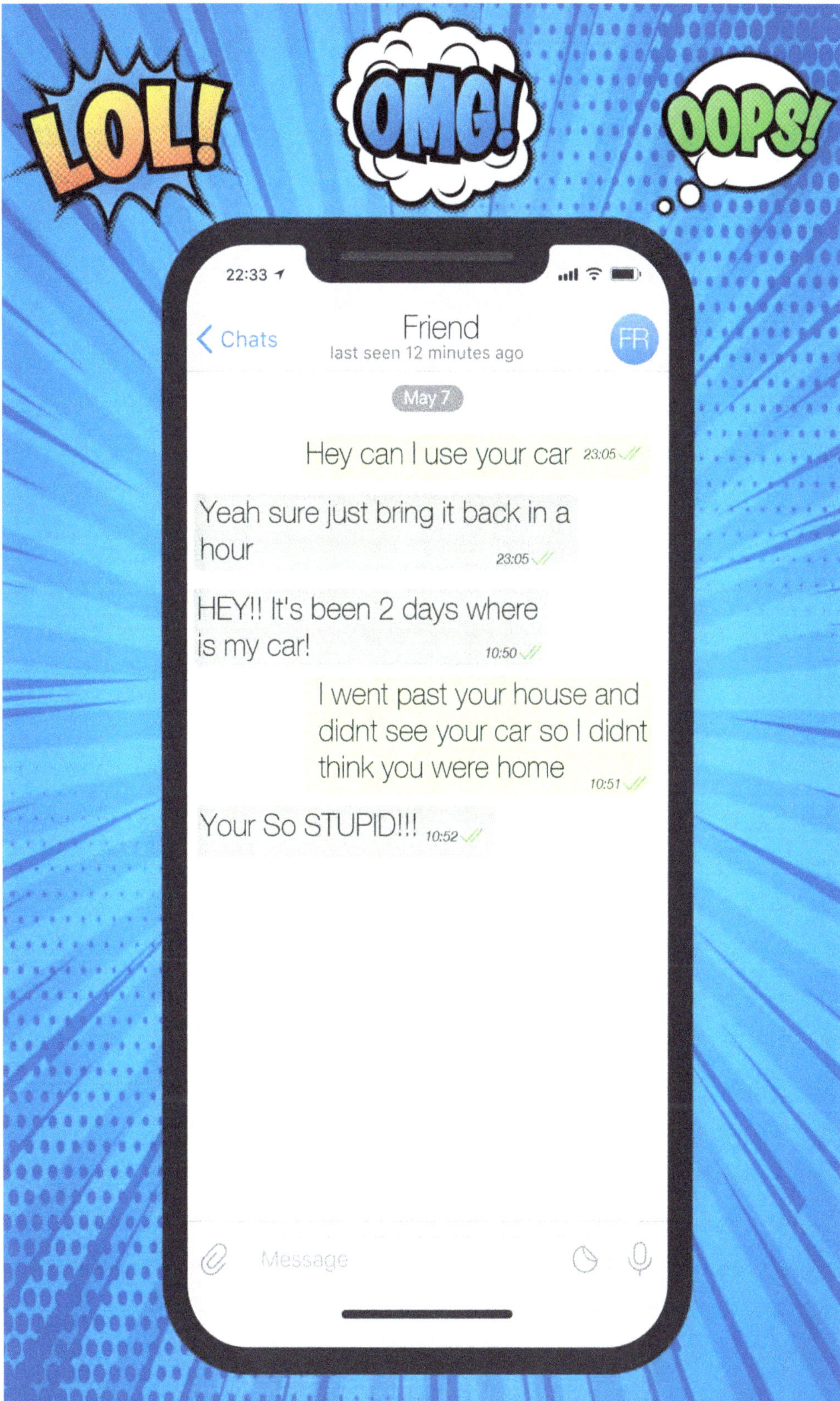
LOL!
OMG!
OOPS!
22:33
Chats
Friend
last seen 12 minutes ago
FR
May 7
Hey can I use your car 23:05
Yeah sure just bring it back in a hour 23:05
HEY!! It's been 2 days where is my car! 10:50
I went past your house and didnt see your car so I didnt think you were home 10:51
Your So STUPID!!! 10:52
Message

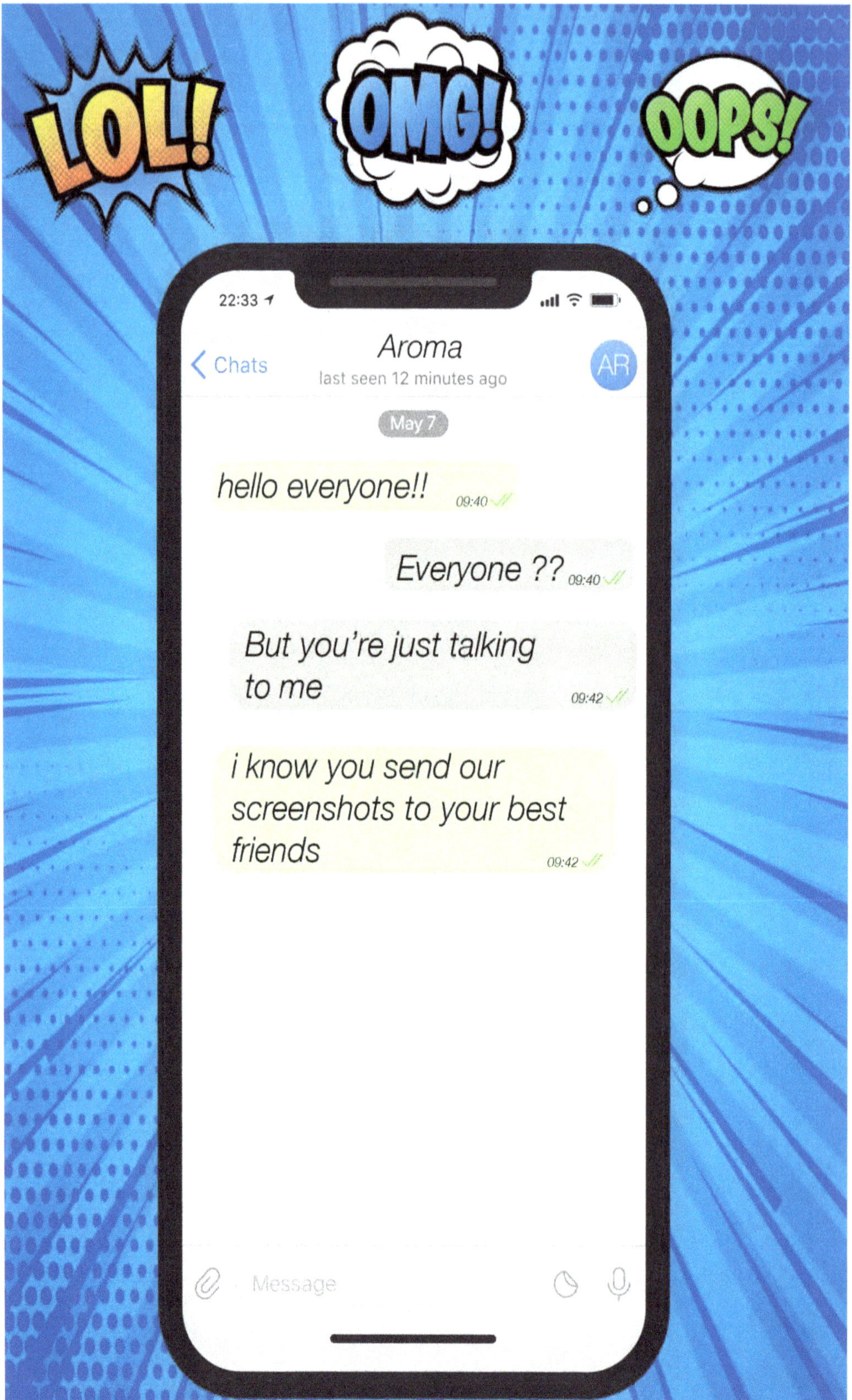

LOL!
OMG!
OOPS!
22:33
Chats
Aroma
last seen 12 minutes ago
AR
May 7
hello everyone!! 09:40
Everyone ?? 09:40
But you're just talking to me 09:42
i know you send our screenshots to your best friends 09:42
Message

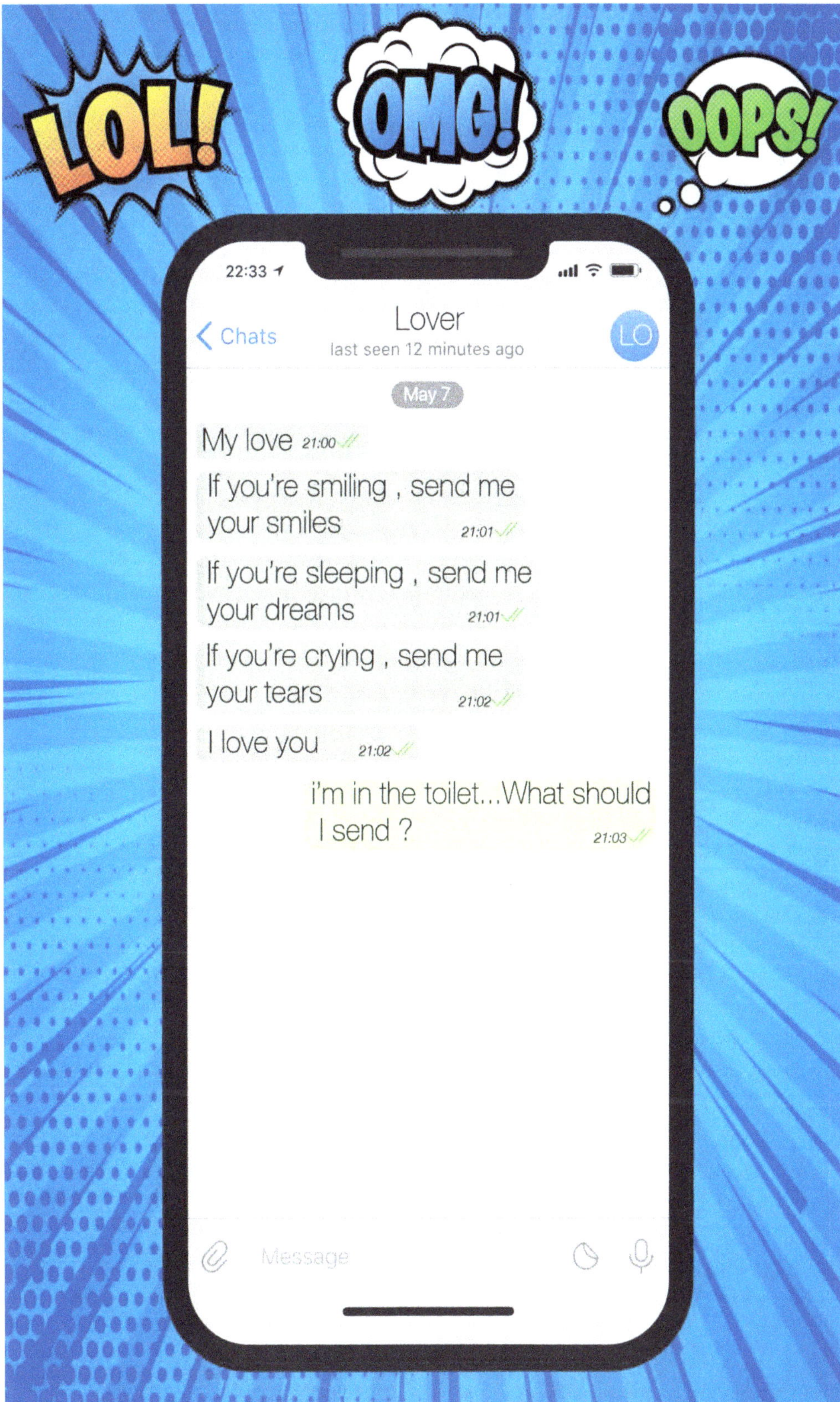
LOL!
OMG!
OOPS!
22:33
Chats
Lover
last seen 12 minutes ago
LO
May 7
My love 21:00
If you're smiling , send me your smiles 21:01
If you're sleeping , send me your dreams 21:01
If you're crying , send me your tears 21:02
I love you 21:02
i'm in the toilet...What should I send ? 21:03
Message

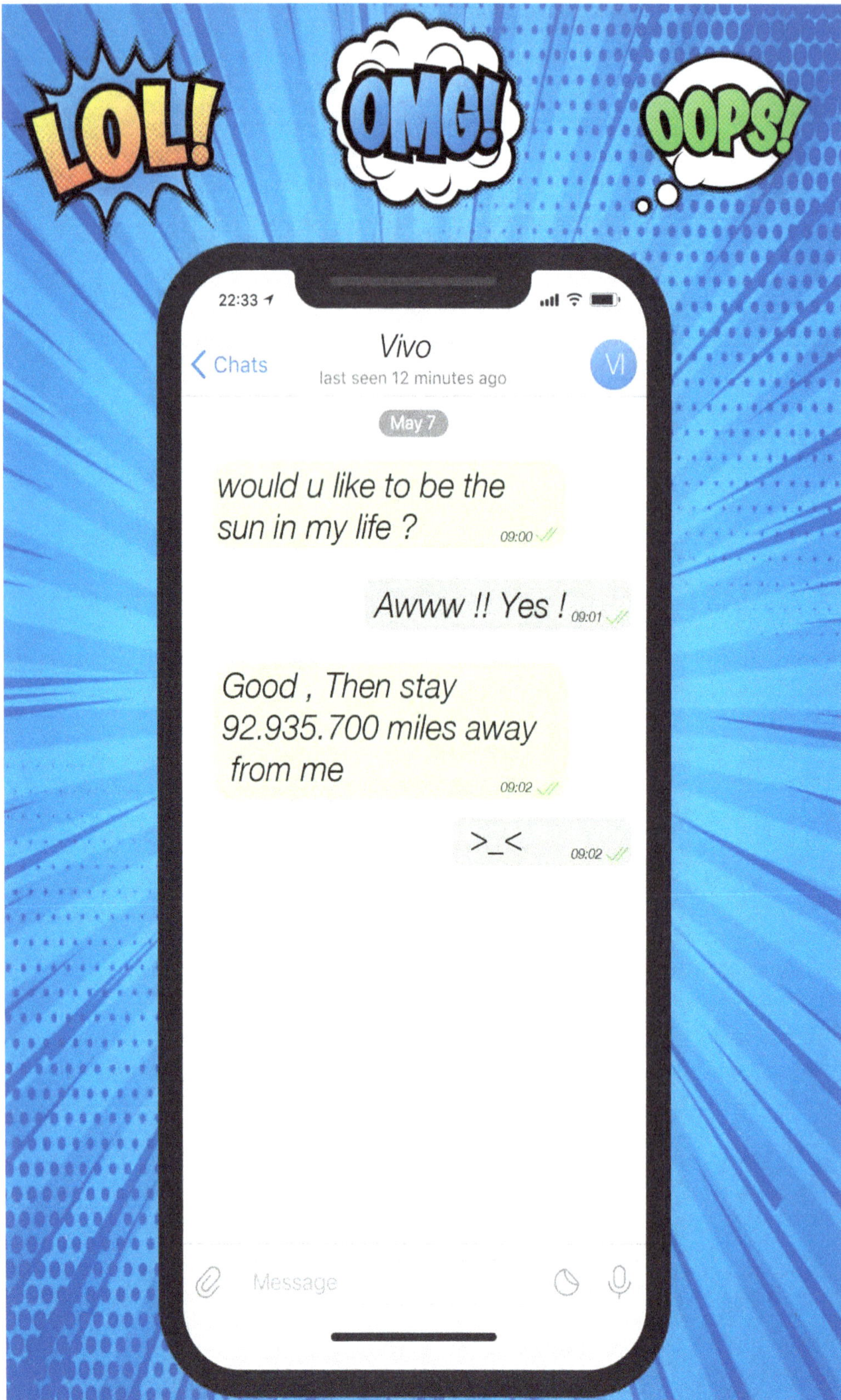
LOL!
OMG!
OOPS!
22:33
Chats
Vivo
last seen 12 minutes ago
VI
May 7
would u like to be the sun in my life ?
09:00
Awww !! Yes !
09:01
Good , Then stay 92.935.700 miles away from me
09:02
>_<
09:02
Message

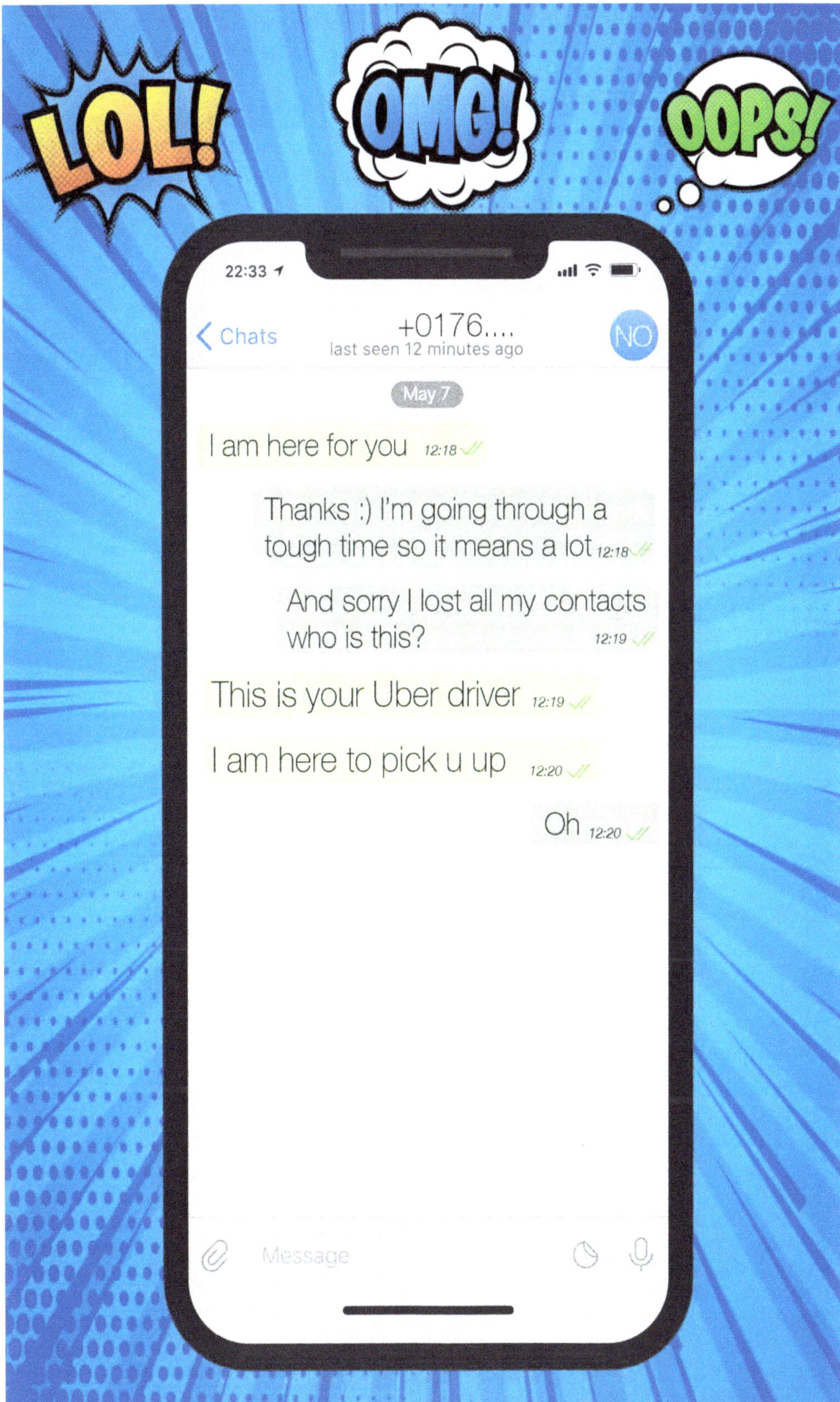
LOL!
OMG!
OOPS!
22:33
Chats
+0176....
last seen 12 minutes ago
NO
May 7
I am here for you 12:18
Thanks :) I'm going through a tough time so it means a lot 12:18
And sorry I lost all my contacts who is this? 12:19
This is your Uber driver 12:19
I am here to pick u up 12:20
Oh 12:20
Message

LOL!
OMG!
OOPS!
22:33
Chats
Dude
last seen 12 minutes ago
DE
May 7
How do you manage to be cool all the time? 05:42
Bcuz I don't get into arguments with stupid people, I just cut it short and say:" you are right" 05:43
But that's completely irrational and wrong 05:45
You are right 05:47
Message

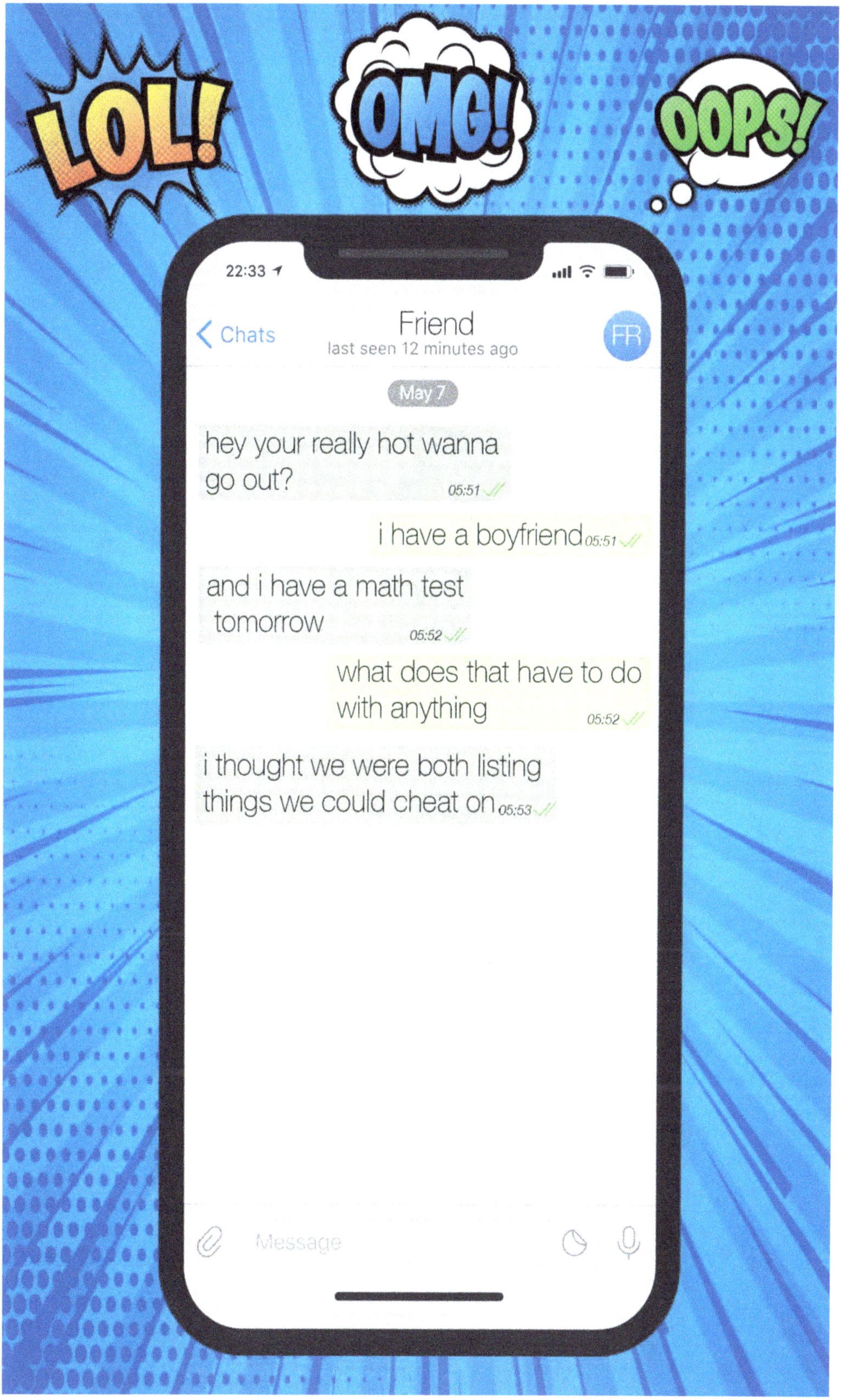
LOL!
OMG!
OOPS!
22:33
Chats
Friend
last seen 12 minutes ago
FR
May 7
hey your really hot wanna go out? 05:51
i have a boyfriend 05:51
and i have a math test tomorrow 05:52
what does that have to do with anything 05:52
i thought we were both listing things we could cheat on 05:53
Message

LOL!
OMG!
OOPS!
22:33
Chats
Friend
last seen 12 minutes ago
FR
May 7
What's ur major 09:42
Communications ,Yours? 09:43
I'm doing biology I want to be a pedestrian 09:45
A what lmfao 09:47
Like I want to be a doctor for kids 09:47
Pediatrician? 05:49
Message

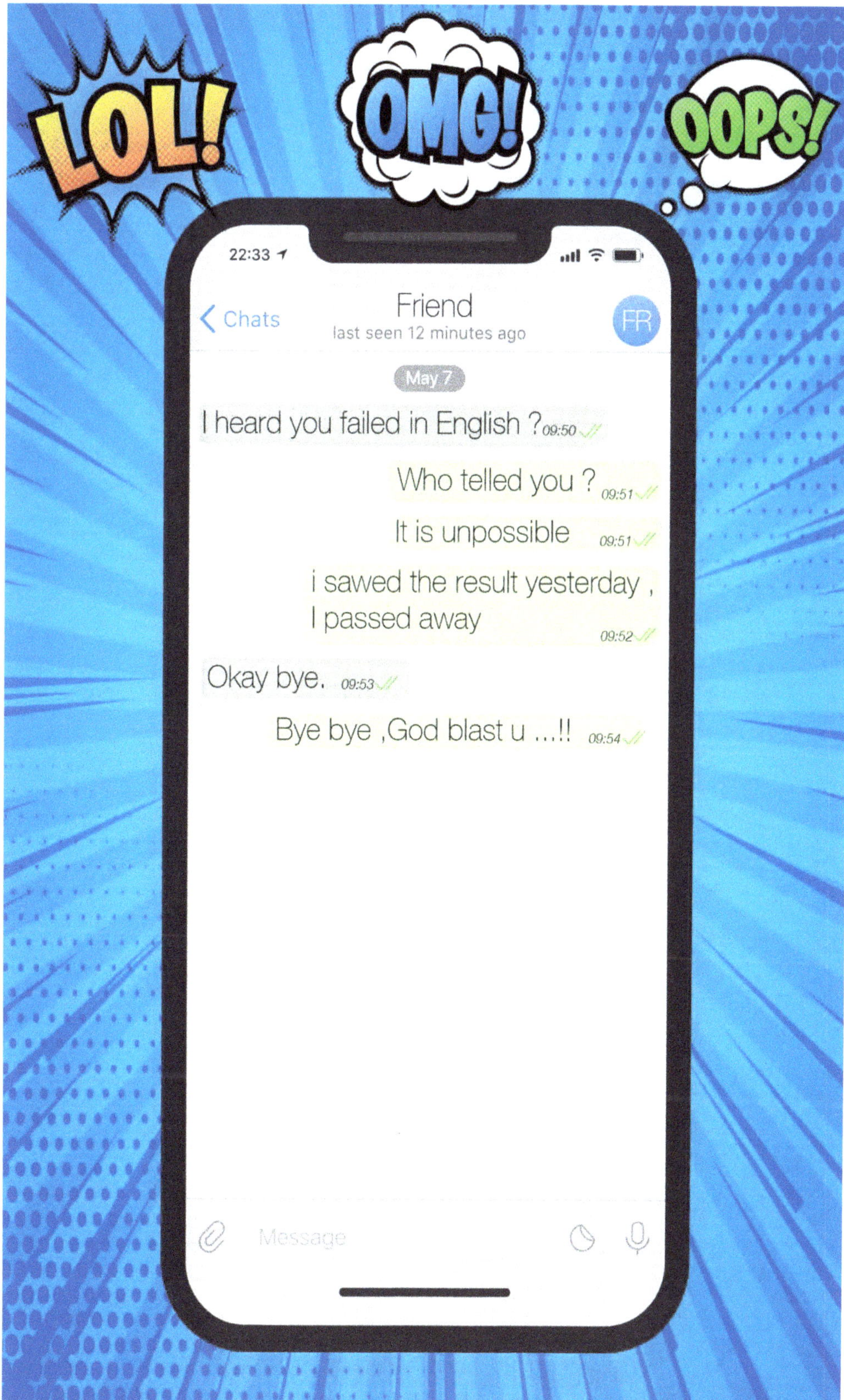

LOL!
OMG!
OOPS!
22:33
Chats
Friend
last seen 12 minutes ago
FR
May 7
I heard you failed in English ? 09:50
Who telled you ? 09:51
It is unpossible 09:51
i sawed the result yesterday ,
I passed away 09:52
Okay bye. 09:53
Bye bye ,God blast u ...!! 09:54
Message

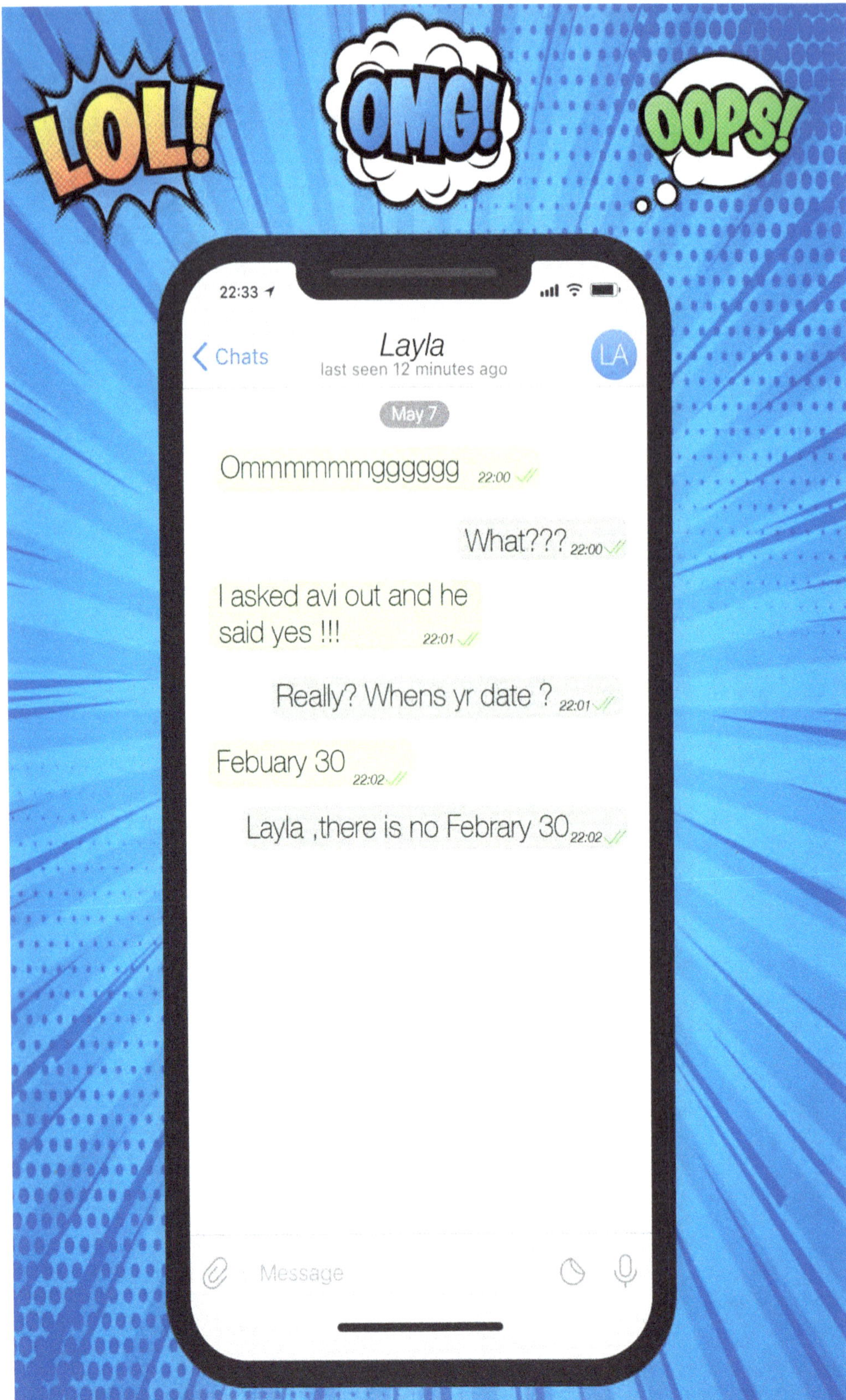
LOL!
OMG!
OOPS!
22:33
Chats
Layla
last seen 12 minutes ago
LA
May 7
Ommmmmmgggggg 22:00
What??? 22:00
I asked avi out and he said yes !!! 22:01
Really? Whens yr date ? 22:01
Febuary 30 22:02
Layla ,there is no Febrary 30 22:02
Message

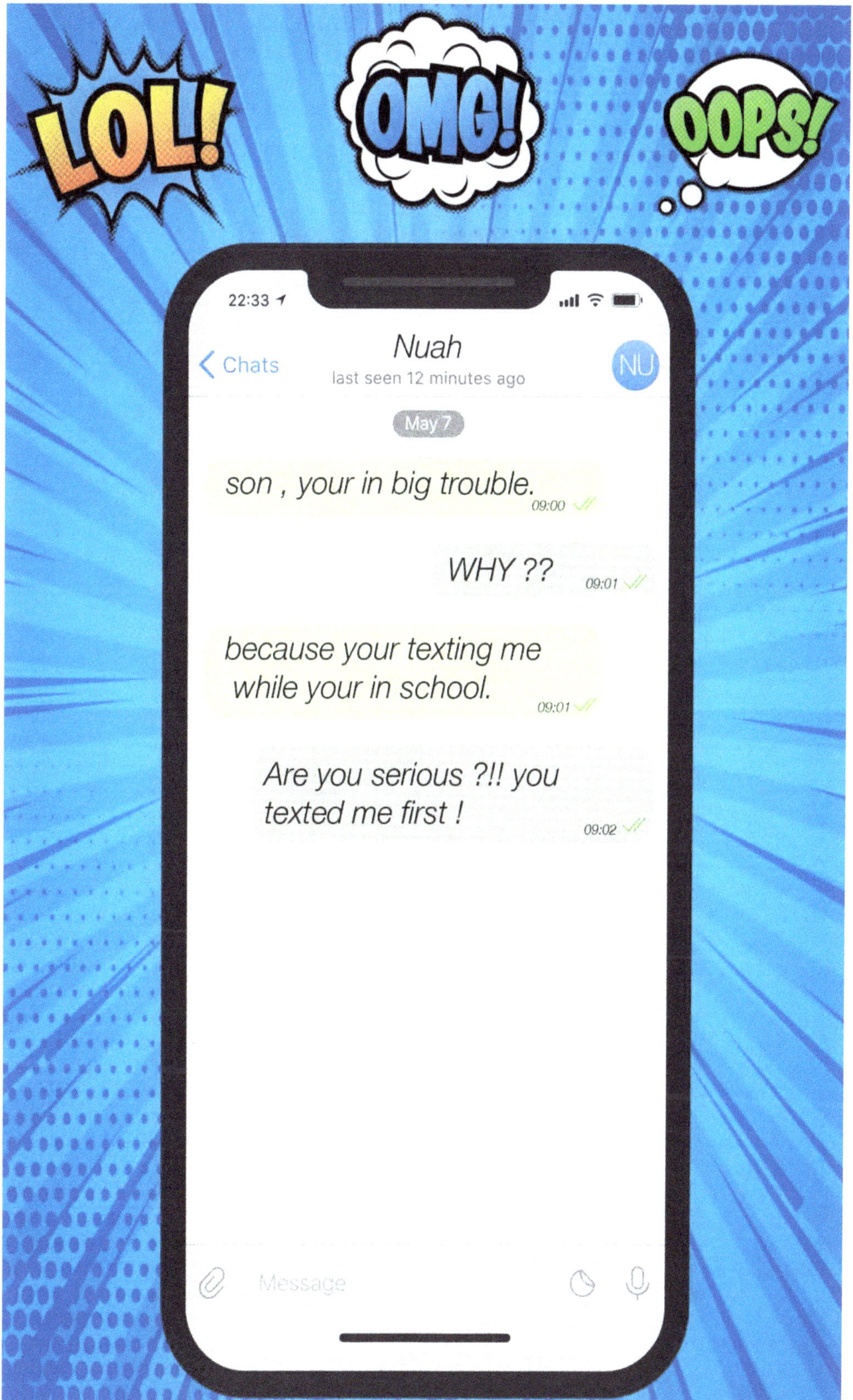
LOL!
OMG!
OOPS!
22:33
Nuah
last seen 12 minutes ago
Chats
NU
May 7
son , your in big trouble.
09:00
WHY ??
09:01
because your texting me while your in school.
09:01
Are you serious ?!! you texted me first !
09:02
Message

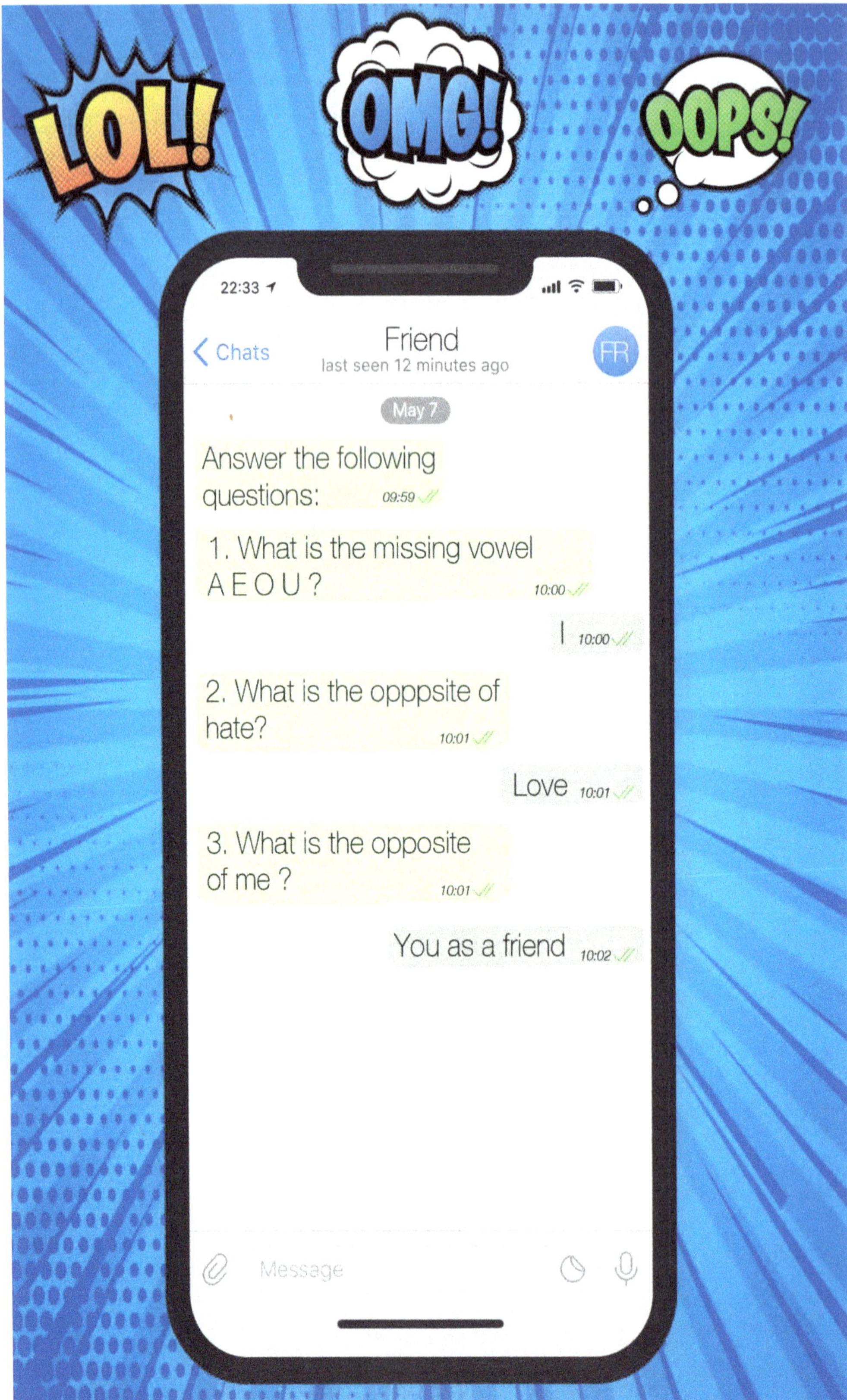
LOL!
OMG!
OOPS!
22:33
Chats
Friend
last seen 12 minutes ago
FR
May 7
Answer the following questions: 09:59
1. What is the missing vowel A E O U ? 10:00
I 10:00
2. What is the opppsite of hate? 10:01
Love 10:01
3. What is the opposite of me ? 10:01
You as a friend 10:02
Message

LOL!
OMG!
OOPS!
22:33
Chats
Safae
last seen 12 minutes ago
SA
May 7
How is Our Pregnant Little Daughter ?
15:07
Mom .How did you know?
15:08
I Meant Perfect
15:09
Wait WHAT !!
15:09
Message

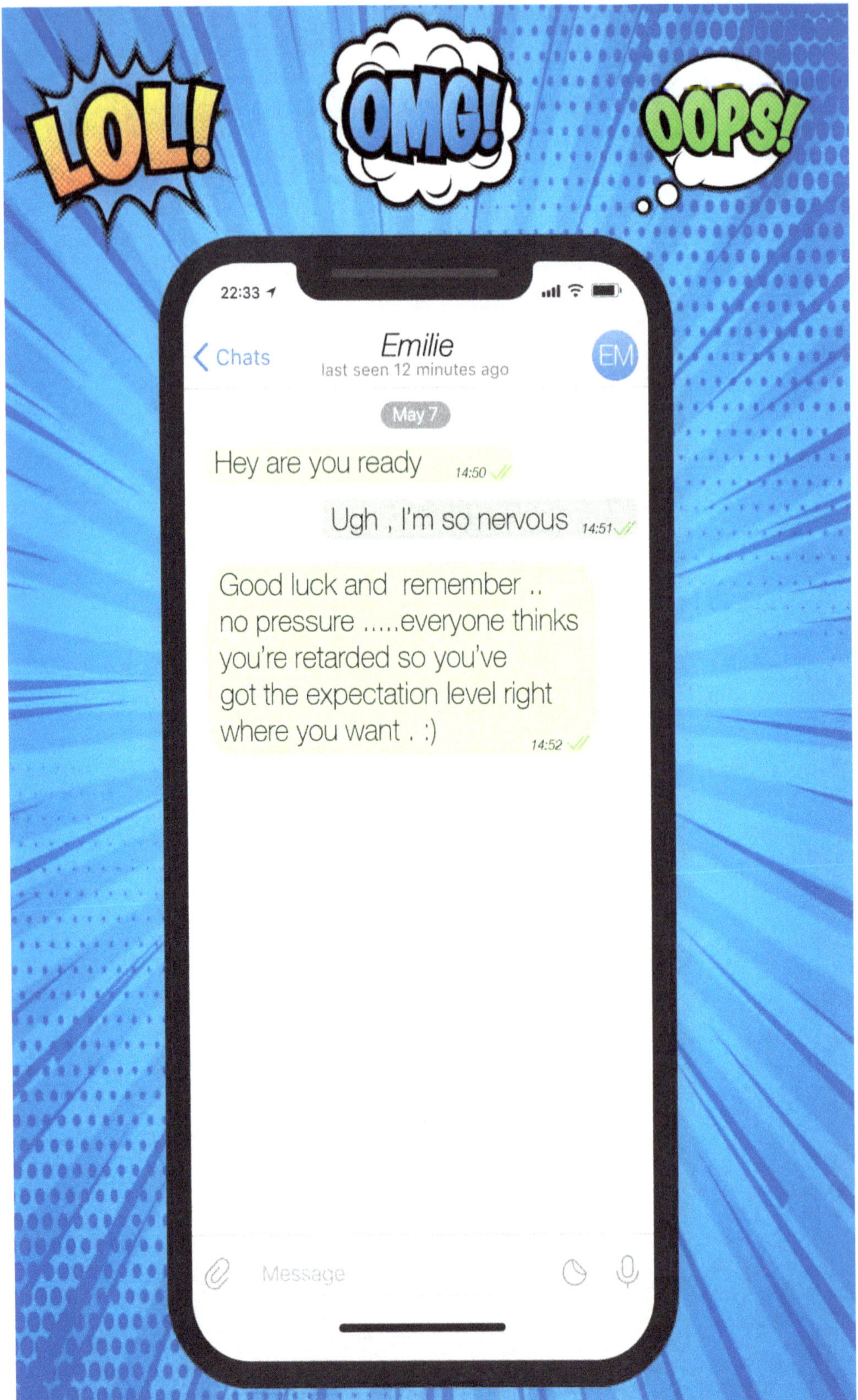
LOL!
OMG!
OOPS!
22:33
Chats
Emilie
last seen 12 minutes ago
EM
May 7
Hey are you ready 14:50
Ugh , I'm so nervous 14:51
Good luck and remember .. no pressure .....everyone thinks you're retarded so you've got the expectation level right where you want . :) 14:52
Message

LOL!
OMG!
OOPS!
22:33
Chats
Raychel
last seen 12 minutes ago
RA
May 7
Hey whatcha doing 19:24
Cleaning my boobs,people were stepping all over them 19:25
Uhhh what ? 19:25
hahahhaha OMG I meant boots, They are all scuffed up lol 19:25
Message

LOL!
OMG!
OOPS!
22:33
Chats
Helen
last seen 12 minutes ago
HE
May 7
What's up?? 15:07
I've just ruined a relationship that lasted for 5 years. 15:08
Oh,I'm sorry .. 15:09
It's fine . It wasn't mine. 15:09
Message

LOL!
OMG!
OOPS!
22:33
Chats
Mom
last seen 12 minutes ago
MO
May 7
Uh, Mom this girl keeps telling everyone I'm pregnant with Michael's baby. What should I do? 00:26
Beat her ass, Sophia, beat her ass!! 00:26
I can't! 00:27
Why?!!? It's bad for the baby. 00:28
Message

LOL!
OMG!
OOPS!
22:33
Chats
Dude
last seen 12 minutes ago
DU
May 7
I wasn't even that drunk 07:12
You took out a kitchen knife and made kelly throw vegtables at you. 07:12
and were yelling "I am the fruit ninja!" 07:13
Was i any good? 07:13
Noooo 07:14
Message

LOL!
OMG!
OOPS!
22:33
Chats
Mike
last seen 12 minutes ago
MI
May 7
Could you send me Uncle Bill's adress? 19:11
I caby found Muir gladness giver.Canny text nose. 19:11
Huh? 19:13
I found my glasses! 19:13
Message

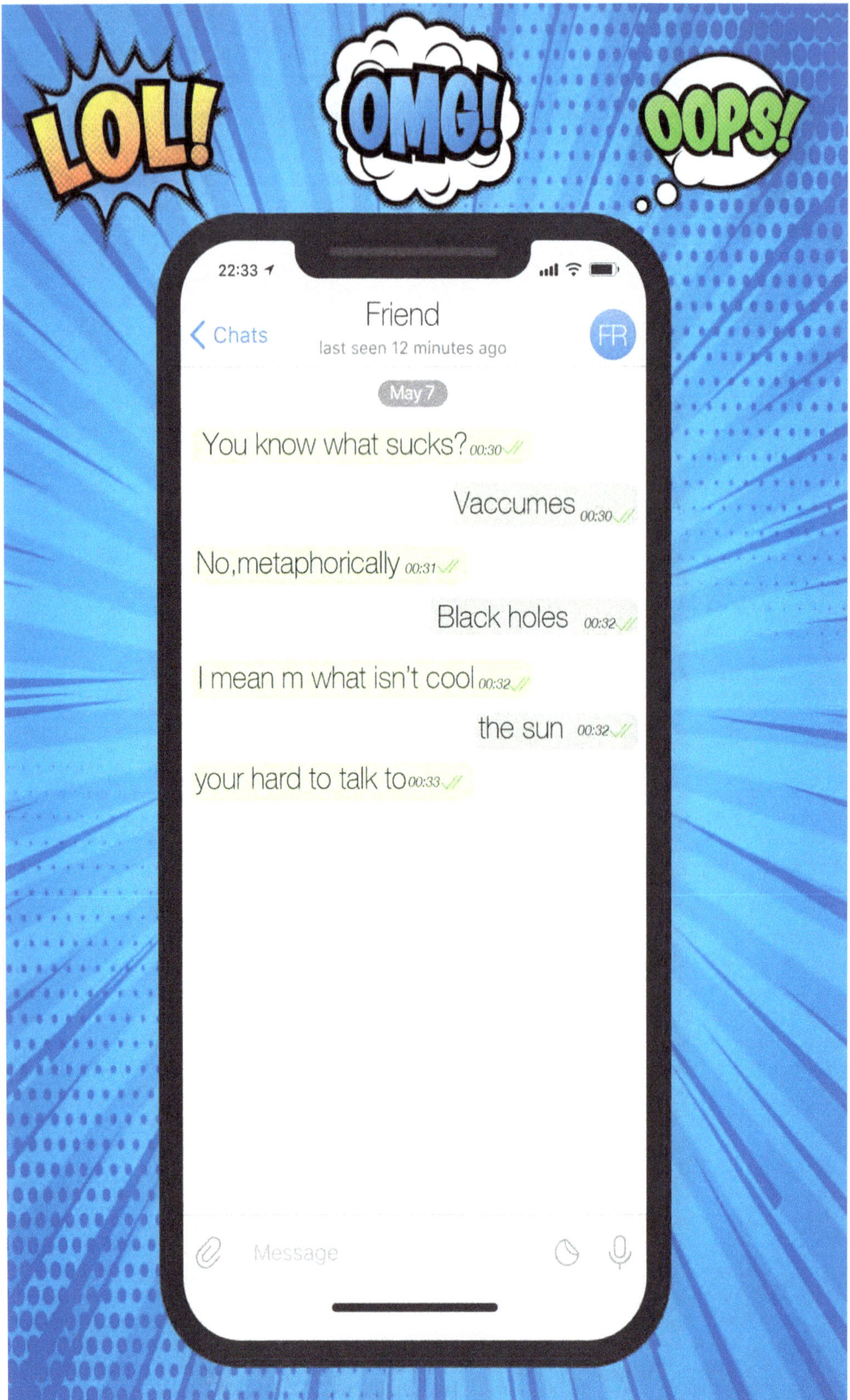

LOL!
OMG!
OOPS!
22:33
Chats
Friend
last seen 12 minutes ago
FR
May 7
You know what sucks? 00:30
Vaccumes 00:30
No,metaphorically 00:31
Black holes 00:32
I mean m what isn't cool 00:32
the sun 00:32
your hard to talk to 00:33
Message

LOL!
OMG!
OOPS!
22:33
Chats
Friend
last seen 12 minutes ago
FR
May 7
Hey wat's up 09:00
I'm at the mall with my bf and he just bought me the prettiest necklace after he told me he loved me 09:02
Reality? 09:02
Sitting on the floor eating mac and cheese because my dog peed on the couch 09:03
HAHA! 09:04
Message

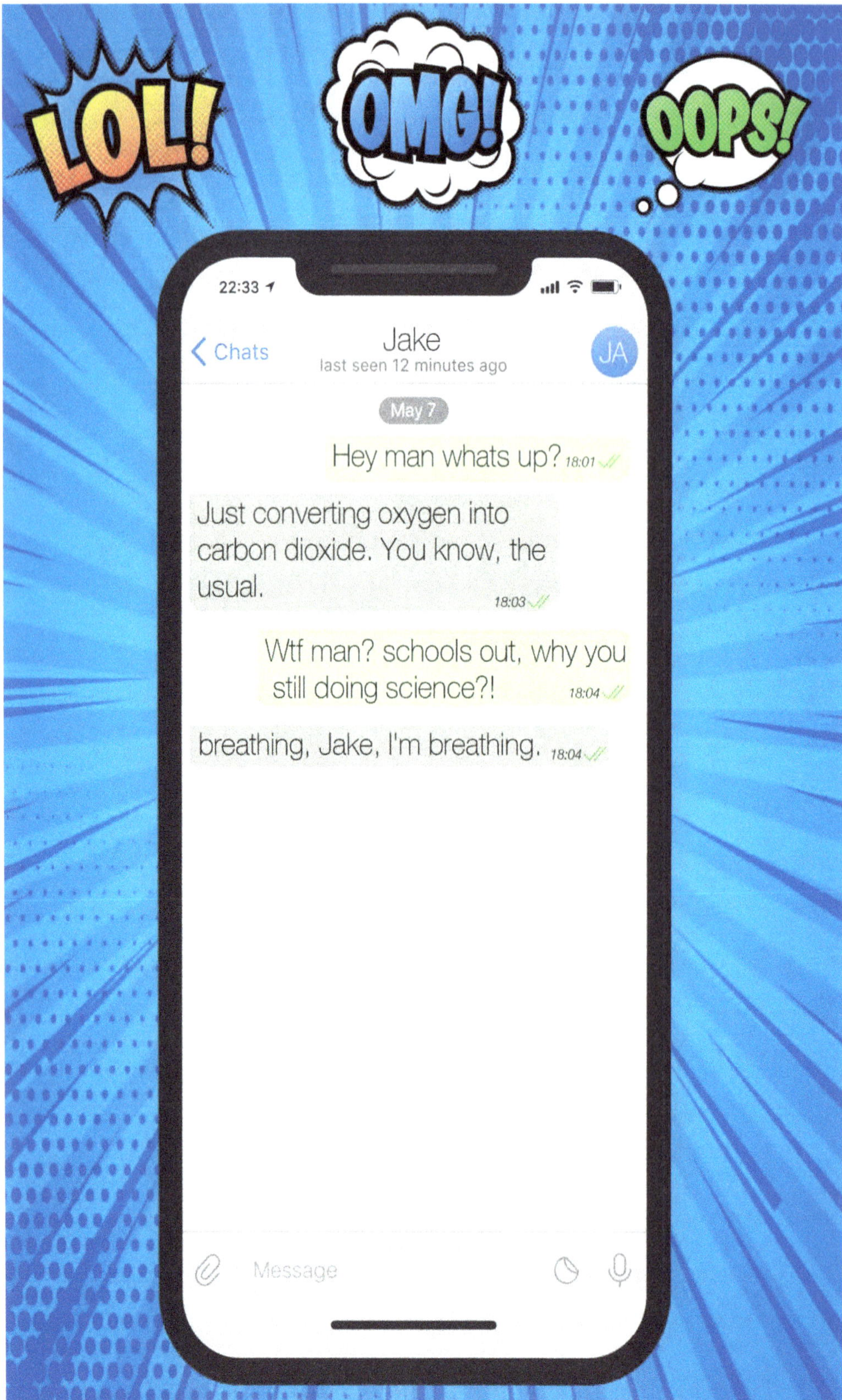
LOL!
OMG!
OOPS!
22:33
Chats
Jake
last seen 12 minutes ago
JA
May 7
Hey man whats up? 18:01
Just converting oxygen into carbon dioxide. You know, the usual. 18:03
Wtf man? schools out, why you still doing science?! 18:04
breathing, Jake, I'm breathing. 18:04
Message

LOL!
OMG!
OOPS!
22:33
Chats
Mom
last seen 12 minutes ago
AN
May 7
Hi sweetie ow is school? :D 22:00
Bad i got detention 22:15
Why 22:16
Cause someone texted me during class 22:16
Who? 22:17
You stupid 22:17
Message

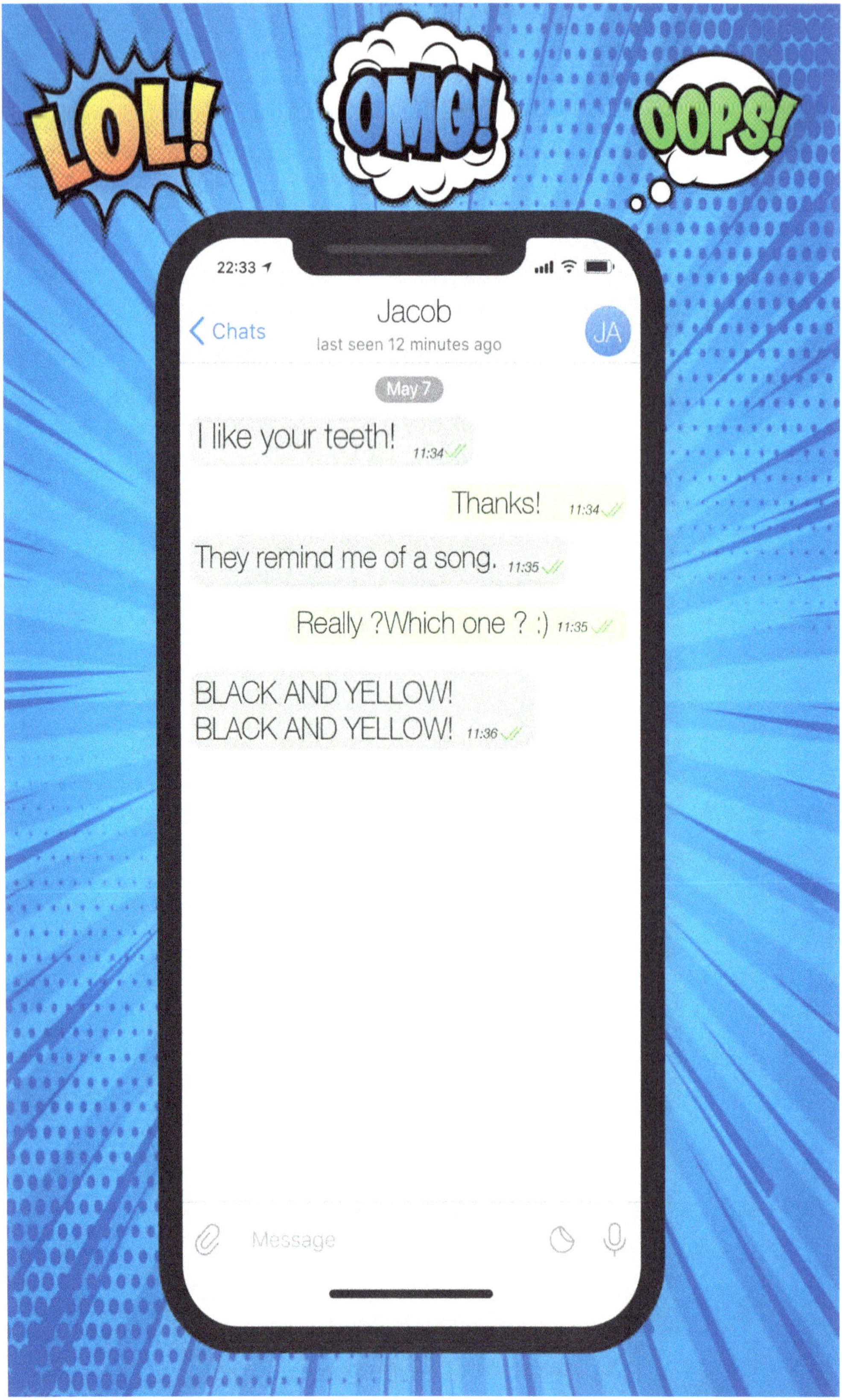
LOL!
OMG!
OOPS!
22:33
Chats
Jacob
last seen 12 minutes ago
JA
May 7
I like your teeth! 11:34
Thanks! 11:34
They remind me of a song. 11:35
Really ?Which one ? :) 11:35
BLACK AND YELLOW!
BLACK AND YELLOW! 11:36
Message

LOL!
OMG!
OOPS!
22:33
Chats
Gary
last seen 12 minutes ago
GA
May 7
Hey can I get my pencil back I have an exam in 30 . 09:33
Yeah I wil got get it out of my lover 09:33
You and Dan are into some kinky stuff,Haha 09:34
* Locker .Love it ! 09:34
Message

LOL!
OMG!
OOPS!
22:33
Chats
Daddy
last seen 12 minutes ago
DA
May 7
Hi sweetie where are you ? 21:15
I'm right upstairs dad... 21:15
Sorry honey,you don't need to pick up condoms ,she's home.I swera that girl needs more friends... 21:16
Still me dad. 21:18
.... 21:18
Message

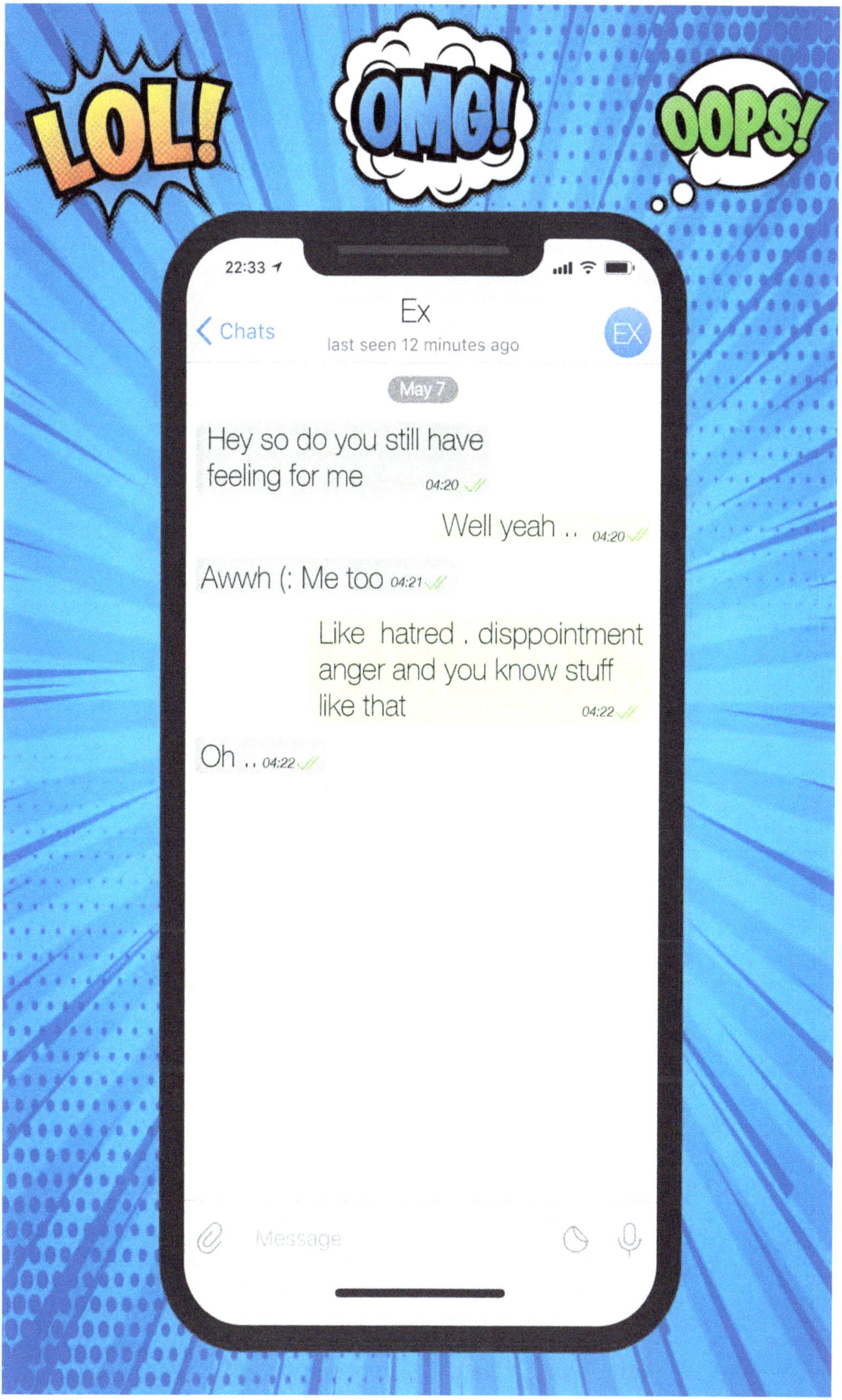

LOL!
OMG!
OOPS!
22:33
Ex
Chats
last seen 12 minutes ago
EX
May 7
Hey so do you still have feeling for me 04:20
Well yeah .. 04:20
Awwh (: Me too 04:21
Like hatred . disppointment anger and you know stuff like that 04:22
Oh .. 04:22
Message

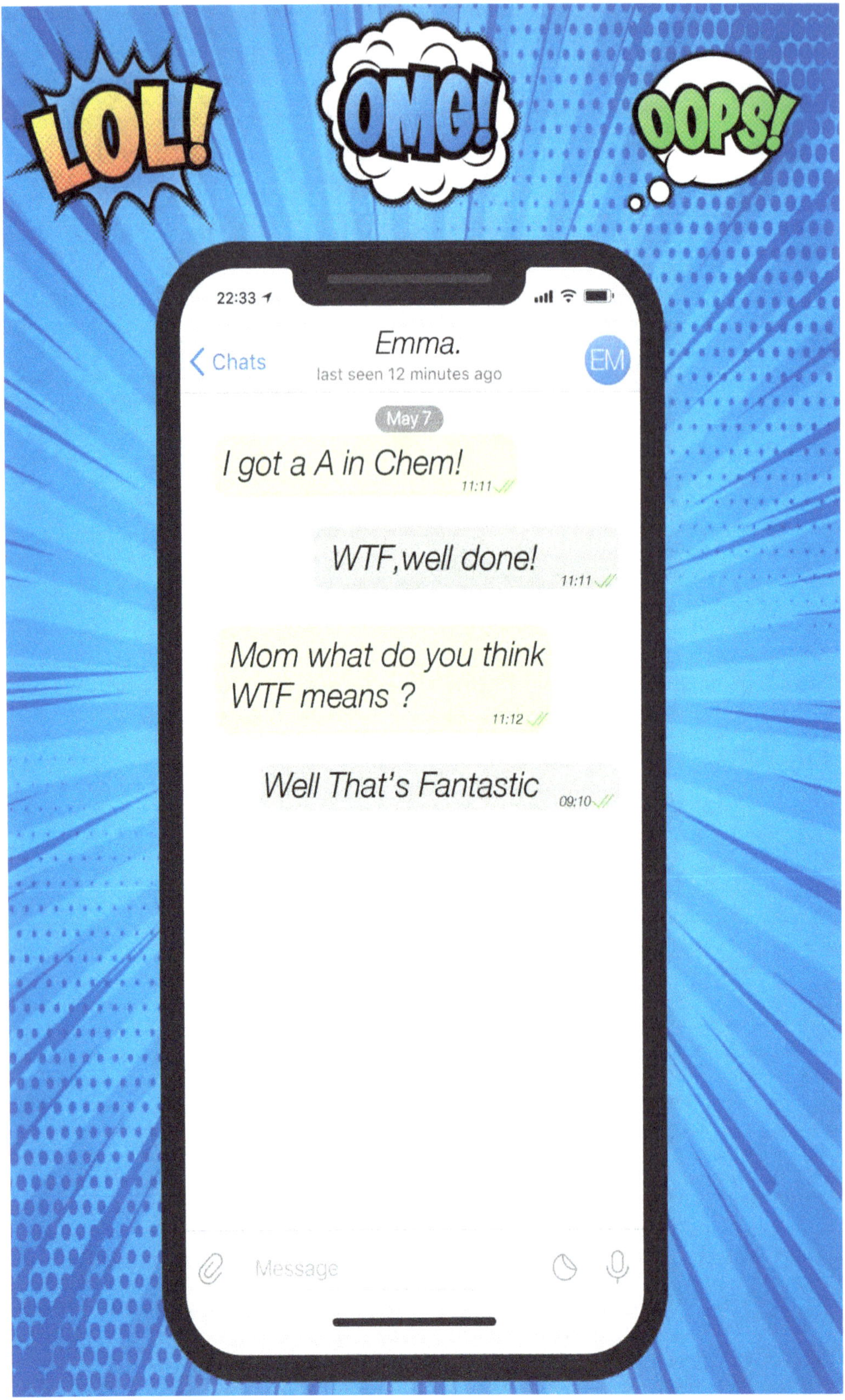
LOL!
OMG!
OOPS!
22:33
Chats
Emma.
last seen 12 minutes ago
EM
May 7
I got a A in Chem!
11:11
WTF,well done!
11:11
Mom what do you think WTF means ?
11:12
Well That's Fantastic
09:10
Message

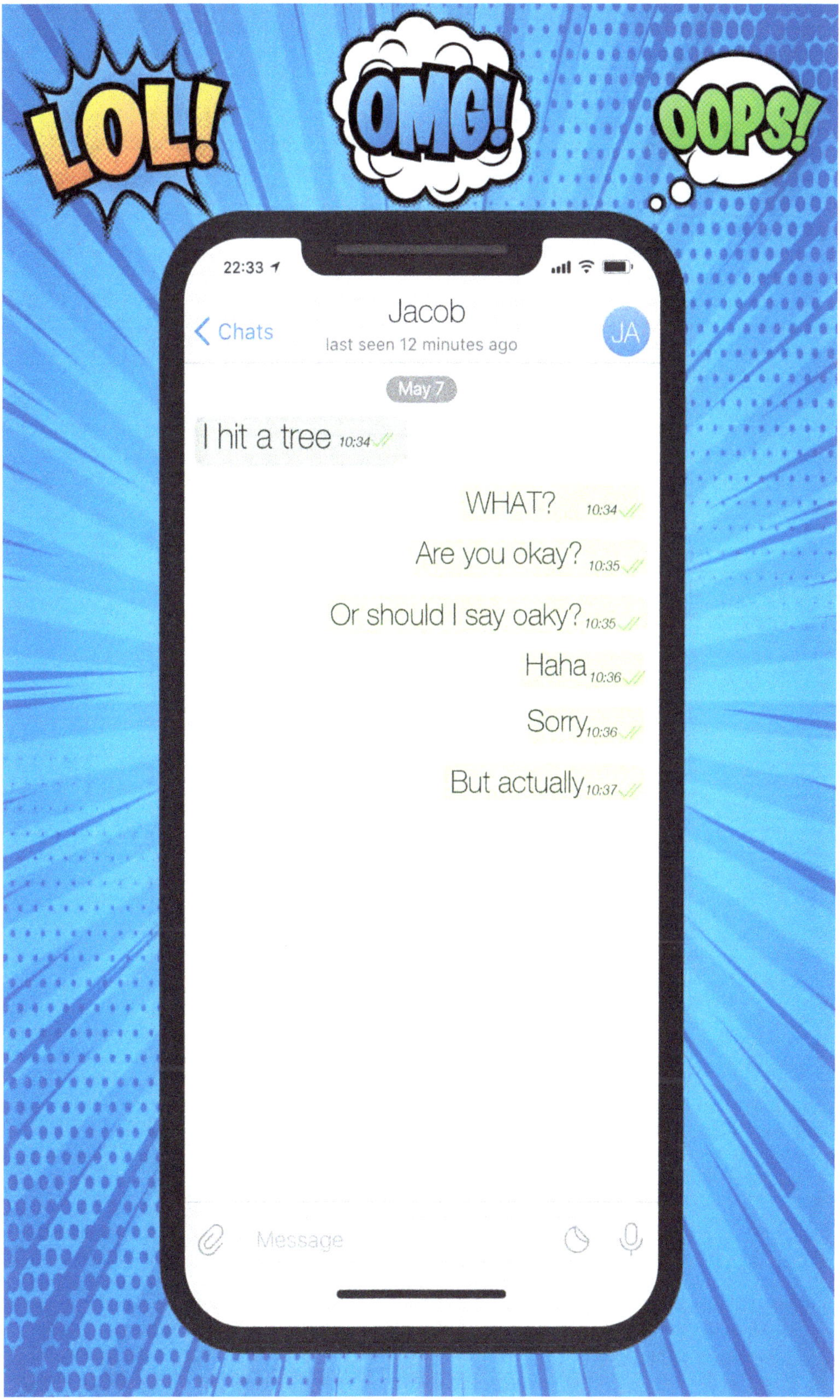
LOL!
OMG!
OOPS!
22:33
Chats
Jacob
last seen 12 minutes ago
JA
May 7
I hit a tree 10:34
WHAT? 10:34
Are you okay? 10:35
Or should I say oaky? 10:35
Haha 10:36
Sorry 10:36
But actually 10:37
Message

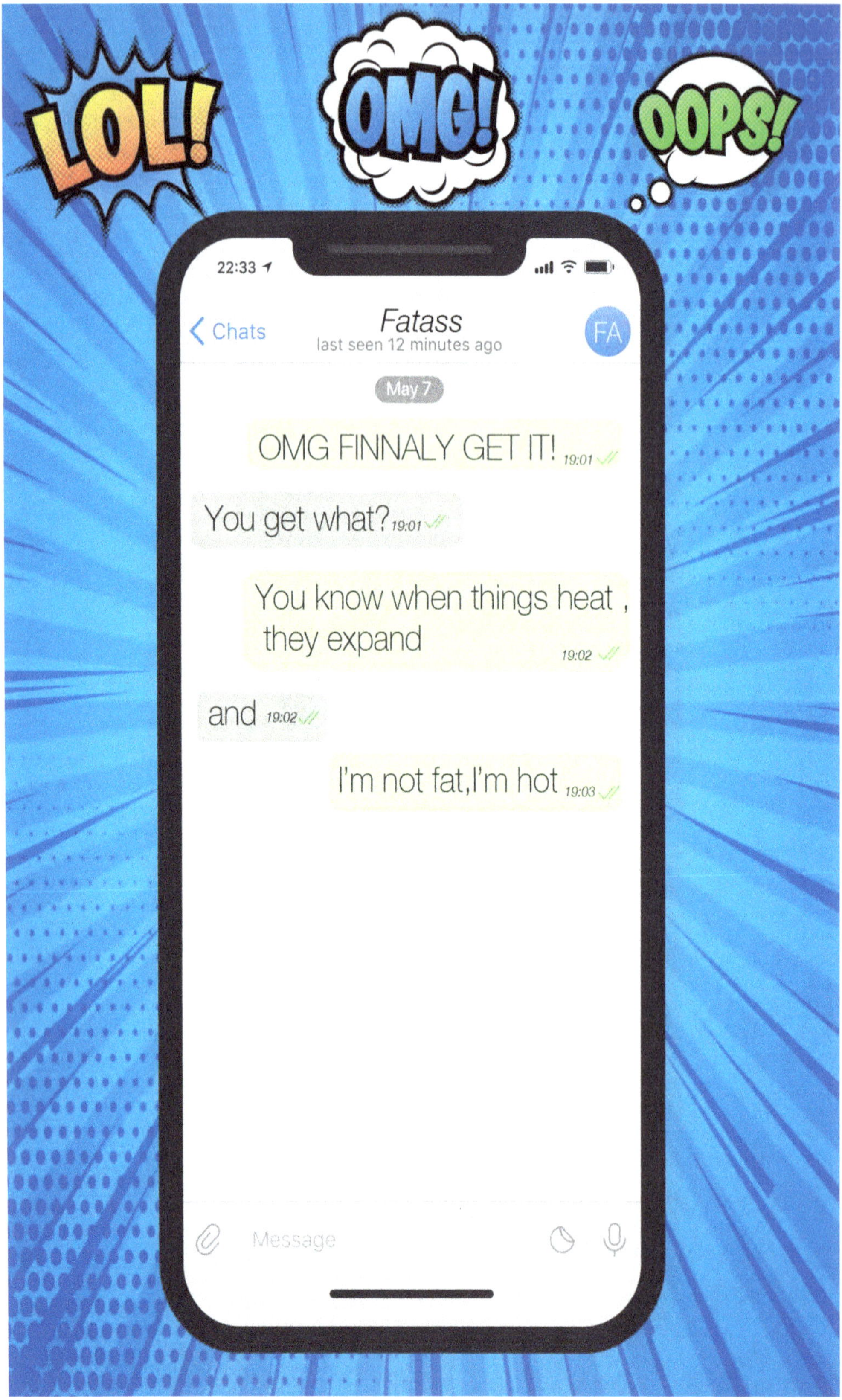
LOL!
OMG!
OOPS!
22:33
Chats
Fatass
last seen 12 minutes ago
FA
May 7
OMG FINNALY GET IT! 19:01
You get what? 19:01
You know when things heat , they expand 19:02
and 19:02
I'm not fat,I'm hot 19:03
Message

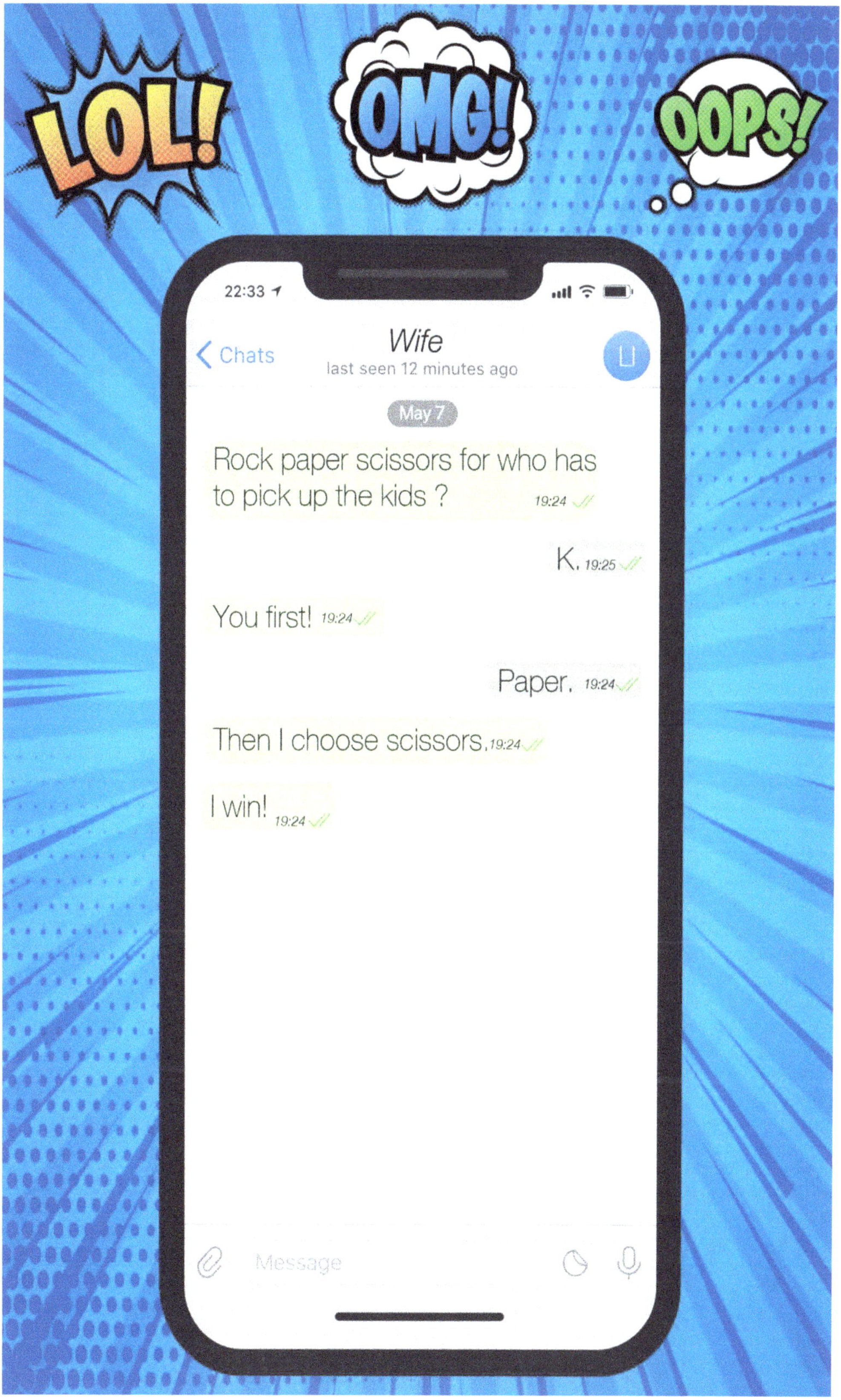

LOL!
OMG!
OOPS!
22:33
Chats
Wife
last seen 12 minutes ago
May 7
Rock paper scissors for who has to pick up the kids ? 19:24
K. 19:25
You first! 19:24
Paper. 19:24
Then I choose scissors. 19:24
I win! 19:24
Message

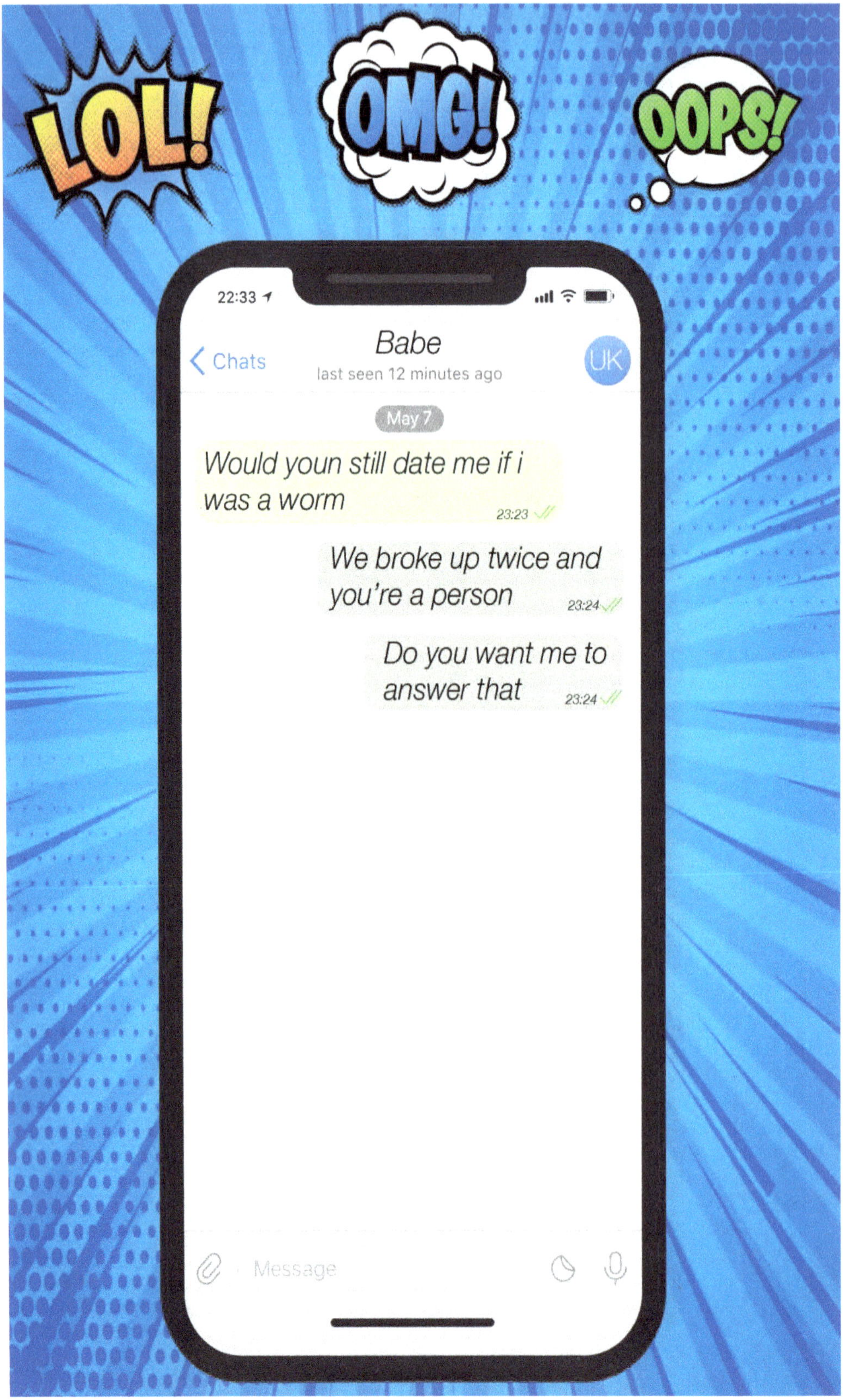

LOL!
OMG!
OOPS!
22:33
Chats
Babe
last seen 12 minutes ago
UK
May 7
Would youn still date me if i was a worm
23:23
We broke up twice and you're a person
23:24
Do you want me to answer that
23:24
Message

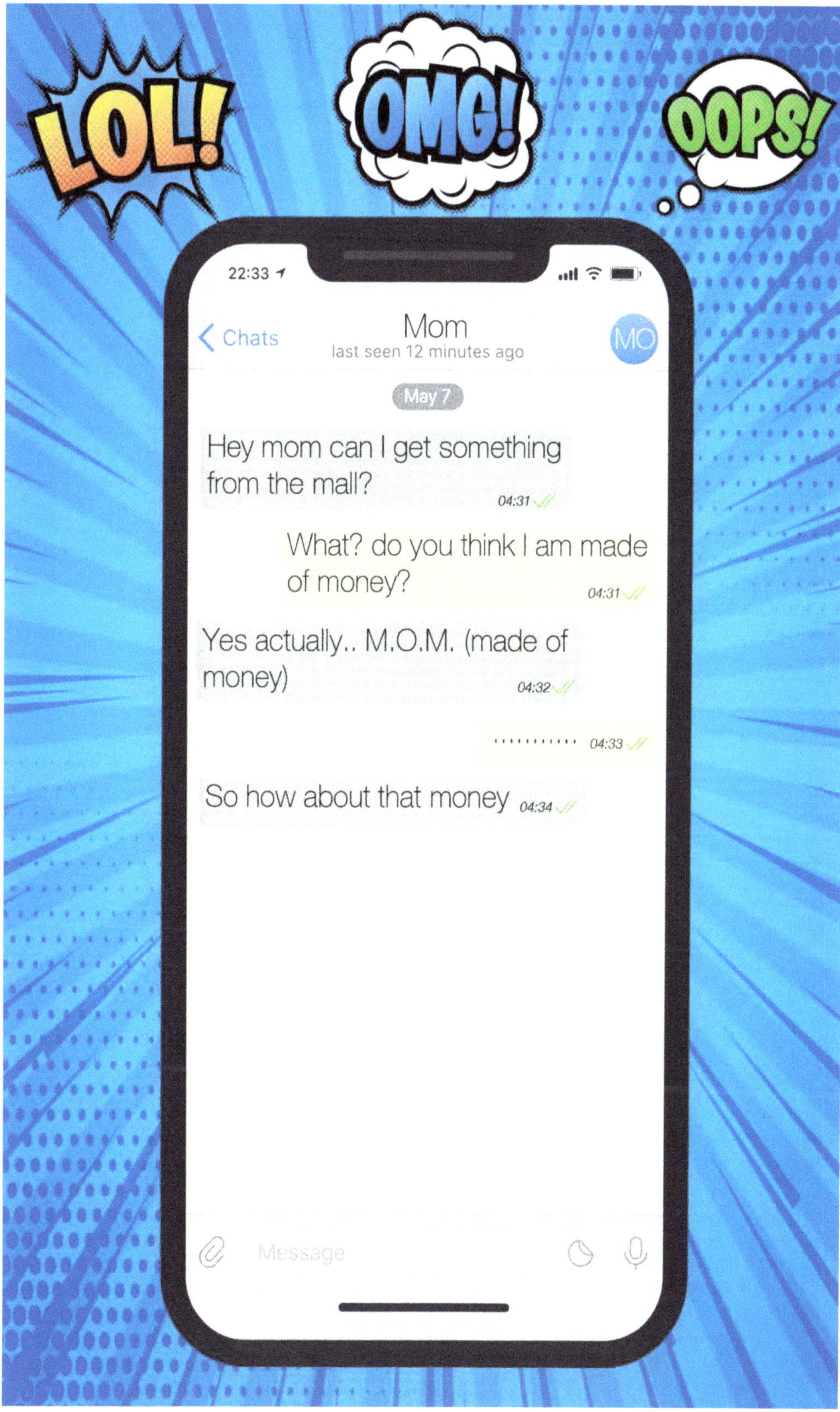
LOL!
OMG!
OOPS!
22:33
Chats
Mom
last seen 12 minutes ago
MO
May 7
Hey mom can I get something from the mall? 04:31
What? do you think I am made of money? 04:31
Yes actually.. M.O.M. (made of money) 04:32
.... 04:33
So how about that money 04:34
Message

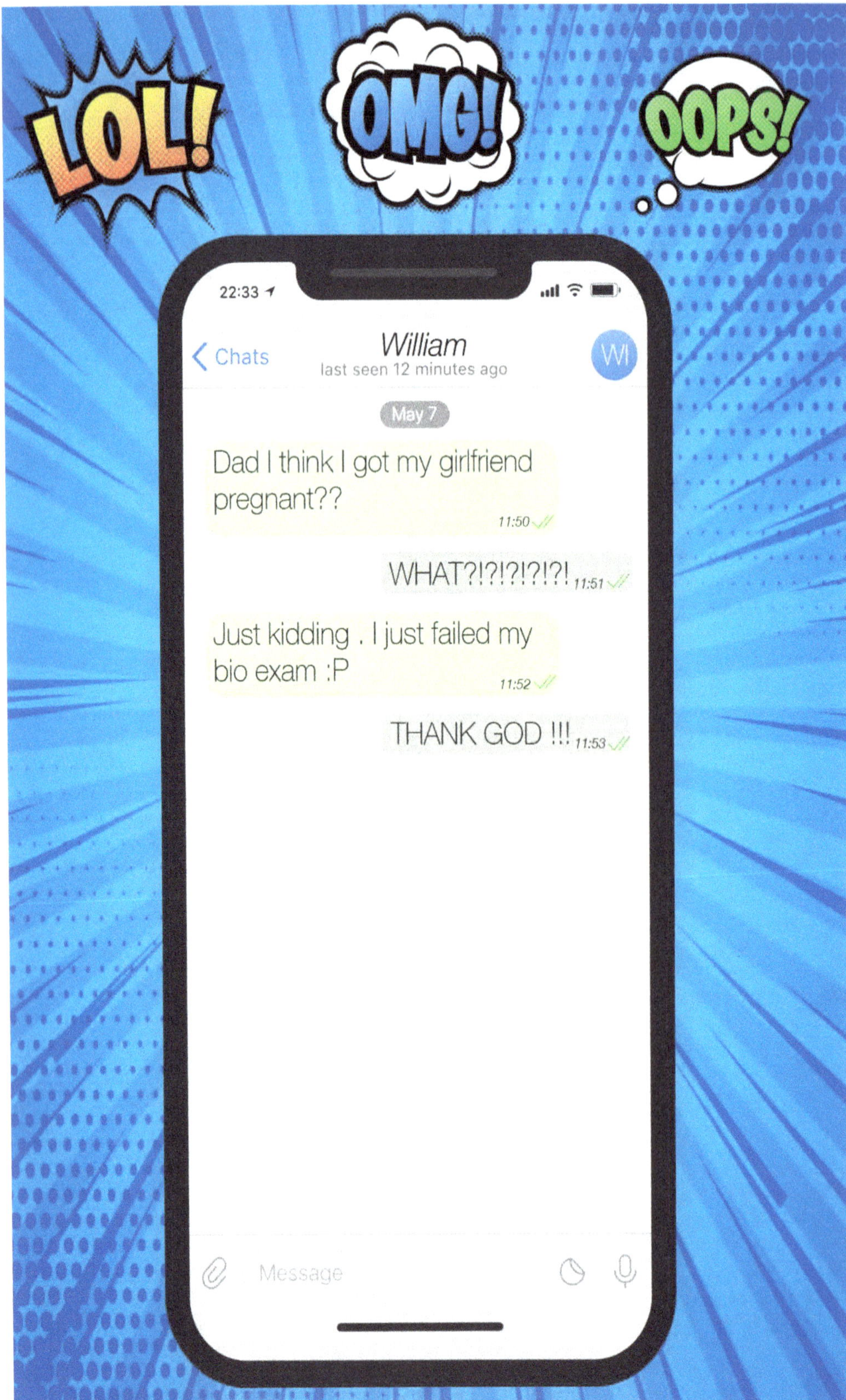
LOL!
OMG!
OOPS!
22:33
Chats
William
last seen 12 minutes ago
WI
May 7
Dad I think I got my girlfriend pregnant??
11:50
WHAT?!?!?!?!?!
11:51
Just kidding . I just failed my bio exam :P
11:52
THANK GOD !!!
11:53
Message

LOL!
OMG!
OOPS!
22:33
Chats
Sarah
last seen 12 minutes ago
SA
May 7
“What does IDK ,LY & TTYL mean?” 15:43
I don’t know,love you, talk to you later . 15:45
Ok , i will ask your sister . 15:50
Message

LOL!
OMG!
OOPS!
22:33
Chats
Mom
last seen 12 minutes ago
MO
May 7
Hey Mom I'm At A Stripper Club :) 02:50
Do you See Anything Your Not suppose To? 02:51
Yeah 02:52
What? 02:53
Dad ... 02:54
Message

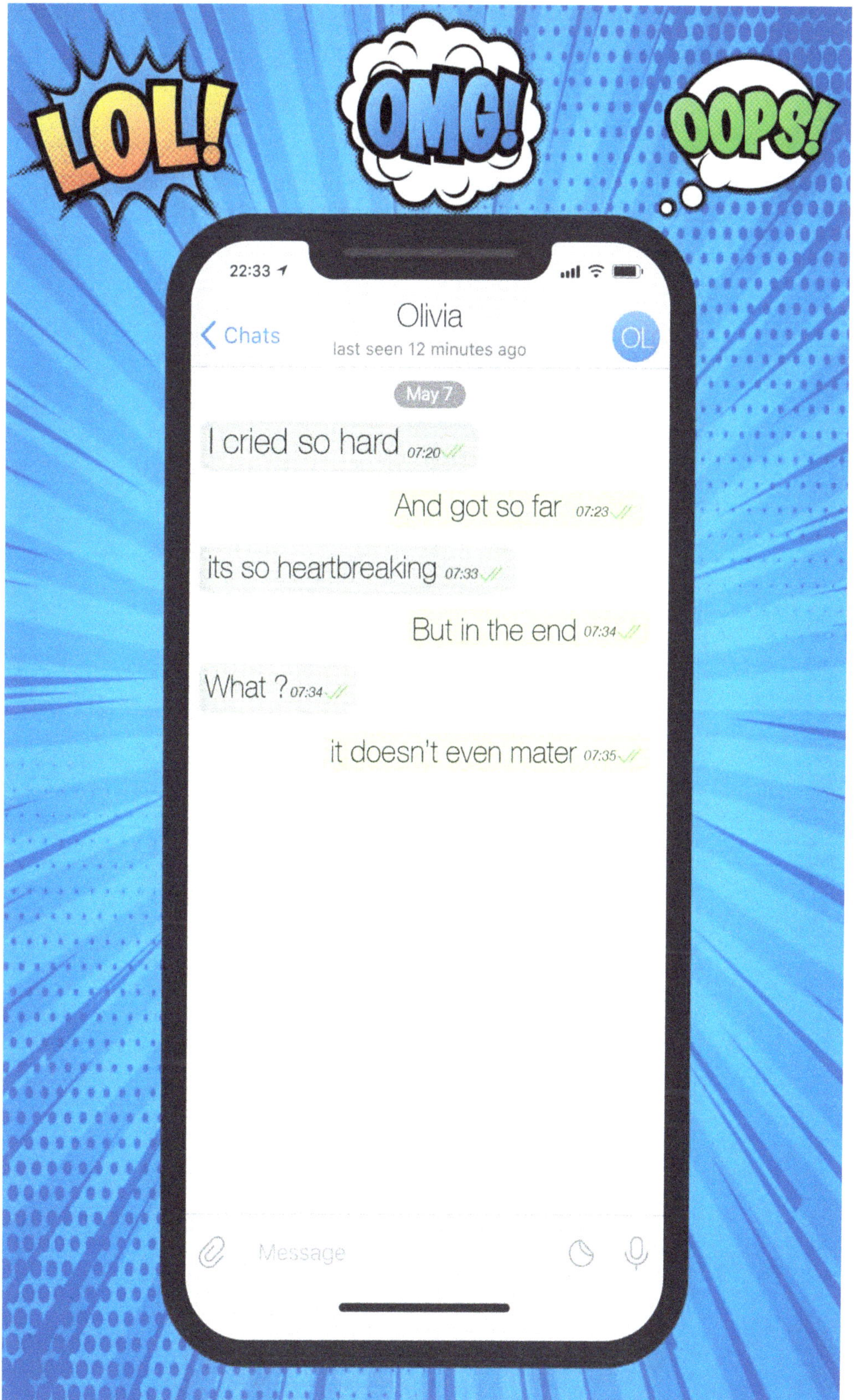

LOL!
OMG!
OOPS!
22:33
Chats
Olivia
last seen 12 minutes ago
OL
May 7
I cried so hard 07:20
And got so far 07:23
its so heartbreaking 07:33
But in the end 07:34
What ? 07:34
it doesn't even mater 07:35
Message

LOL!
OMG!
OOPS!
22:33
Chats
Love
last seen 12 minutes ago
LO
May 7
How much do you love me ?? 09:11
Well .look at the stars and count them.That's how much I love you 09:12
But it's morning 09:12
Exactly 09:13
Message

LOL!
OMG!
OOPS!
22:33
Chats
Charlotte
last seen 12 minutes ago
CH
May 7
So,I hear you like bad boys? 21:21
Yea why ? 21:23
Wel,not trying to impress you or anything,but I press the handicapped button that opens door..I'm not handicapied 21:23
Message

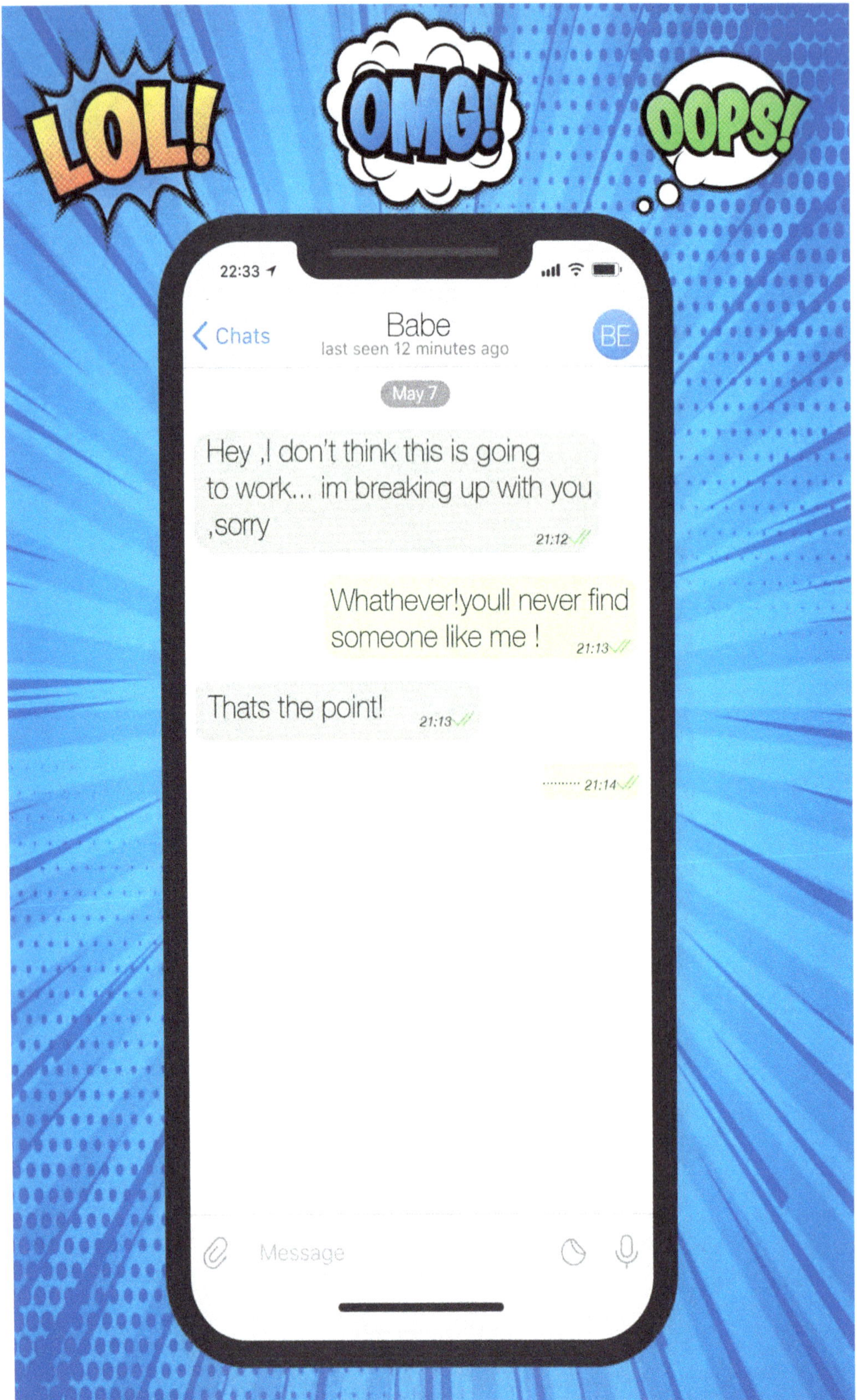
LOL!
OMG!
OOPS!
22:33
Chats
Babe
last seen 12 minutes ago
BE
May 7
Hey ,I don't think this is going to work... im breaking up with you ,sorry 21:12
Whathever!youll never find someone like me ! 21:13
Thats the point! 21:13
.... 21:14
Message

LOL!
OMG!
OOPS!
22:33
Chats
Bobby
last seen 12 minutes ago
BO
May 7
Hey sweetie 23:45
Who? 23:45
You... 23:46
Oh... 370HSSV 0773H 23:46
What?? 23:47
Turn it upside down 23:47
Message

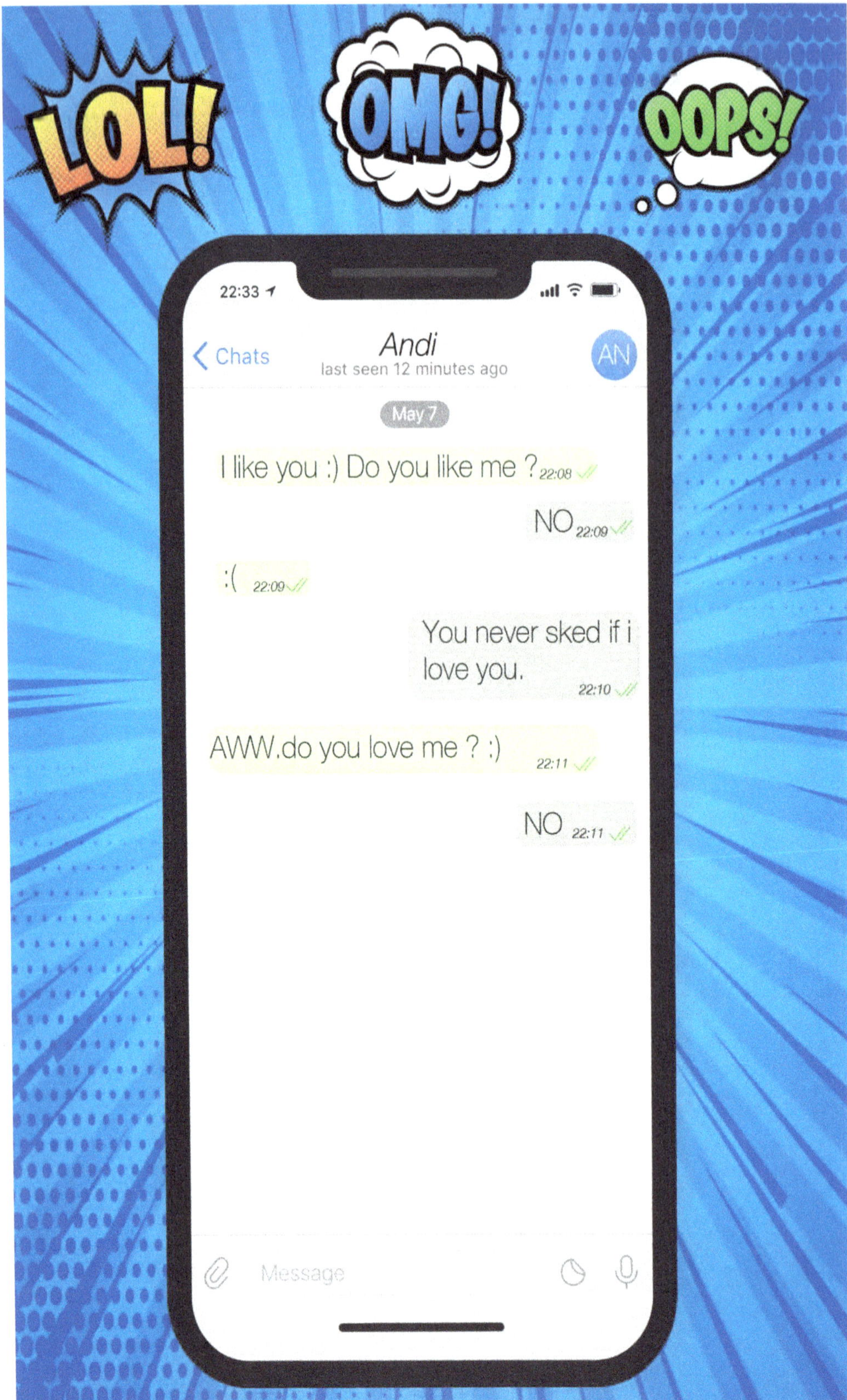
LOL!
OMG!
OOPS!
22:33
Chats
Andi
last seen 12 minutes ago
AN
May 7
I like you :) Do you like me ? 22:08
NO 22:09
:(22:09
You never sked if i love you. 22:10
AWW.do you love me ? :) 22:11
NO 22:11
Message

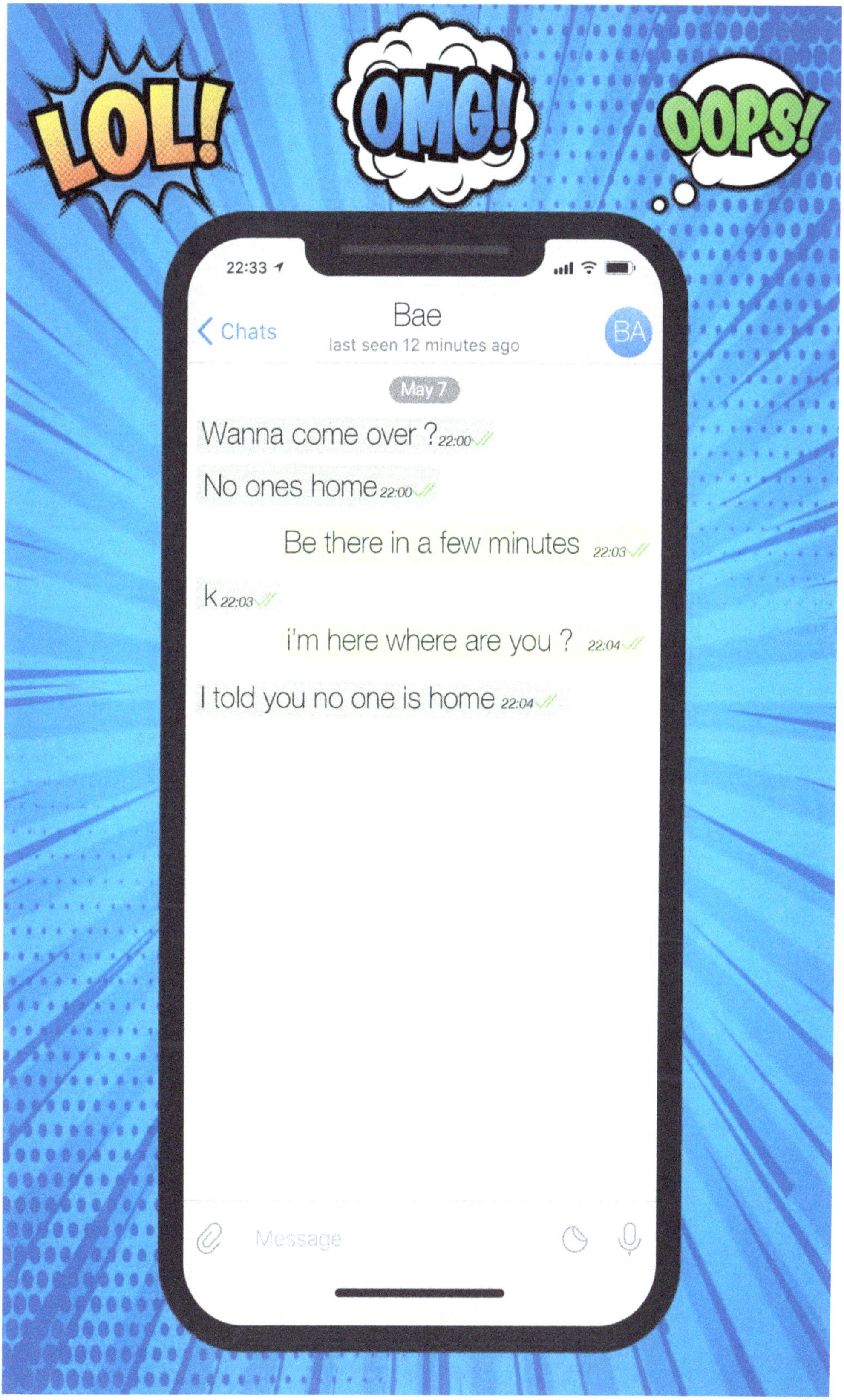
LOL!
OMG!
OOPS!
22:33
Chats
Bae
last seen 12 minutes ago
BA
May 7
Wanna come over ? 22:00
No ones home 22:00
Be there in a few minutes 22:03
k 22:03
i'm here where are you ? 22:04
I told you no one is home 22:04
Message

LOL!
OMG!
OOPS!
22:33
Chats
Crush
last seen 12 minutes ago
CR
May 7
Heyyy 22:50
What are you doing? 22:51
Trying to rearrange the alphabet and put U and I together 22:51
There's no need for that when N and O are already together 22:52
Message

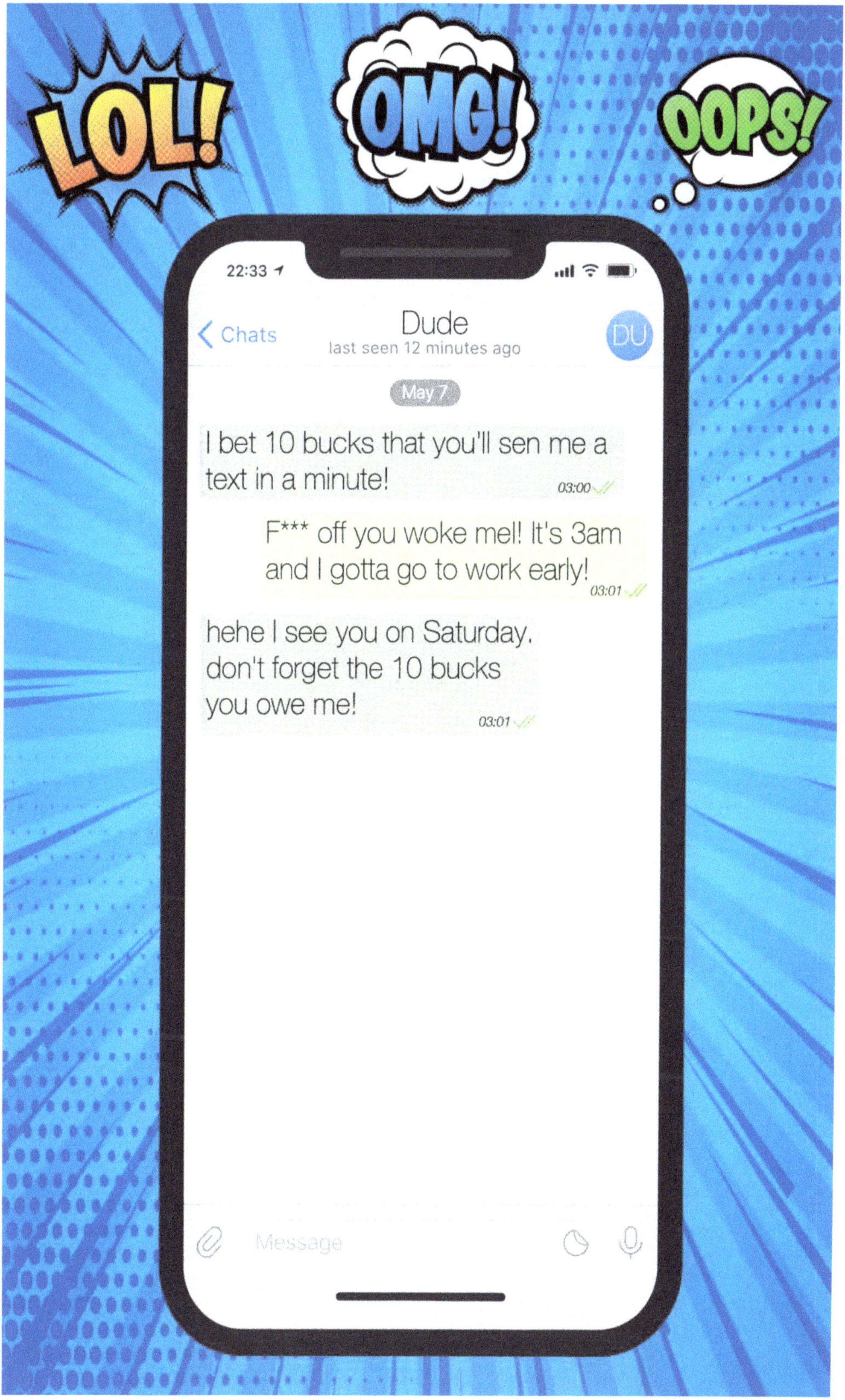
LOL!
OMG!
OOPS!
22:33
Chats
Dude
last seen 12 minutes ago
DU
May 7
I bet 10 bucks that you'll sen me a text in a minute!
03:00
F*** off you woke me!! It's 3am and I gotta go to work early!
03:01
hehe I see you on Saturday, don't forget the 10 bucks you owe me!
03:01
Message

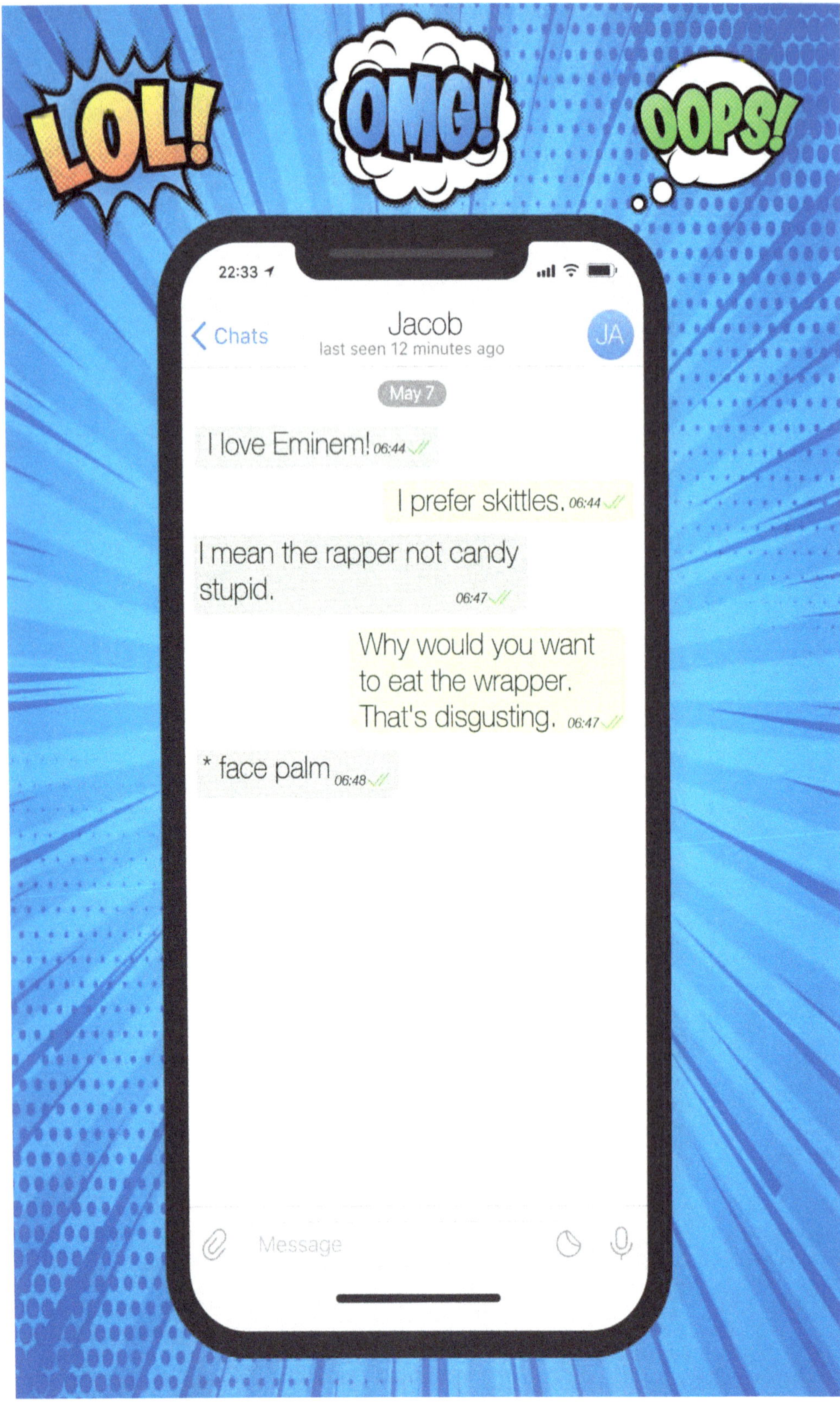
LOL!
OMG!
OOPS!
22:33
Chats
Jacob
last seen 12 minutes ago
JA
May 7
I love Eminem! 06:44
I prefer skittles. 06:44
I mean the rapper not candy stupid. 06:47
Why would you want to eat the wrapper. That's disgusting. 06:47
* face palm 06:48
Message

LOL!
OMG!
OOPS!
22:33
Chats
911
last seen 12 minutes ago
EM
May 7
Hello 911 10:59
Yes, what's your emergency 11:01
Two girls r fighting for me 11:01
What is the problem with it Sir 11:02
The ugly one is winning 11:03
Message

LOL!
OMG!
OOPS!
22:33
Chats
Wiliam
last seen 12 minutes ago
WI
May 7
Clean your room 14:44
Mom,why? 14:45
We're having guests over for dinner 14:45
I didn't realize that dinner will be heldin my room. 14:46
Message

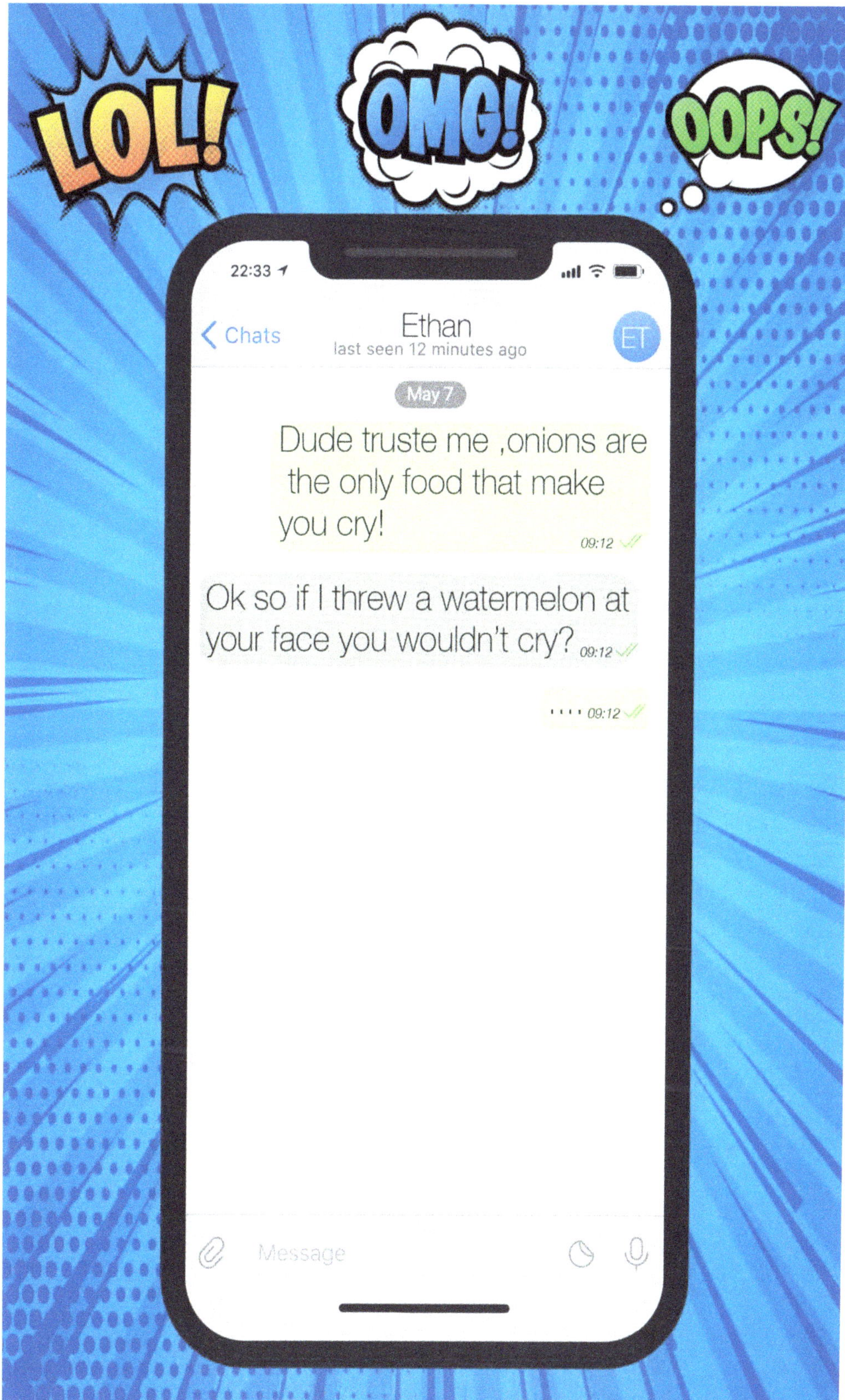
LOL!
OMG!
OOPS!
22:33
Chats
Ethan
last seen 12 minutes ago
ET
May 7
Dude truste me ,onions are the only food that make you cry! 09:12
Ok so if I threw a watermelon at your face you wouldn't cry? 09:12
.... 09:12
Message

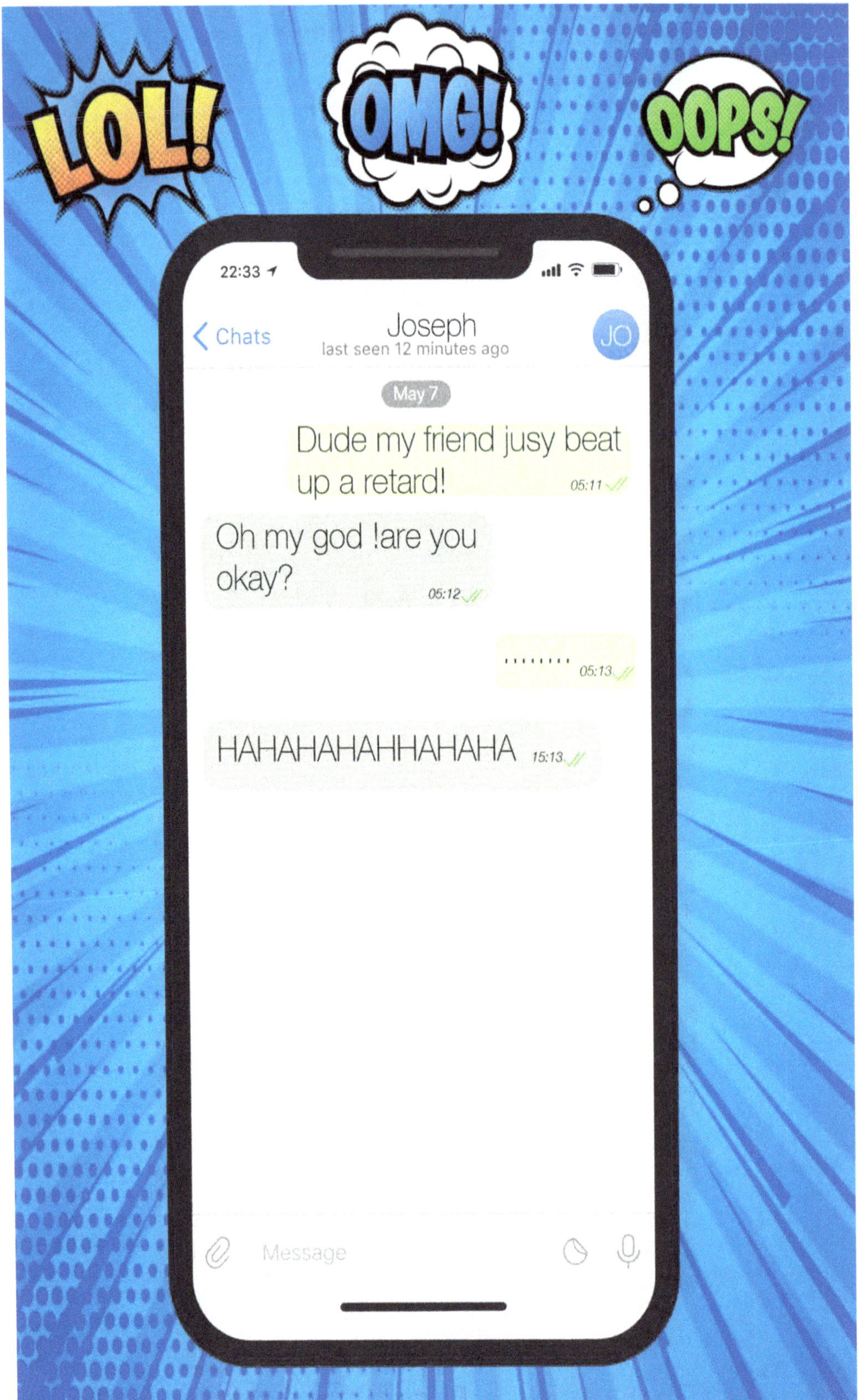
LOL!
OMG!
OOPS!
22:33
Chats
Joseph
last seen 12 minutes ago
JO
May 7
Dude my friend jusy beat up a retard! 05:11
Oh my god !are you okay? 05:12
.... 05:13
HAHAHAHAHHAHAHA 15:13
Message

LOL!
OMG!
OOPS!
22:33
Chats
+0198...
last seen 12 minutes ago
NU
May 7
You're pretty 18:01
Thanks 18:03
I wish there was something between us... 18:04
Me too Really?Like what? 18:04
A wall 18:01
Message

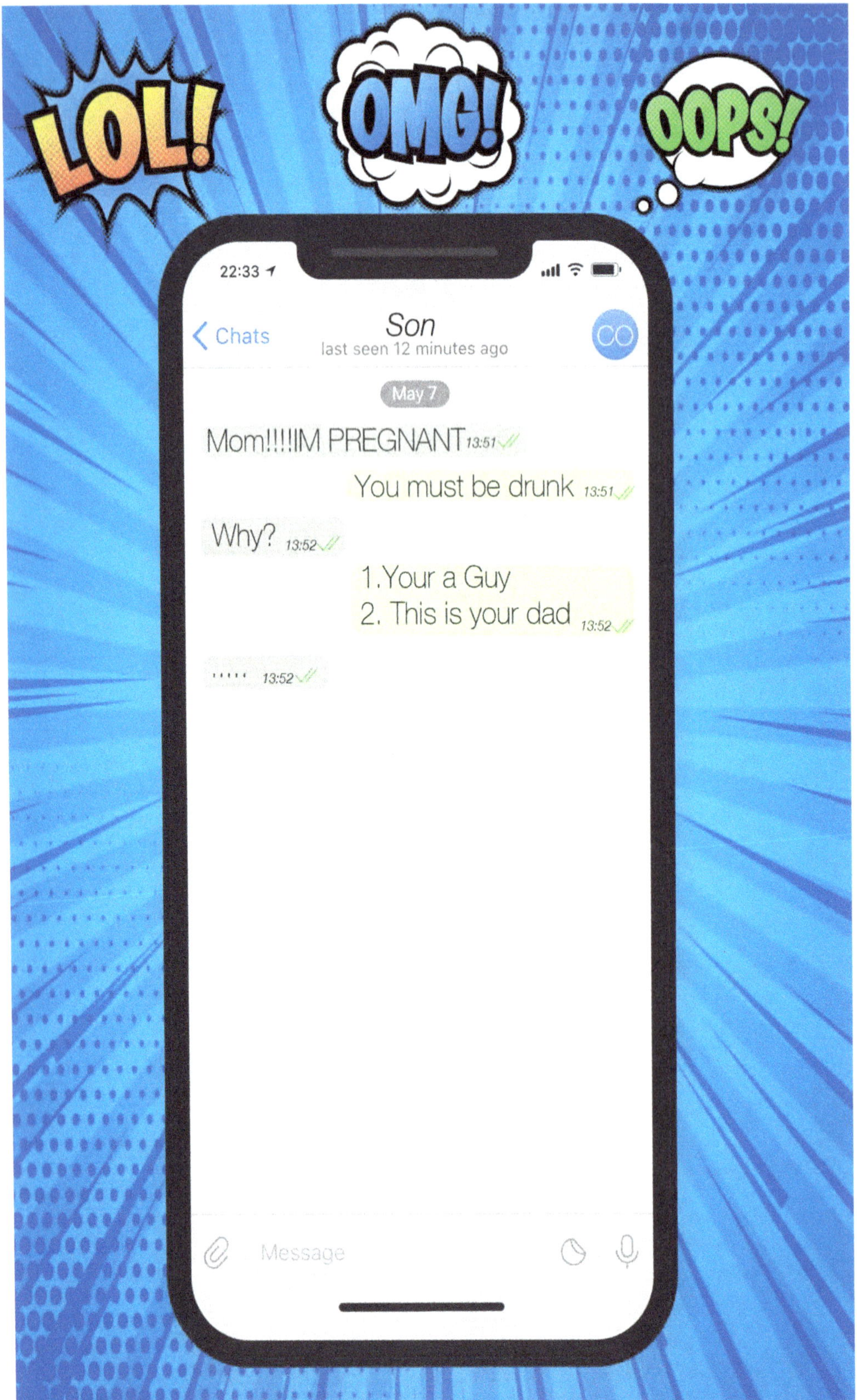
LOL!
OMG!
OOPS!
22:33
Chats
Son
last seen 12 minutes ago
CO
May 7
Mom!!!!IM PREGNANT 13:51
You must be drunk 13:51
Why? 13:52
1.Your a Guy
2. This is your dad 13:52
...... 13:52
Message

LOL!
OMG!
OOPS!
22:33
Chats
Friend
last seen 12 minutes ago
FR
May 7
Your Mom and I are going to divorce next month 13:13
What???Why !call me please? 13:14
I wrote Disney and this phone changed it.We are going to Disney. 13:15
Message

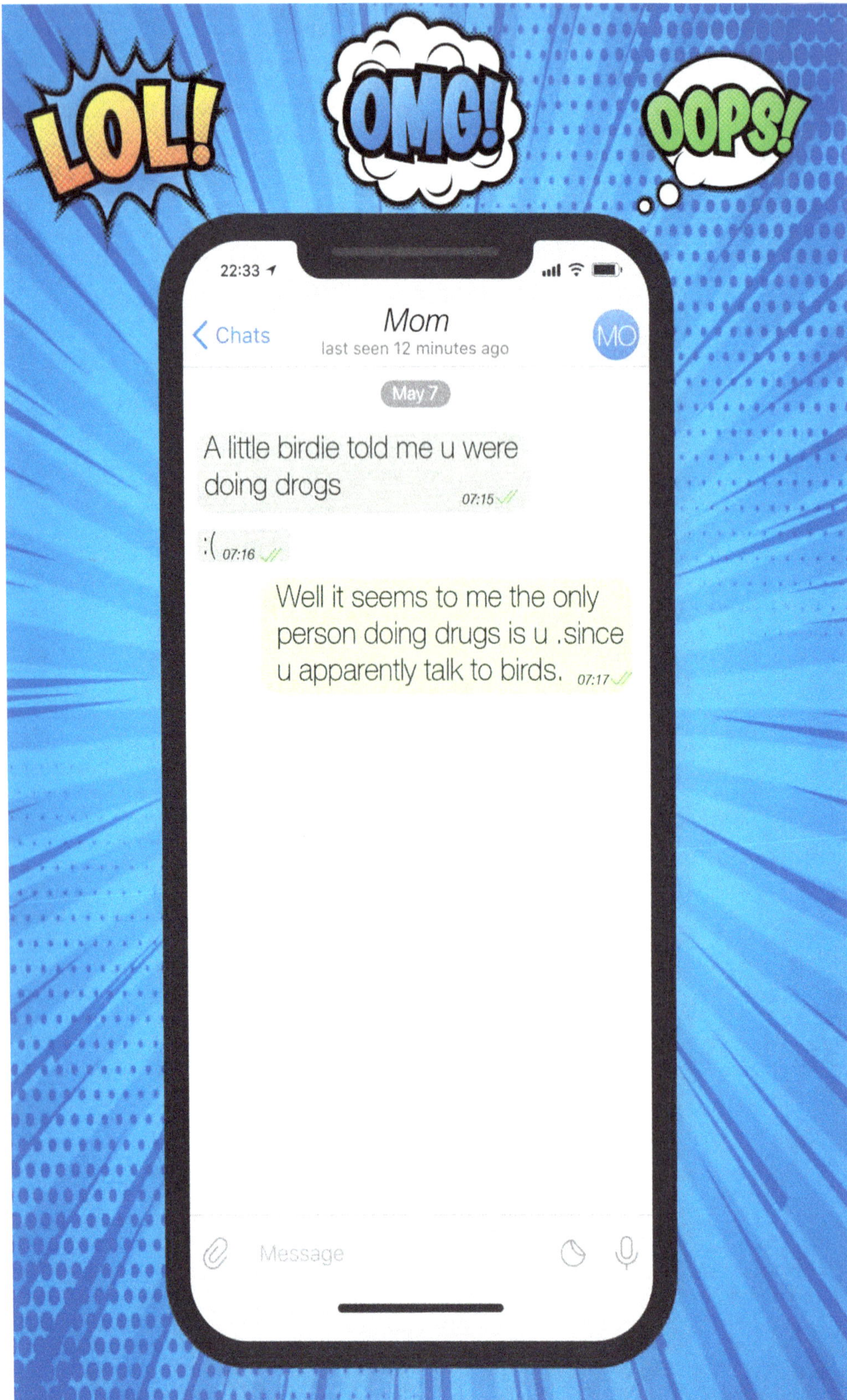
LOL!
OMG!
OOPS!
22:33
Chats
Mom
last seen 12 minutes ago
MO
May 7
A little birdie told me u were doing drogs 07:15
:(07:16
Well it seems to me the only person doing drugs is u .since u apparently talk to birds. 07:17
Message

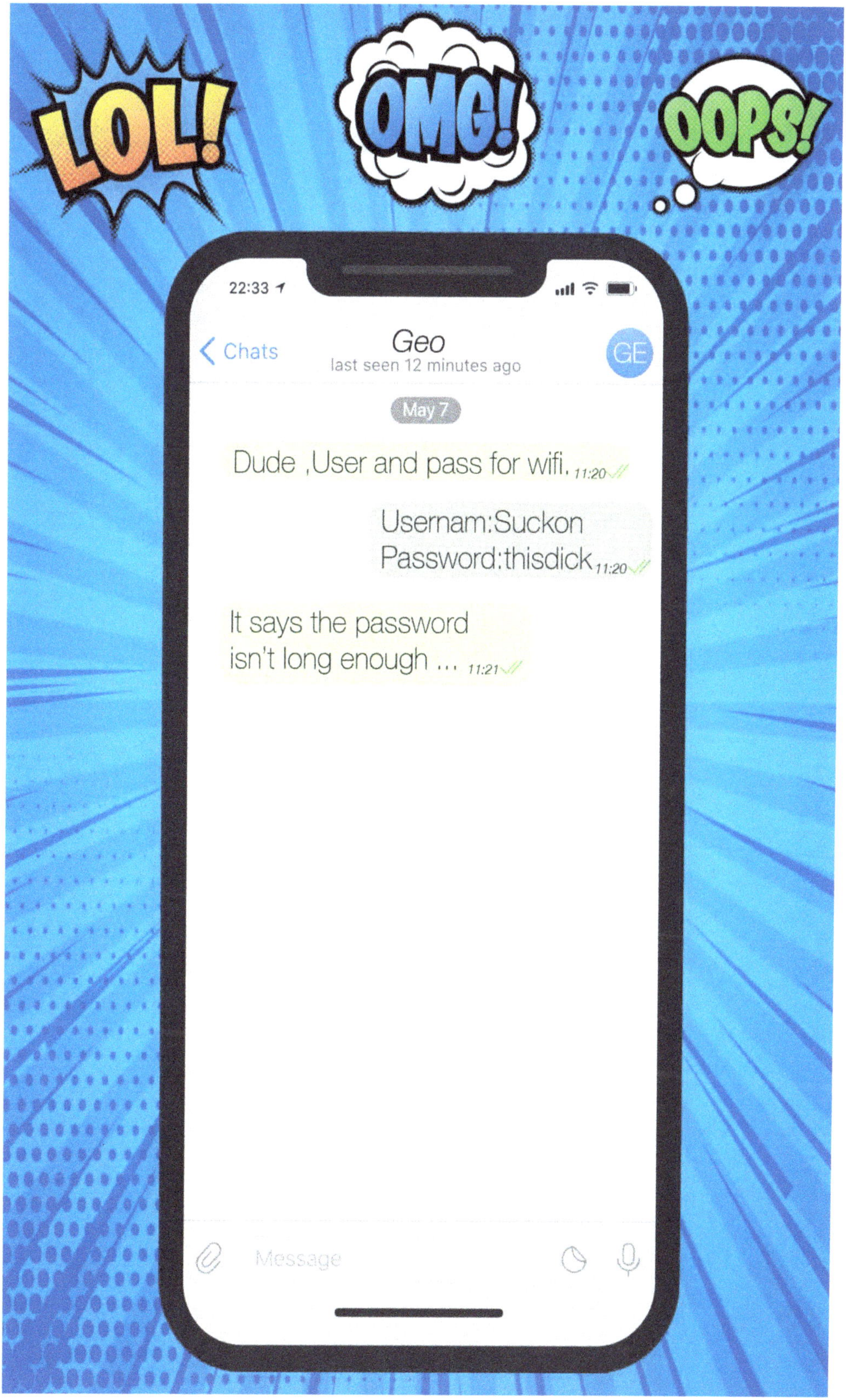
LOL!
OMG!
OOPS!
22:33
Chats
Geo
last seen 12 minutes ago
GE
May 7
Dude ,User and pass for wifi. 11:20
Usernam:Suckon
Password:thisdick 11:20
It says the password
isn't long enough ... 11:21
Message

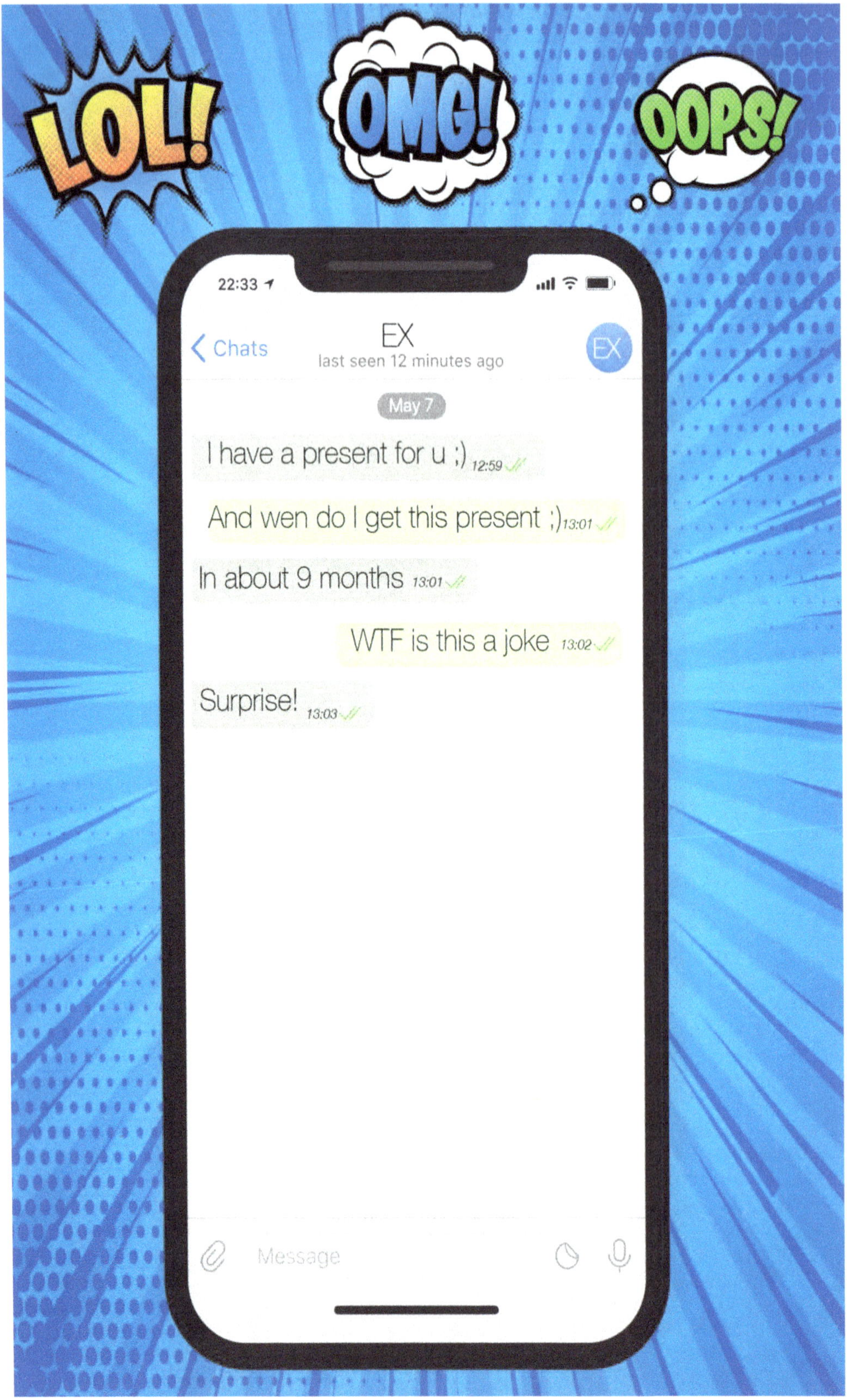
LOL!
OMG!
OOPS!
22:33
Chats
EX
last seen 12 minutes ago
EX
May 7
I have a present for u ;) 12:59
And wen do I get this present ;) 13:01
In about 9 months 13:01
WTF is this a joke 13:02
Surprise! 13:03
Message

LOL!
OMG!
OOPS!
22:33
Chats
Friend
last seen 12 minutes ago
FR
May 7
I'l be back in a minute 11:46
Huh??!! 11:46
I meant BACK,Freaking autocorrect. i'll be BACK.As far as i know I won't beblack anytime soon.Lolz 11:47
Message

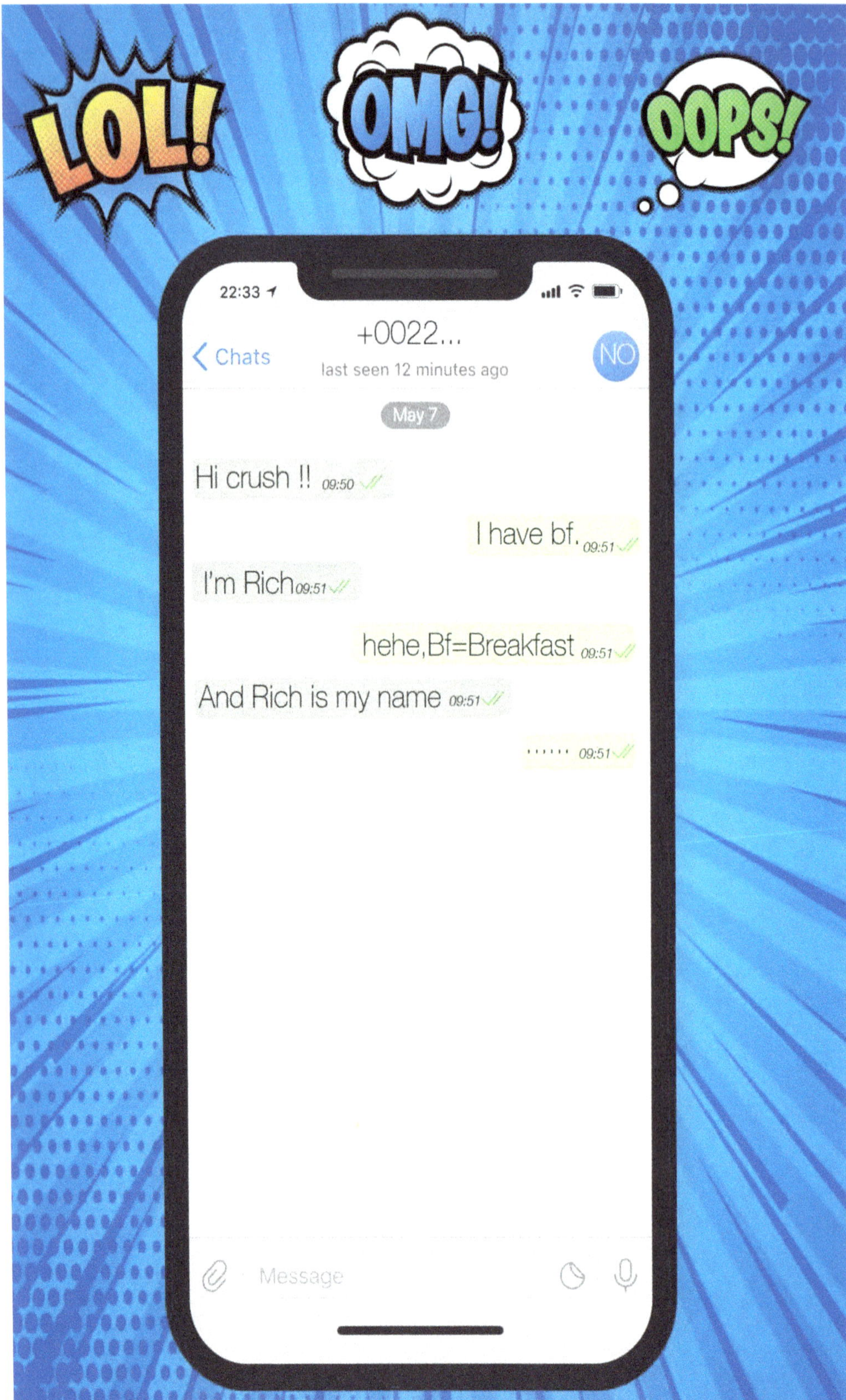
LOL!
OMG!
OOPS!
22:33
Chats
+0022...
last seen 12 minutes ago
NO
May 7
Hi crush !! 09:50
I have bf. 09:51
I'm Rich 09:51
hehe,Bf=Breakfast 09:51
And Rich is my name 09:51
...... 09:51
Message

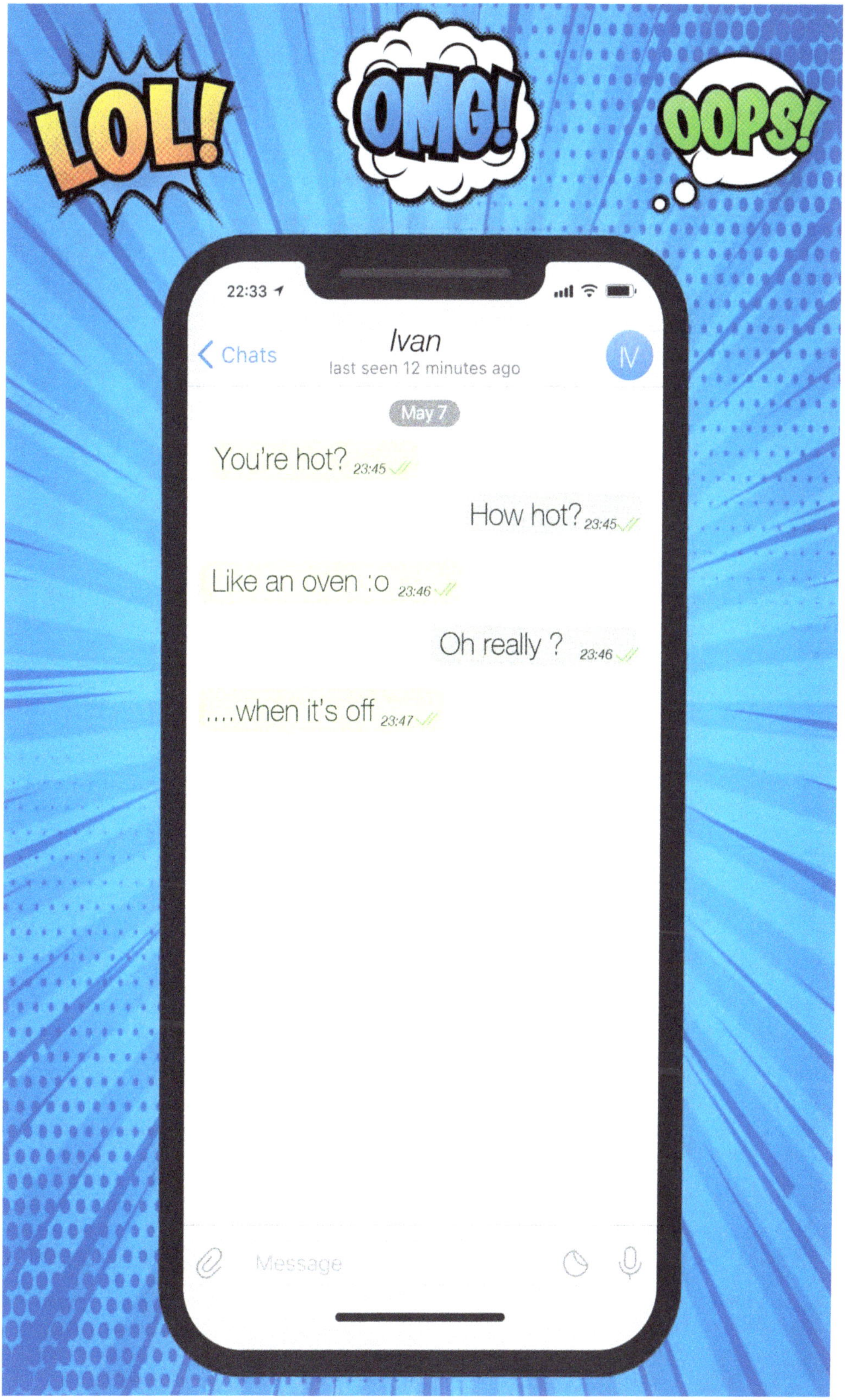
LOL!
OMG!
OOPS!
22:33
Chats
Ivan
last seen 12 minutes ago
IV
May 7
You're hot? 23:45
How hot? 23:45
Like an oven :o 23:46
Oh really ? 23:46
....when it's off 23:47
Message

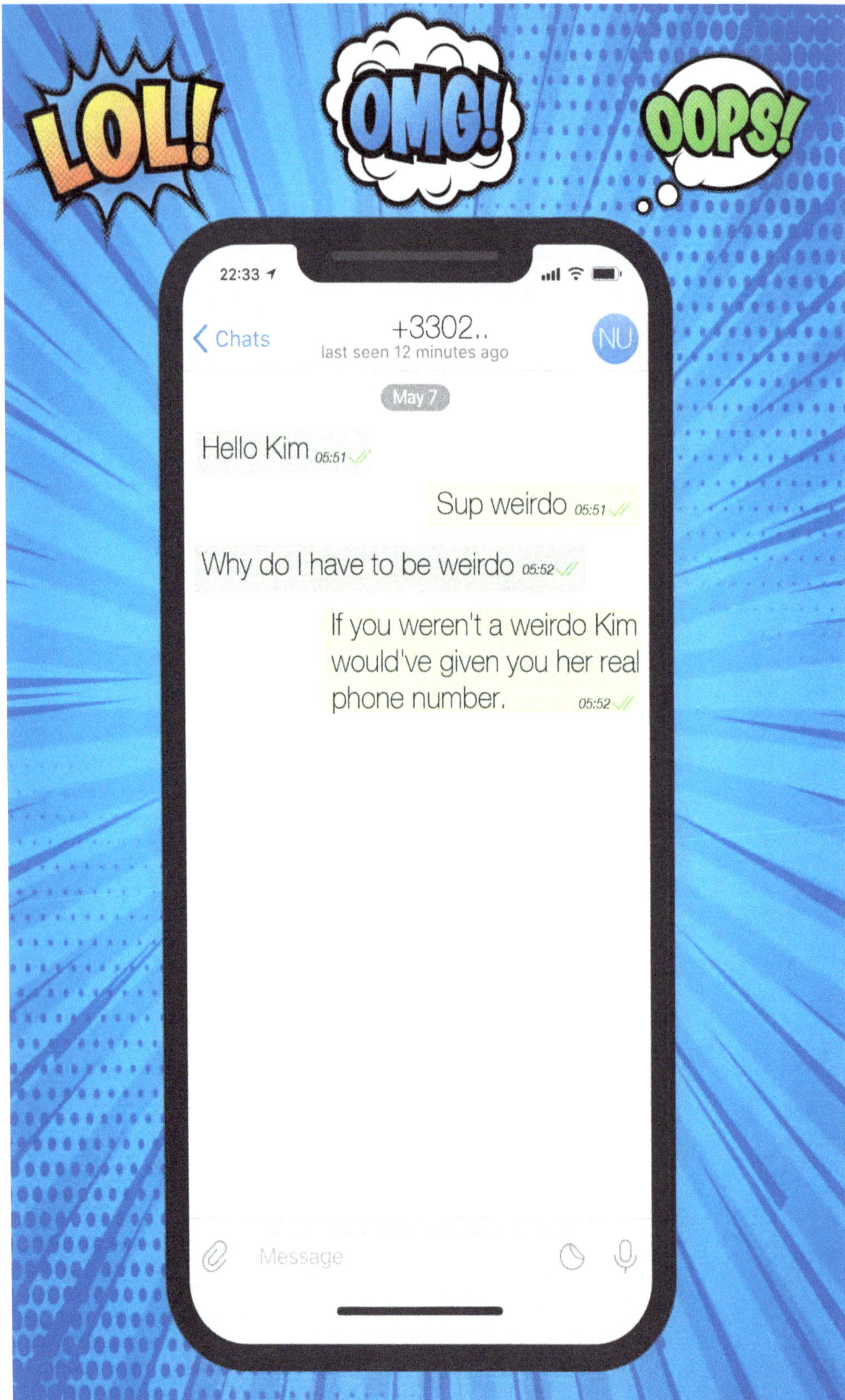
LOL!
OMG!
OOPS!
22:33
Chats
+3302..
last seen 12 minutes ago
NU
May 7
Hello Kim 05:51
Sup weirdo 05:51
Why do I have to be weirdo 05:52
If you weren't a weirdo Kim would've given you her real phone number. 05:52
Message

LOL!
OMG!
OOPS!
22:33
Chats
Asshole
last seen 12 minutes ago
AS
May 7
Hey 23:10
Who is this ... I have like 10 of my ex's names changed to asshole.which one are you ? 23:11
Its your father 23:14
Message

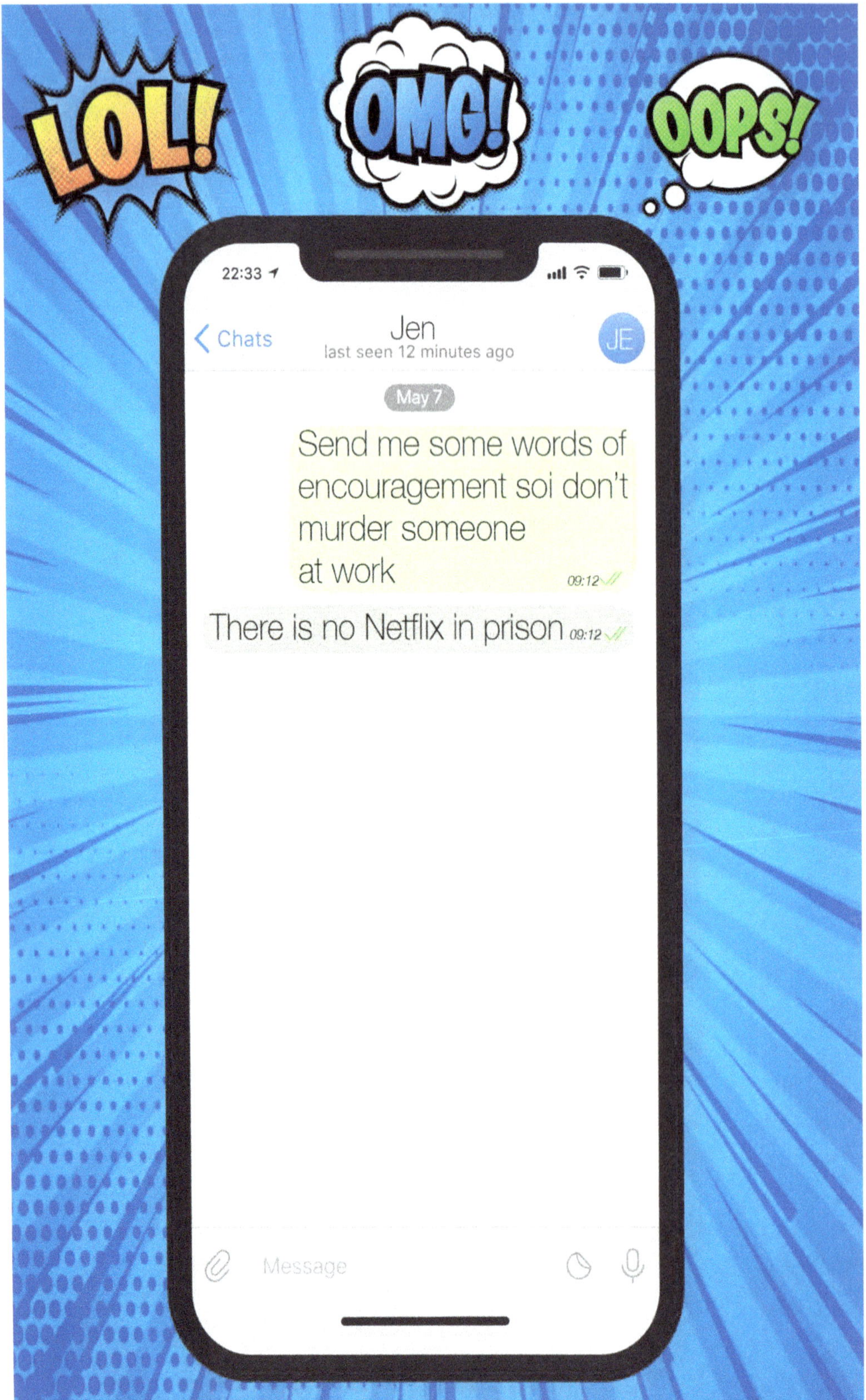
LOL!
OMG!
OOPS!
22:33
Chats
Jen
last seen 12 minutes ago
JE
May 7
Send me some words of encouragement soi don't murder someone at work 09:12
There is no Netflix in prison 09:12
Message

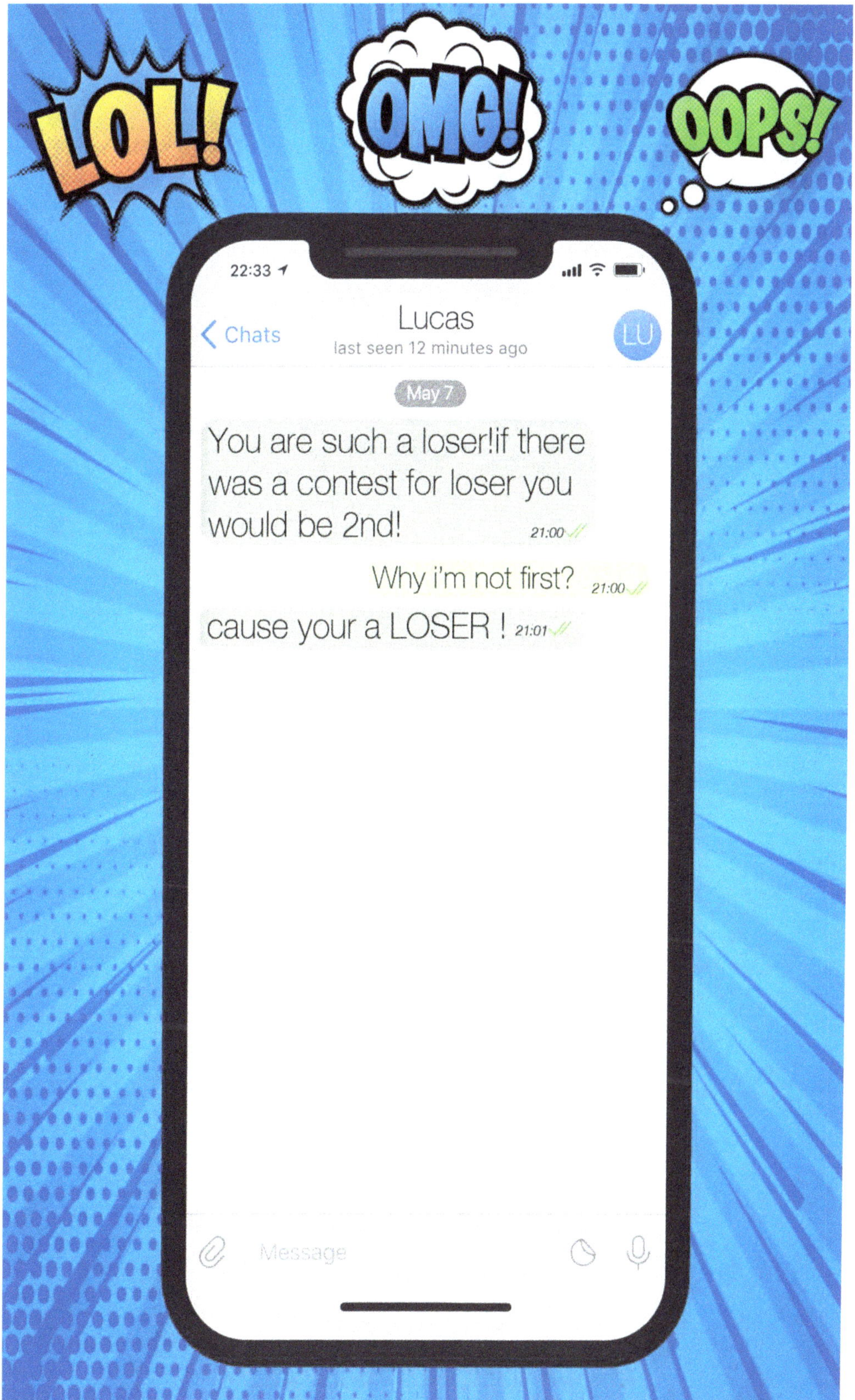
LOL!
OMG!
OOPS!
22:33
Chats
Lucas
last seen 12 minutes ago
LU
May 7
You are such a loser!if there was a contest for loser you would be 2nd! 21:00
Why i'm not first? 21:00
cause your a LOSER ! 21:01
Message

LOL!
OMG!
OOPS!
22:33
Chats
Sarah
last seen 12 minutes ago
SA
May 7
Hey you remind me of the sun 15:21
why,is it because I brighten your day 15:23
No it's because I can't look at u directly 15:23
Message

LOL!
OMG!
OOPS!
22:33
Chats
David
last seen 12 minutes ago
DA
May 7
Dude I wasn't THAT drunk. 07:15
Dyude ,you gave a mushroom to a midget and kept yelling "GROW MARIO GROW" 07:17
Message

LOL!
OMG!
OOPS!
22:33
Chats
Friend
last seen 12 minutes ago
FR
May 7
So I heard you like bad boys. 22:50
Yeah? 22:51
I don't mean ro brag but when I play Wii.I don't put the safety strap on 22:51
Message

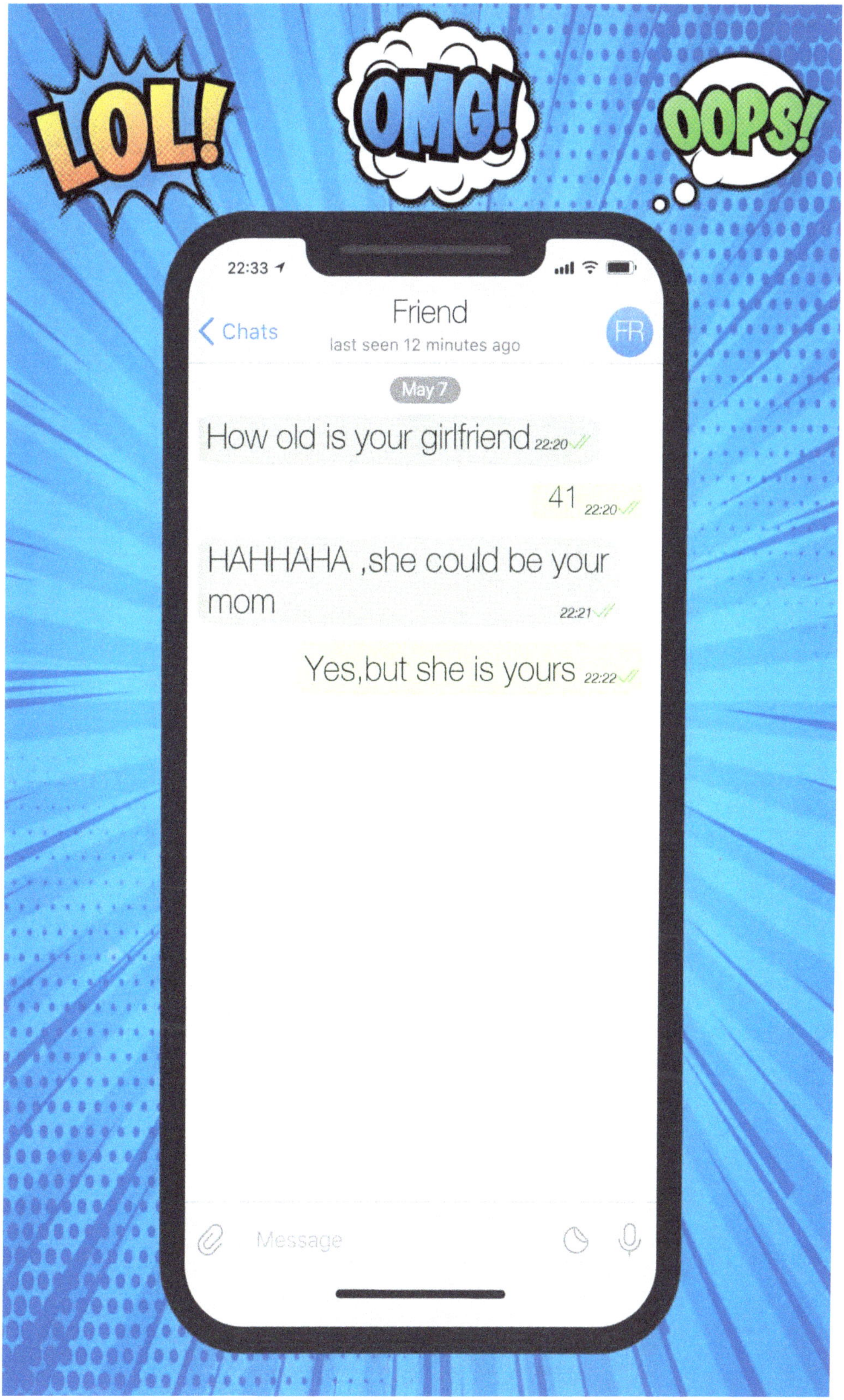
LOL!
OMG!
OOPS!
22:33
Chats
Friend
last seen 12 minutes ago
FR
May 7
How old is your girlfriend 22:20
41 22:20
HAHHAHA ,she could be your mom 22:21
Yes,but she is yours 22:22
Message

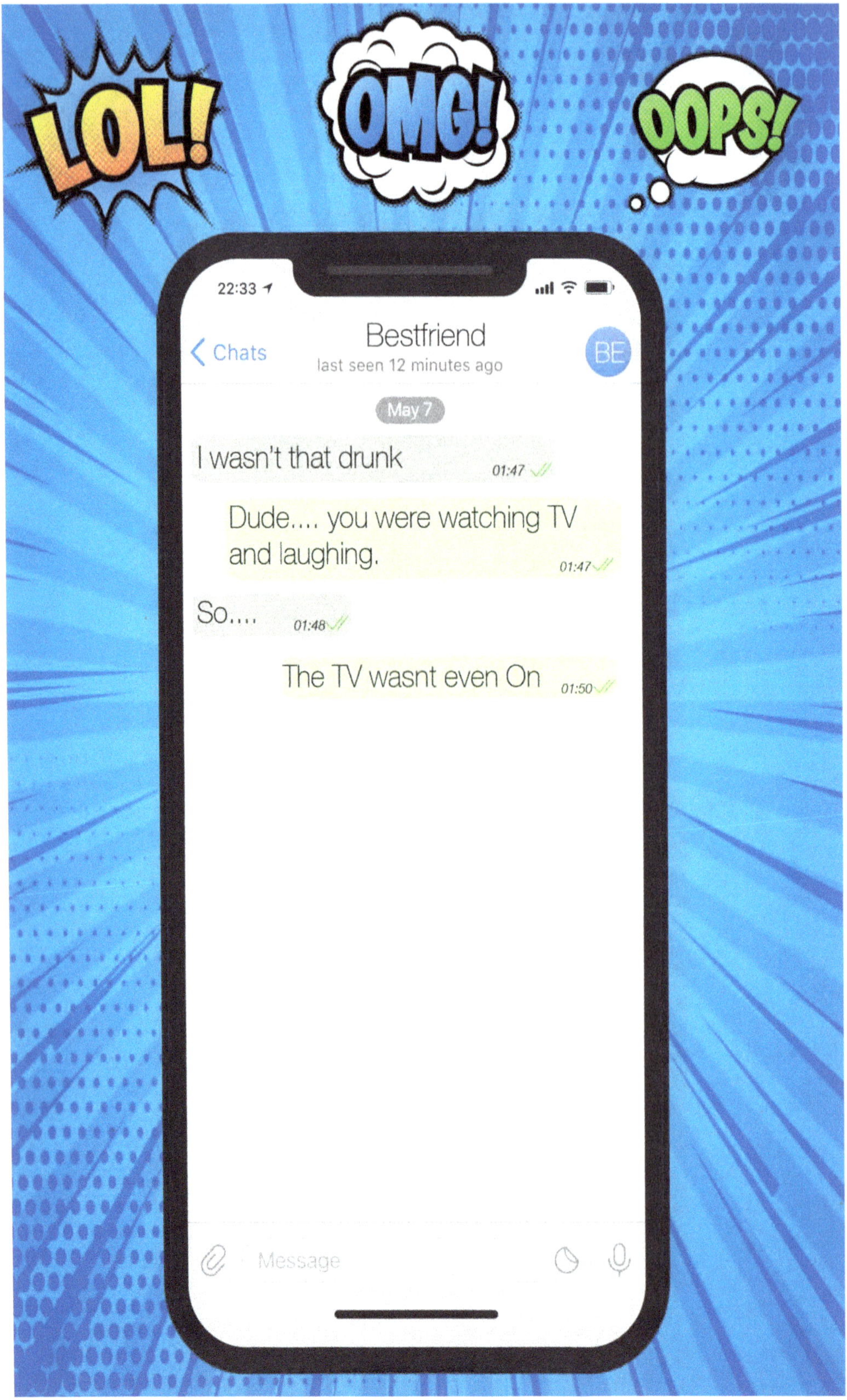
LOL!
OMG!
OOPS!
22:33
Chats
Bestfriend
last seen 12 minutes ago
BE
May 7
I wasn't that drunk 01:47
Dude.... you were watching TV and laughing. 01:47
So.... 01:48
The TV wasnt even On 01:50
Message

LOL!
OMG!
OOPS!
22:33
Chats
Luke
last seen 12 minutes ago
LU
May 7
Why arent you returning my calls?!!?! 01:47
i can explain 01:47
Then explain !!! 01:48
I like my ringtone 01:50
Message

LOL!
OMG!
OOPS!
22:33
Chats
Dad
last seen 12 minutes ago
DA
May 7
Dad,can take a look at your computer ??
15:07
Of course . Just don't turn it on.
15:08
Message

LOL!
OMG!
OOPS!
22:33
Chats
David
last seen 12 minutes ago
DA
May 7
Wemen are the best!! 13:18
Thank you
But actually it's "o" not "e" 13:18
actualy I forget the space
after first "e" 13:19
Message

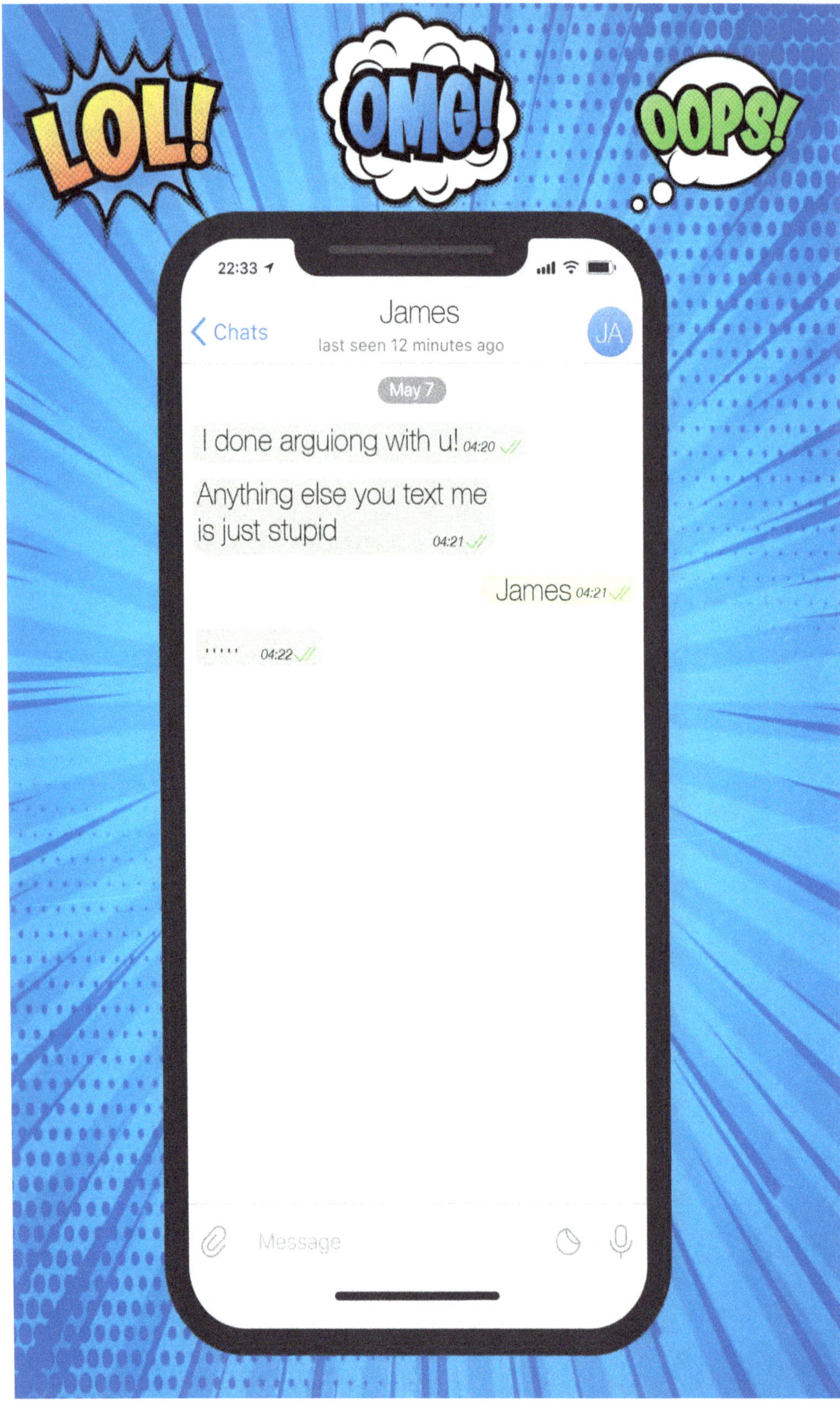
LOL!
OMG!
OOPS!
22:33
James
Chats
last seen 12 minutes ago
JA
May 7
I done arguiong with u! 04:20
Anything else you text me is just stupid 04:21
James 04:21
''''' 04:22
Message

LOL!
OMG!
OOPS!
22:33
Chats
Brother
last seen 12 minutes ago
BR
May 7
Pick me up 03:20
I'm drunk 03:22
Send me your location 03:23
I love that song 03:33
Message

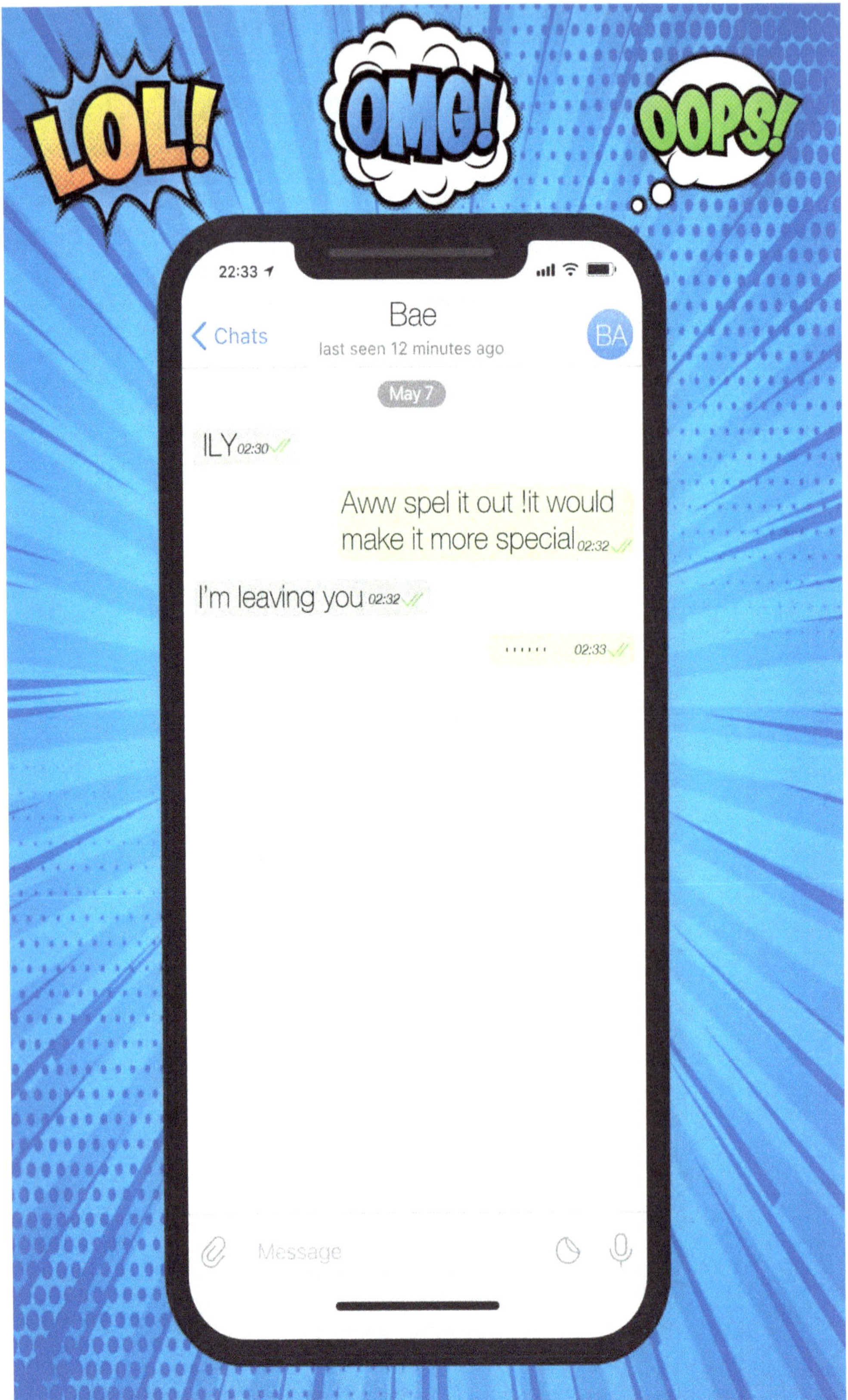
LOL!
OMG!
OOPS!
22:33
Chats
Bae
last seen 12 minutes ago
BA
May 7
ILY 02:30
Aww spel it out !it would make it more special 02:32
I'm leaving you 02:32
...... 02:33
Message

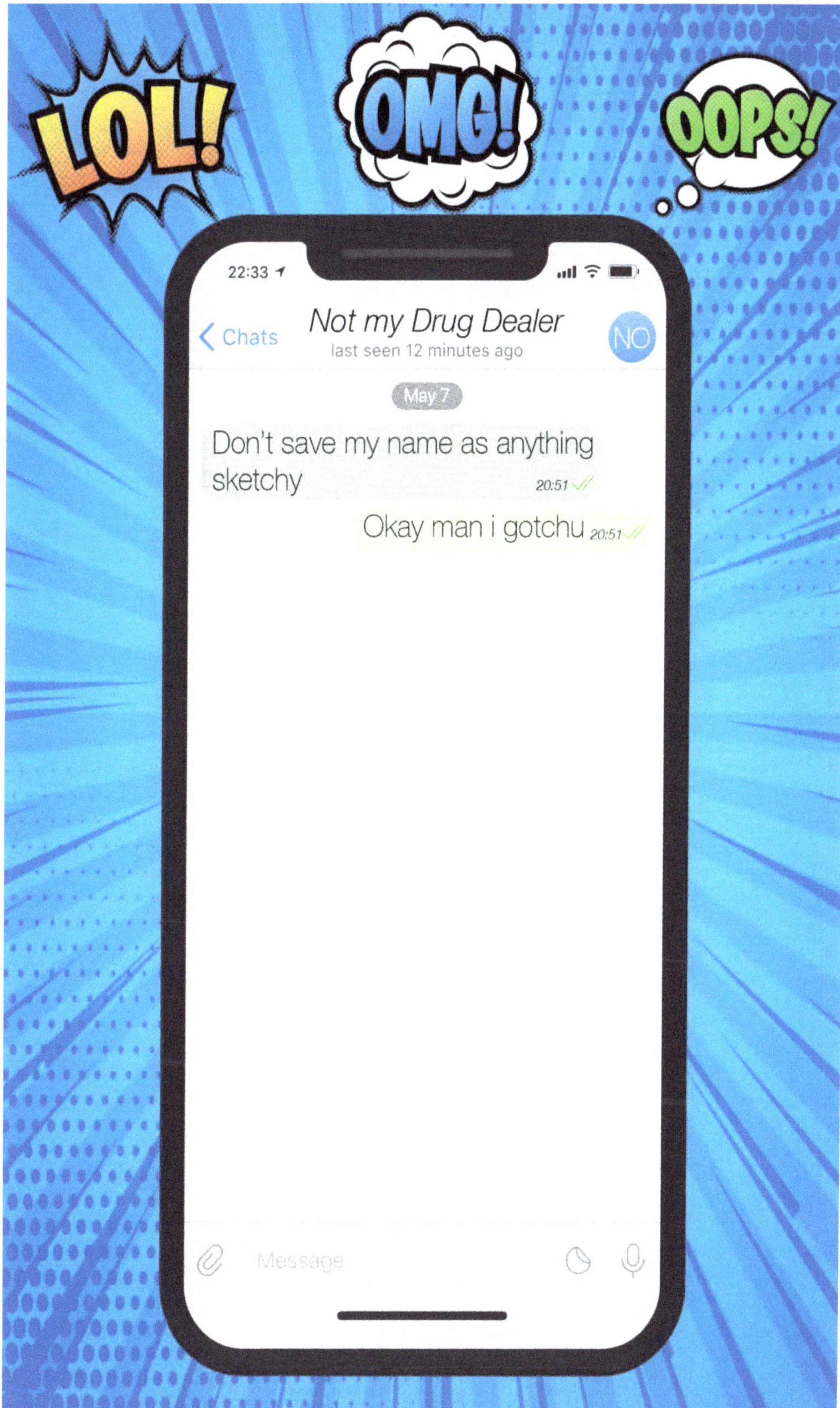
LOL!
OMG!
OOPS!
22:33
Chats
Not my Drug Dealer
last seen 12 minutes ago
NO
May 7
Don't save my name as anything sketchy 20:51
Okay man i gotchu 20:51
Message

LOL!
OMG!
OOPS!
22:33
Chats
Dad
last seen 12 minutes ago
DA
May 7
Can I throw a party this weekend? 22:23
Don't you need friends to throw a party ? 22:23
Message

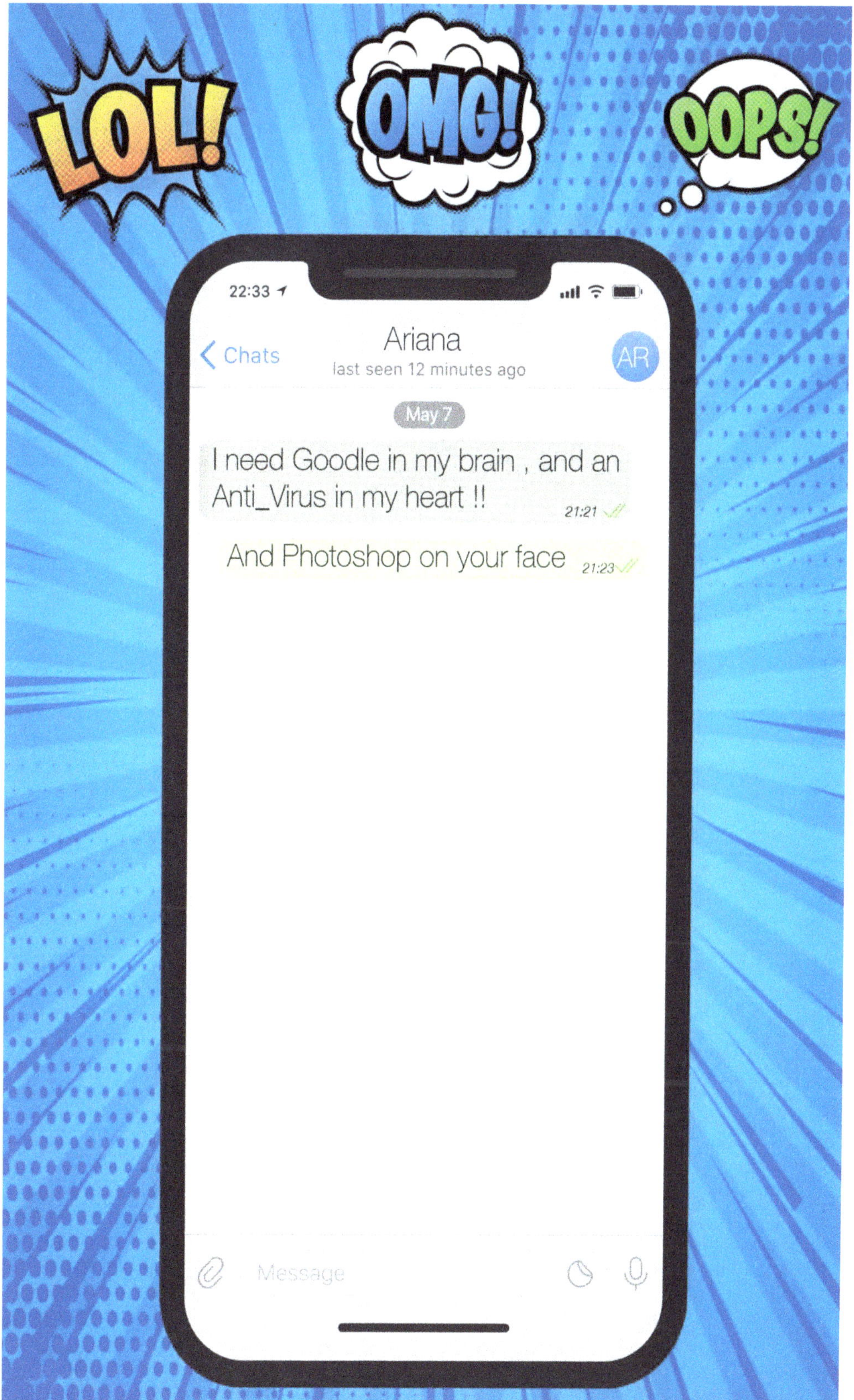
LOL!
OMG!
OOPS!
22:33
Chats
Ariana
last seen 12 minutes ago
AR
May 7
I need Goodle in my brain , and an Anti_Virus in my heart !!
21:21
And Photoshop on your face
21:23
Message

LOL!
OMG!
OOPS!
22:33
Chats
Kristen
last seen 12 minutes ago
CO
May 7
I lost 5 pounds! 23:00
Did you take off your makeup? 23:01
Message

CPSIA information can be obtained
at www.ICGtesting.com
Printed in the USA
BVHW060034260221
601128BV00005B/203

9 781638 360032